On the Plains, and
Among the Peaks

TIMBERLINE BOOKS

STEPHEN J. LEONARD AND THOMAS J. NOEL, EDITORS

ON THE PLAINS, AND AMONG THE PEAKS

OR, HOW MRS. MAXWELL MADE HER
NATURAL HISTORY COLLECTION

Mary Dartt

EDITED, AND WITH AN INTRODUCTION
BY JULIE MCCOWN

UNIVERSITY PRESS OF COLORADO
Louisville

© 2021 by University Press of Colorado

Published by University Press of Colorado
245 Century Circle, Suite 202
Louisville, Colorado 80027

 The University Press of Colorado is a proud member of
the Association of University Presses.

The University Press of Colorado is a cooperative publishing enterprise supported, in part, by Adams State University, Colorado State University, Fort Lewis College, Metropolitan State University of Denver, Regis University, University of Alaska Fairbanks, University of Colorado, University of Denver, University of Northern Colorado, University of Wyoming, Utah State University, and Western Colorado University.

∞ This paper meets the requirements of the ANSI / NISO Z39.48-1992 (Permanence of Paper).

ISBN: 978-1-64642-196-1 (paperback)
ISBN: 978-1-64642-197-8 (ebook)
https://doi.org/10.5876/9781646421978

Library of Congress Cataloging-in-Publication Data

Names: Thompson, Mary Emma Dartt, 1842–1940, author. | McCown, Julie, editor, writer of introduction.
Title: On the plains, and among the peaks : or, how Mrs. Maxwell made her natural history collection / Mary Dartt ; edited, and with an introduction by Julie McCown.
Other titles: How Mrs. Maxwell made her natural history collection
Description: Louisville : University Press of Colorado, [2021] | Includes index.
Identifiers: LCCN 2021034797 (print) | LCCN 2021034798 (ebook) | ISBN 9781646421961 (paperback) | ISBN 9781646421978 (ebook)
Subjects: LCSH: Maxwell, Martha, 1831–1881. | Taxidermists—Colorado—Biography. | Taxidermy—Colorado—19th century. | Natural history—Catalogs and collections—Colorado. | Women naturalists—Colorado—Biography.
Classification: LCC QH31.M36 T48 2021 (print) | LCC QH31.M36 (ebook) | DDC 508.788—dc23
LC record available at https://lccn.loc.gov/2021034797
LC ebook record available at https://lccn.loc.gov/2021034798

The University Press of Colorado gratefully acknowledges the support of Southern Utah University toward the publication of this volume.

Cover image credits: courtesy, History Colorado Center, Denver (*front*); courtesy, Boulder Historical Society / Museum of Boulder (*back*).

Contents

Foreword

STEPHEN J. LEONARD

Martha Dartt Maxwell (1831–1881), "the Colorado Huntress," ranked high among the most famous Colorado women in 1876, the year Colorado became a state. Many of the era's other well-known women shone in part by virtue of light reflected from their prominent husbands. James Maxwell, Martha's husband, a widower twenty years her senior, dutifully supported her unorthodox pursuits for years but by 1876 was obscured by her. A naturalist, hunter, and taxidermist, Martha generated her own light and made her own fame.

Invited by Colorado to stage part of its exhibit at the 1876 Centennial International Exposition, she trundled hundreds of dead birds and other stuffed animals—many of which she had shot or poisoned—to Philadelphia. There, thousands of visitors learned about Colorado wildlife and got to meet the diminutive taxidermist, a rifle-toting, buckskin-clad, deer slayer who her half-sister, Mary Dartt, portrayed as "a wee, modest, tender-hearted woman."

Two years later, Mary Dartt recounted Maxwell's accomplishments in *On the Plains, and Among the Peaks*. Although it received good reviews, the book did not sell well enough to repair Maxwell's sagging fortunes. Beset by marital, financial, and health problems, she died at age fifty in 1881. Her huge stuffed collection, an albatross in many ways, outlived her by some years until it, too, was gradually tossed into to the dustbin of time.

As her birds lost their feathers, as her mammals shed their hair, Martha Maxwell's fame shriveled into a small, nearly dead ember. In 1949, when LeRoy R. Hafen, executive director of the State Historical Society of Colorado, published his four-volume *Colorado and Its People*, its chapter on "Women in Colorado," written by Eudochia Bell Smith, did not mention Maxwell. Fortunately, a few people kept her memory alive. In 1981, Maxine Benson, then the Colorado State Historian, penned a chapter on Maxwell in *A Taste of the West* (1981), a festschrift honoring historian Robert G. Athearn. In 1985, Maxwell became one of the original inductees into the Colorado Women's Hall of Fame, and in 1986 Benson published a biography of Maxwell. Her place in history, albeit less exalted than those of some other Colorado women—such as the flamboyant, buoyant *Titanic* survivor Margaret (Molly) Tobin Brown—was secure, especially among fans of Colorado's past.

Martha's half-sister, Mary, despite outliving Martha by nearly sixty years, was likewise nearly forgotten until Martha's accomplishments were again recognized. Even then, Mary Dartt's 1878 book was usually simply regarded as an account of Martha's story, not as a considerable accomplishment in its own right.

Fortunately, Julie McCown, steeped in literature and contemporary scholarship and blessed with multidisciplinary insights, has taken up Mary's cause by producing this book. In her engaging introduction, McCown ponders important questions. How did Dartt view women's roles and how did she tailor her portrayal of Martha, a defier of stereotypes, to fit nineteenth-century gender expectations? What does her text indicate about then current views of Native Americans? How are animals, the supporting cast in the saga, portrayed?

In addition to accolades for resurrecting Martha and reintroducing Mary, McCown merits readers' thanks for her scholarship. In nearly 150 notes, she elucidates and expands on the original text, identifies people, clarifies Colorado geography, and defines obscure words and phrases. Read on and enjoy an enlightening account of two luminous women.

Acknowledgments

I would like to thank the anonymous peer reviewers of this work for their insightful feedback and suggestions that strengthened my introduction and editorial notes. I also thank University Press of Colorado editors Charlotte Steinhardt and Rachael Levay for their assistance and guidance with the submission and review process. Thank you also to the staff at the Stephen H. Hart Research Center of the History Colorado Center in Denver for granting me access to Martha Maxwell's papers. Thank you to Southern Utah University for funding my research trip to Denver to conduct research on Maxwell. Finally, I would like to thank two of my mentors: Dr. Cedrick May for first introducing me to the world and principles of scholarly editing and Dr. Stacy Alaimo for being an inspiring teacher and scholar who encouraged my interest and work in animal studies and natural history.

On the Plains, and Among the Peaks

Introduction

At the end of an 1873 hunting trip on the plains southeast of Boulder, Colorado, Martha Maxwell encountered a mother skunk nervously protecting her young: "The young one could run but slowly, and the mother would not leave it; but, in her solicitude, ran back and forth, always keeping her body between it and their foes" (Dartt 1879, 150). Maxwell expressed admiration for the mother skunk, declaring "it is a shame to kill anything capable of manifesting so much affection. But she must die some time, and if that time is now, she may be saved the pangs that are so often caused by ungrateful children" (150). Maxwell then unceremoniously shot the two animals, with the promise that she would transform them into specimens for her taxidermy collection. This episode, one of several such scenes in *On the Plains, and Among the Peaks*, highlights how, as the book's subtitle explains, *Mrs. Maxwell Made Her Natural History Collection*. The foregrounding of the mother-child skunk relationship complicates what would otherwise have been a straightforward hunt. The book's author, Mary Dartt, could have easily edited out those details and merely informed readers that Maxwell acquired two skunk specimens. In choosing, however, to anthropomorphize the animals before dispatching them, Dartt creates a compelling and exciting narrative that explores the tensions and contradictions in the life and work of one of America's pioneering naturalists.

American naturalist and taxidermist Martha Maxwell became famous in the 1870s for her skill and expertise in collecting and preserving specimens of Colorado's wildlife. Despite her notoriety in the late nineteenth century, Maxwell is virtually unknown today. Her work and the accompanying book describing it, *On the Plains, and Among the Peaks; or, How Mrs. Maxwell Made Her Natural History Collection* (1879), written by her half-sister Mary Dartt, provides a fascinating case study of how women practiced natural history and taxidermy, as well as a look at the early exploration and settlement of Colorado.

While not the first American woman naturalist, Maxwell is the earliest extant example of one who acquired and prepared animal specimens. Earlier American female naturalists such as Jane Colden and Almira Phelps focused on botany, leaving the messy, dangerous, and bloody work of animal study to their male counterparts. In contrast, Maxwell's life's work in natural history shows her drive to demonstrate that a woman was every bit as capable as a man at excelling at the artistic and scientific endeavor of taxidermy. The small body of scholarship on Maxwell echoes this sentiment, including Karen Jones's (2015, 253; italics in the original) assessment that "Maxwell's extraordinary collection of mounted animal life in the Rockies points to an important insider story of taxidermy, in other words, a story *in* the West as well as *of* it. Her work also serves to mediate the myth of female subservience on the frontier as well as highlighting (yet) another public outing of the hunter heroine." What remains relatively unremarked upon is *On the Plains, and Among the Peaks* itself; Dartt's book should be regarded as a significant literary artifact in its own right rather than simply as a source of information on Maxwell and her taxidermy. While the book does indeed serve that purpose, it also stands on its own, providing an account of the nineteenth-century American West as a contested and contradictory space for humans and nonhumans alike in which women both conform to and break out of gendered expectations, Native Americans are regarded with both romanticized nostalgia and generalized annoyance and irritation, and animals are both sentient, intelligent beings and raw organic material that promotes scientific progress.

BIOGRAPHICAL SKETCH OF MARTHA MAXWELL

Martha Ann Dartt was born on July 21, 1831, in northern Pennsylvania to Amy and Spencer Dartt. After Spencer's death from scarlet fever in 1833, Amy married his first cousin Josiah Dartt in 1841, and the couple had two daughters, Martha's half-sisters, Mary Emma (b. 1842) and Sarah Elizabeth (b. 1844). Martha's love of nature and passion for education were encouraged and supported by two family members in particular: her maternal grandmother, Abigail Sanford, and her stepfather, Josiah Dartt. The Dartt family settled in Wisconsin in 1845, and in 1853, Martha met her future husband, James A. Maxwell, a prominent businessman in Baraboo, Wisconsin. James Maxwell, twenty years Martha's senior, was a widower with six children. He initially asked Martha to serve as companion and chaperone to his two oldest children at Lawrence University in Appleton, Wisconsin, in exchange for him paying for her to go to the university as well. Shortly thereafter, James wrote to Martha, soliciting her hand in marriage. Reluctant at first, Martha wrote in a reply to James a few weeks later: "Think you that I am capable of bearing the responsibilities of *Mother* in a family like yours? As you very justly conclude I 'have neither gifts or graces above many,' but I think that I should *need* to have were I to enter this responsible situation, for I know of *no* one of my age, who is, (in my opinion) capable of filling it" (quoted in Benson 1986, 39; italics in the original). After their marriage in 1854, the birth of their only child, Mabel, in 1857, and James's financial devastation caused by the Panic of 1857, Martha and James Maxwell moved to Boulder, Colorado, in 1859 in hopes of cashing in on the Colorado Gold Rush. They left two-year-old Mabel in Wisconsin in the care of her maternal grandparents, Amy and Josiah Dartt. Mabel, along with Mary Dartt, eventually joined the Maxwells in Boulder in 1868.

Although James Maxwell never found financial success in prospecting, the move to Colorado introduced Martha Maxwell to the new and varied wildlife of the American West that would become her life's work. Maxwell's first stay in Colorado was cut short in 1862 when she had to return to Wisconsin to attend to her sick mother, as well as care for her husband's family. While in Wisconsin, Maxwell first learned and discovered her extraordinary skill in taxidermy, a story that is recounted in *On the Plains, and Among the Peaks*. After Maxwell's return to Boulder in 1868, she began her work of collecting and preparing specimens of Colorado's wildlife. She was an avid, even obsessive, collector of specimens, and her taxidermy mounts were renowned for their lifelike appearance and their placement in natural habitat groupings. Her taxidermy techniques were cutting-edge at the time and seemed to have developed simultaneously, although not in concert, with those of better-known taxidermy pioneers William Hornaday and Frederic Webster. Indeed, she was highly skilled and made advancements to the art that future taxidermists would copy, including using natural poses for animal specimens, placing animals in natural surroundings, inventing a special pickling solution that both softened and preserved hides and protected against insect predation, and creating plaster body molds (Moring 2005, 177–179). In discussing Maxwell's taxidermy, an 1876 article in *New Century for Woman* observes Maxwell's skill and innovation:

> She learned something of the arts of the taxidermist, but satisfied neither with their results nor her own, she set to work to do better, and succeeded in making improvements, that if she had been self-appreciative and "had known at the time," might have been patented with profitable results. But now her "way" is copied by many. Which "way" was, not to stuff the skin to any shape it would assume, but to take careful measurement of the animal, construct a model and then clothe it with its own skin. She first used plaster, but finding this too heavy for transportation and liable to crack, she has since found a more desirable material for her models. ("The Colorado Naturalist" 1876)

Maxwell was also an accomplished naturalist, discovering a new species of owl that would be named after her, *Scops asio* var. *maxwellæ*, or Mrs. Maxwell's owl, and acquiring some of the first specimens of the black-footed ferret, an elusive animal initially identified and described by John James Audubon. Maxwell corresponded regularly with noted scientists of her day, including Robert Ridgway, a Smithsonian Institution ornithologist who named the owl after Maxwell and contributed the catalog of birds included as an appendix to *On the Plains, and Among the Peaks,* and Spencer Fullerton Baird, a naturalist and curator at the Smithsonian, to whom Maxwell sent bird specimens and in return received catalogs of birds and mammals to continue her study of the natural sciences.

As Maxwell's taxidermy collection grew, so did her reputation as a highly skilled taxidermist. In addition to adding to her own ever-expanding collection, she would mount specimens for others as a way to earn money; she also began to exhibit her collection at fairs, including the Colorado Agricultural Society fair in 1868 and 1870. By 1870, the Maxwell family's financial situation had worsened, and Maxwell made the difficult decision to sell her collection of around 600 specimens for $600 to Shaw's Garden (now known as the Missouri Botanical Garden) in St. Louis, Missouri. The money allowed the Maxwell family to purchase land and build a new house in Boulder. Maxwell immediately set about rebuilding her collection, and it quickly grew so large that she could no longer contain it in her home and taxidermy studio (which her family referred to as her "den"). Maxwell soon decided to open a museum, both to accommodate her extensive collection and to, she hoped, alleviate some of her family's financial problems, which while temporarily eased by the sale of specimens never entirely went away. Transforming personal collections into public museums was not uncommon at the time; as Sarah Amato (2015, 205–207) notes, museums in the Victorian age often "were formed out of private collections, . . . displaying diverse objects that were amassed according to the tastes of an individual collector." The Rocky Mountain Museum opened in Boulder, Colorado, in June 1874. Maxwell intended the museum to serve multiple functions, simultaneously contributing to scientific knowledge, educating the public (especially children and young women), and providing popular entertainment and curiosities—all common aims of natural history museums at the time.[1]

The centerpiece of the museum was Maxwell's taxidermy placed in her signature habitat groupings, which, while novel at the time, would soon become, as Rachel Poliquin (2012, 81) phrased it, "the zenith of artistic taxidermic skill."[2] In a letter dated November 11, 1874, Maxwell wrote to Marianne Dascomb, the principal of the Oberlin Female Department (in Ohio), where Mabel had recently enrolled, explaining what she hoped to gain by turning her collection into a museum: "I am anxious to make it a pecuniary success for two reasons, first that we may be able to give our daughter as good an education as she is capable of receiving, and my next ambition is to build up a temple of science that shall be a credit to *our sex* and an acquisition to the world." Maxwell goes on to note: "A determined will and strong muscles have been my principle [*sic*] capital."[3] The museum was moved to the more populous and tourist-heavy Denver in 1875 in an effort to make it more profitable, but the museum was never financially successful. Its lack of financial success, despite praise from both the general and scientific communities,[4] can be ascribed to multiple factors. In her biography of Martha Maxwell, Maxine Benson (1986, 111) notes that "the receipts from the sale of the twenty-five-cent tickets did not go far to meet the other expenses such as light and fuel." In addition, tourism in Colorado outside of the summer season was low, and Boulder's population wasn't big enough to support the museum, "particularly considering the depressed economy in the mid-1870s" (111). These problems persisted even when the museum moved to more populous Denver.

Maxwell achieved her highest level of fame with her exhibit at the Philadelphia Centennial International Exposition of 1876. She re-created her taxidermy tableaux as part of Colorado's exhibit in the Kansas and Colorado Building. Her massive exhibit, titled *Woman's Work*, included 47 mammal species and 224 bird species arranged in natural groupings on an artificial landscape of mountain ledges, plains, and running water. *Woman's Work* proved enormously popular with both the general public and the scientific community. Reactions to the exhibit from two of the country's foremost ornithologists at the time are included in the appendix of *On the Plains, and Among the Peaks*. First, Robert Ridgway (1879, 226) comments that the collection's specimens are "excellently mounted" and that the collection "illustrates very fully the avian fauna of Colorado" and "bears testimony . . . to the success which has crowned the enthusiastic and intelligent efforts of a 'woman Naturalist.'" Second, Elliott Coues, a prominent ornithologist and author of *Key to North American Birds* (1872), writes in "Notice of Mrs. Maxwell's Exhibit of Colorado Mammals" (1879, 217)—included as an appendix to *On the Plains, and Among the Peaks*—that *Woman's Work* gave him "both pleasure and instruction": "I was glad to see a collection of our native animals mounted in a manner far superior to ordinary museum work, and to know that there was at least one lady who could do such a thing and who took pleasure in doing it." In addition to its scientific value, Coues notes that *Woman's Work* is a means of "popularizing Natural History, and making the subject attractive to the public; this desirable object being attained by the artistic manner in which the specimens were mounted and grouped together" (217). The high praise for Maxwell continued into the early twentieth century. Writing in 1915, Junius Henderson asserts that Maxwell's taxidermy is "well worthy of the high commendation it received, not only from the general public, but also from naturalists whose opinions command high respect," and that it marks "one of the earliest efforts in America to exhibit the animals of a large area in imitation of their natural environment" (88, 89). Alongside his praise, Henderson laments the waning recognition of Maxwell's work: "Forty years have elapsed, and those who are familiar with Mrs. Maxwell's work at first hand are rapidly dwindling in numbers" (89). Her lack of recognition is also due in part, Henderson argues, to the fact that "published accounts of her work are meager and obscure, hence apt to escape the attention of future museum workers" (90). Importantly, Henderson notes that while it is impossible to accurately measure Maxwell's influence, "even those who never heard of the estimable lady are perhaps to a greater or less extent reaping the results of her stimulating example" (90).

Despite massive public interest and favorable reviews from the popular press and the scientific community, Maxwell's exhibit was not financially successful. The financial disappointment of *Woman's Work* can be largely attributed to two factors. First, the Colorado legislature had promised Maxwell that it would reimburse her for the transportation costs of shipping her collection to Philadelphia; however, the legislature refused to honor that promise, and by June 1876 it still owed her around $733. Second, the primary source of income for Maxwell at the exposition was selling photos of herself and her collection. The Centennial Photographic Company, which had a virtual monopoly on photographs at the exposition, could not keep up with the high demand for photos of Maxwell's exhibit; when Maxwell tried to sell her own copies to meet demand, the company threatened to close her photo stands completely. In the following years, Maxwell's continued efforts to make her collection profitable failed. Following her death from an ovarian tumor in 1881, the logistics and cost of shipping and storing Maxwell's enormous collection eventually resulted in its loss and destruction by the early years of the twentieth century. Written descriptions and photographs are all that remain of her groundbreaking taxidermy work.

COMPOSITION AND PUBLICATION OF
ON THE PLAINS, AND AMONG THE PEAKS

Onc of the efforts undertaken after the centennial to both raise Maxwell's status as a naturalist and taxidermist and earn much-needed money, *On the Plains, and Among the Peaks* was a collaboration between Maxwell and her half-sister Mary Dartt Thompson, with whom Maxwell maintained a close friendship throughout her life. Mary Dartt graduated from the Baraboo Collegiate Institute in Wisconsin in 1865 and then taught at Catharine Beecher's Milwaukee Female College until she moved to Boulder to join the Maxwells. While in Colorado, she frequently accompanied Maxwell and her husband on their excursions in the Rocky Mountains to collect specimens. Dartt moved to Massachusetts in 1875 with her husband, Nathan Thompson, a minister she had married in 1870. Dartt had some experience as a published writer, having contributed poems and essays to the *Baraboo Republic* newspaper between 1865 and 1867.

Dartt began writing *On the Plains, and Among the Peaks* in 1877, working with Maxwell in composing the book. It was published in 1878 by the Philadelphia firm Claxton, Remsen and Haffelfinger. As Dartt explains in the opening section of the book (9), which is set at the Centennial International Exposition and features a litany of questions from visitors about Maxwell and her taxidermy, Dartt wrote *On the Plains, and Among the Peaks* as an answer to the repeated questions from visitors to the *Woman's Work* exhibit: "Do tell us who she is, and how she did it?" Following her promise to do just that, Dartt first describes the Rocky Mountain Museum by way of a lengthy excerpt from Helen Hunt's review "Mrs. Maxwell's Museum," published in the *New York Independent* on September 23, 1875. She then backtracks to introduce us to Maxwell when she was living in Wisconsin between 1862 and 1868 and first learned taxidermy. From there, Dartt recounts several episodes of Maxwell hunting and procuring animals, crafting taxidermy specimens, and creating her Rocky Mountain Museum. Along the way, Dartt introduces her readers to the landscape and wilderness of the Rocky Mountains and Colorado Territory, explaining the territory to non-Coloradans and providing a vicarious experience to readers. *On the Plains, and Among the Peaks* concludes with a description of Maxwell's creation and installation of *Woman's Work* at the Centennial International Exposition. *The book* ends with an appendix featuring two catalogs of Maxwell's specimens: Elliott Coues's "Notice of Mrs. Maxwell's Exhibit of Colorado Mammals" and Robert Ridgway's "Mrs. Maxwell's Colorado Museum. Catalogue of the Birds."

As with Maxwell's taxidermy, the book was well reviewed by both the press and the scientific community; yet it was not the financial success for which Dartt and Maxwell had hoped. A four-page pamphlet published by Claxton,

Remsen and Haffelfinger as a promotion piece for *On the Plains, and Among the Peaks* includes snippets of reviews of the book from twenty-six newspapers and publications. The reviews frequently praise Dartt's "pleasant," "entertaining," and "unpretending" writing style, as well as the exciting and vivid adventures of Maxwell's hunting expeditions. Notable reviews in the pamphlet include the *Chicago Tribune*'s assertion that "the work has been well done, and it makes a fascinating story" and the *Sunday Post*'s observations that "the style and intellectual atmosphere of the little volume is pleasant throughout" and that "Miss Dartt manifests no less talent and skill in her style of dressing up abstruse scientific facts than did Mrs. Maxwell in preparing her numerous subjects for the Centennial levee" ("A Suitable Book for Holiday Presents"). In his 1879 review of *On the Plains, and Among the Peaks*, Joel A. Allen notes that the book is "a very intelligent and pleasantly written account" (113). Like most discussions of the book, the review quickly moves past Dartt's writing and focuses on Maxwell and her taxidermy. In praising *Woman's Work*, Allen calls the exhibit "a startling revelation of what a woman can do in one of the most difficult fields of art" (113). Maxwell, Allen writes, was "more than a successful and enthusiastic taxidermist; she [was] an ardent and thorough student of nature, and her explorations of the zoology of Colorado have revealed the existence of many species in that State not previously known to occur there, and contributed many new facts regarding the habits and distribution of others" (113). The combined sensationalism and novelty of a woman taxidermist and Maxwell's undisputed mastery and skill at her craft invariably (and somewhat understandably) overshadowed Dartt's writing.

Although it makes no mention of *On the Plains, and Among the Peaks*, Nina Baym's comprehensive study, *Women Writers of the American West, 1833–1927* (2012), helps situate Dartt's book in its literary and historical context. Baym notes that of the 343 women writers in her study, "at least two-thirds were literary professionals or semiprofessionals—mainly journalists or women who freelanced for newspapers and periodicals. There were also editors, teachers, community activists, clubwomen, local historians, and novelists" (5). Dartt fits comfortably within this pattern. Moreover, Baym draws the following general conclusion about the women writers she analyzed: "I found these writers showing women making western lives for themselves and their families by achieving domesticity in a new place, improving over what they'd known before but still accepting a domestic agenda . . . Women are seen to be crucial to the western development of families, farms, and business. In exchange for their work, the West made women healthier, more active, more useful, more engaged than their sisters back East" (2). When specifically examining writings about Colorado, Baym notes that as the prospecting of the early Gold Rush "quickly gave way to heavily capitalized mines and turned miners into day-laborers, many of them immigrants," many writers in Colorado "were keen to portray the place as manly, traditional, and truly western," leaving women's place in that vision less than certain (116). In *On the Plains, and Among the Peaks*, Dartt creates a carefully crafted image of Martha Maxwell "as a feminine artistic woman devoted to the study of natural history" (Benson 1986, 168). Dartt achieves that image by scrupulously balancing riveting hunting expeditions on the Colorado frontier, descriptions of the meticulous study and practice of natural history, and scenes of motherly care and concern for Maxwell's daughter, Mabel.

CRITICAL INTERPRETATIONS OF
ON THE PLAINS, AND AMONG THE PEAKS

There are no extended analyses of *On the Plains, and Among the Peaks* specifically and only limited discussions of Maxwell and her taxidermy, much of which focuses on her gender and how it relates to her taxidermy and scientific pursuits. The publication of this new edition presents an opportunity for renewed interest in and appreciation of *On the Plains, and Among the Peaks* and Martha Maxwell, as well as representing a text for scholars to study and analyze. The critical interpretations that follow are by no means exhaustive, and Dartt's book presents many more areas for further study and analysis than I address here. My intention is to open a conversation about the possibilities for critical analysis with the hope that other literary scholars and historians will join in and further situate Dartt's and Maxwell's work within the numerous disciplines to which it speaks, including nineteenth-century American literature, women's history, the history of the American West, natural history, museum studies, animal studies, environmental history, and many others.

Gender

Even with all the various fields of interest related to *On the Plains, and Among the Peaks*, Maxwell's gender consistently draws the most attention, both from her contemporaries and from twentieth- and twenty-first-century scholars. *On the Plains, and Among the Peaks*, in its descriptions of Maxwell's work, provides a meaningful glimpse of how women both practiced and wrote about natural history. In her book *"Good Observers of Nature": American Women and the Scientific Study of the Natural World, 1820–1885*, Tina Gianquitto (2010) charts the changes in how women wrote about nature over the course of the nineteenth century.[5] She observes that the use of nature "as a platform for discussing issues of domesticity, education, morality, and the nation" (1), which was common in early nineteenth-century natural theology writing, was challenged by developing scientific understanding as the century progressed, especially Charles Darwin's *On the Origin of Species* (1859) in which he argues, as Gianquitto states, "for a directionless evolutionary process that was determined by natural and sexual selection mixed with a heady dose of chance and adaptation" (10). Other factors also "influenced the ways in which women wrote about nature, including women's education reform and the attendant challenges to conventional notions of domesticity, the shift to literary realism after the Civil War, and the rise of professionalism in the sciences in the latter part of the century" (2). Gianquitto's study of four women writers—Almira Phelps, Margaret Fuller, Susan Fenimore Cooper, and Mary Treat—focuses almost exclusively on botany, with the only animals the insects and arachnids of Treat's work. While botanical education became quite common in school curricula for girls, as it "was seen to serve several valuable ends: it led girls outside, exercising in the fresh air; it trained them to look for scientific connections among objects in the natural world; and it showed them how to translate those connections into pious lessons for the home" (5), the kind of scientific work undertaken by Maxwell (both her hunting expeditions and her taxidermy work) was outside the normal bounds for a nineteenth-century woman naturalist.

In Maxwell's case, being in the American West afforded her additional benefits, as the West was a region that, as Baym (2012, 9) points out, "was seen to allow women to become capable, physically active, independent, honest, and forthright. Ideas of bigness and spaciousness, of freedom from convention, of physical development, contribute to a sense of the western heroine as a new kind of person." However, the new western heroine did not mean a rejection of traditional femininity; in fact, western books, Baym argues, "portray their local heroines in opposition to their overcultivated and too-often manipulative sisters from Boston or New York as the thoroughly American development of true womanhood" (9). Maxwell embodies this model of the new western heroine, whose scientific pursuits exercised both her body and her mind. Yet Maxwell's engagement with natural science resulted in behaviors that could have been judged by her peers as a dereliction of her motherly and domestic duties. She left young Mabel behind in Wisconsin when she and James initially moved to Boulder; once reunited with Mabel, Maxwell took her along on hunting trips that often turned dangerous, including a perilous descent down a mountain in a raging storm (see chapter 10). Mabel appears to have harbored lingering resentment and bitterness toward her mother and her single-minded focus on her work. In Mabel Maxwell Brace's 1948 book *Thanks to Abigail*, she states that Maxwell "lacked any very strong maternal qualities. They may have been swallowed up in her artistic and scientific interests" (n.p.). The fraught dynamics of Maxwell and Mabel's relationship are conspicuously absent from Dartt's book, reflecting both Dartt's and Maxwell's efforts to present a particular image of Maxwell as the ideal model of a woman naturalist.

Maxwell's status as a woman naturalist and how it spoke to broader ideas about women and their place in society was a key focus for both Dartt and Maxwell. In a passage in *On the Plains, and Among the Peaks* discussing Maxwell's decision to take up shooting to acquire animal specimens, Dartt (1879, 25) makes a broader claim about women's abilities, noting "that *capacity* and *ability*, rather than birth, color, sex, or anything else, should determine where individuals belong, and what they shall do. If they can use a gun, and are so inclined, what is to hinder their doing it?" Dartt capitalizes on Maxwell's gun usage, turning it into an opportunity to make a broader claim about women's abilities and their right to pursue their own interests. This sentiment about women's abilities is mirrored in Maxwell's own writings and correspondence. In a letter to Spencer Baird from 1875, Maxwell writes, "The greatest desire of my life is to help inspire women with confidence in their own resources and abilities" (quoted in Benson 1986, 119). In an undated note, Maxwell observes that "woman's selfdenial[,] will and muscle has brought [the collection] to its present status—and I am unwilling it should loose [*sic*] its feminine identity" (quoted in Benson 1986, 136). In addition to her passion for natural history, Maxwell displayed an acute appreciation for how her work would symbolically and materially affect society's attitudes and behaviors toward women in general, a responsibility she did not take lightly. Perhaps most obvious, Maxwell naming her centennial exhibit *Woman's Work* shows her awareness of and savvy regarding how inseparable her gender was from her work. Leslie Madsen-Brooks (2009, 17) posits that Maxwell's choice of the title was an effort "perhaps to capitalize on the novelty of her gender as well as on the scope of her talent." Madsen-Brooks suggests that *Woman's Work* offered "a (possibly unintentional) critique of science-as-usual" by eschewing the at-the-time standard museum triad display of one male, one female, and one juvenile of a species—opting instead for a display that highlighted an ecosystem, "a landscape alive with stories of species diversity, cohabitation, and interdependence" (17, 18). Not content with merely following the example set by the male naturalists of the day, Maxwell used her perspective and knowledge gained from hours of careful observation in the Colorado wilderness to innovate, showing that women could provide valuable contributions to scientific knowledge.

At the Philadelphia Centennial International Exposition, Maxwell spent hours answering countless questions from the public about her work. Dartt includes a sampling of those questions in the opening section of *On the Plains, and Among the Peaks*: "How could a woman do it?" "Did she kill any of the animals?" "What did she do it for?" "What sort of woman is she?" "If she's married why isn't it called Mr. Maxwell's collection?" (5–9). These questions reveal the public's preoccupation with and concern for Maxwell as a woman, as well as an inability to ever fully divorce her work from her gender. Perhaps the most salient point of discussion in terms of Maxwell's gender was her use of guns to hunt and kill her animal specimens. In *Her Best Shot: Women and Guns in America*, Laura Browder (2009, 1) notes that "throughout much of American history, the gun has served as a recurrent symbol that links violence and masculinity. For over two centuries, there have been women who have escaped conventional gender roles by picking up guns." In discussing Maxwell specifically, Browder examines Maxwell's use of guns, arguing that it led the American public to question "both her whiteness and her femininity," as spectators and press at the centennial identified Maxwell "as variously white, Native American, a hunter, a housewife, a lady, and an amazon" (57). Browder also observes that Maxwell's combined gun usage and scientific acumen might offer an explanation for her lack of lasting recognition: "The armed woman as scientist was not a figure that endured, for an intellectual woman hunter was an uncomfortable combination of things—too smart, too violent—for the public to assimilate" (65). Maxwell was a gun-toting naturalist, and her identity threatened to unsettle not just one but two gender expectations of her time, which only served to compound people's interest in her gender as such.

Many contemporary reviews of Maxwell's exhibit at the centennial emphasize her bodily appearance and identity as a "little lady" of "refined sensibility" (Browder 2009, 61–63). An 1876 review in *Harper's Bazaar* notes: "Mrs. Maxwell is a quiet little blue-eyed woman, shy and unassuming in mien, and not at all like the Amazon that one might expect to find in the Rocky Mountain huntress" ("Mrs. Maxwell's Rocky Mountain Museum," 730). An 1876 newspaper clipping from the *American Register* moves quickly from an overview of *Woman's Work* to Maxwell herself, focusing at length on her physical appearance: "Admirable as the collection is in taxidermic skill and landscape arrangement, the most wonderful of all is the little Rocky Mountain woman herself, who killed most of the animals and prepared them all. She is still young, rather small, her face is somewhat bronzed, but not at all unpleasantly so; her blue eyes dance with sweetness and intelligence, and the mixture of gentleness, courage, and capabilities is so blended in her appearance as to make her very attractive."[6] Returning to Junius Henderson's essay (1915, 91) praising Maxwell's scientific skill, he concludes his discussion of Maxwell by drawing attention to her gender and her body: "She was not a coarse, angular, western giantess, imbued with a desire to kill. Acquaintances have described her as slight, not strapping; refined, not coarse; modest, not brazen; tenderhearted, not bloodthirsty." Even while conceding Maxwell's skill with a gun, Henderson is careful to assert that she used a gun "not because of a thirst for innocent blood, for she loved the creatures whose lives she took; but she was determined to bring about results pleasing to her artistic and nature-loving eye and instructive to those who were unacquainted with wildlife in its native haunts" (91). For these and many other reviewers, Maxwell's body is worthy of as much, if not more, attention as the taxidermied bodies of the animals she prepared, and, in their view, it is vital that her body be represented as "appropriately" feminine.

This careful positioning of Maxwell's feminine identity can be explained in part when put alongside the big game hunting narratives of men in the Victorian age. In discussing the narratives of Victorian big game hunters,

Harriet Ritvo (1987, 254) argues: "If the spoils of the big game hunter powerfully evoked the conquest and domination of exotic territories, written accounts made his exploits seem still more inspiring and more widely accessible. The connection between triumphing over a dangerous animal and subduing unwilling natives was direct and obvious, and the association of the big game hunter with the march of empire was literal as well as metonymic." Ritvo further asserts that "even more than trophy collections, narratives written by the potent protagonists fanned public appreciation of the heroic big game hunter" (255). To avoid readers equating Maxwell with these male big game hunters, reviewers like Henderson reminded readers of Maxwell's "proper" femininity.

Dartt also takes great care to position Maxwell as almost the antithesis of the Victorian big game hunters. For example, Dartt (1879, 118) presents a conversation in which a female friend asks Maxwell, "You fearful woman! how can you have the heart to take so many lives?" Maxwell replies: "I suppose you think me very cruel, but I doubt if I am as much so as you! There isn't a day you don't tacitly consent to have some creature killed that you may eat it. I never take life for such carnivorous purposes! All must die some time; I only shorten the period of consciousness that I may give their forms a perpetual memory; and, I leave it to you, which is the more cruel? to kill to eat, or kill to *immortalize*" (118–119). In explaining herself, Maxwell justifies her hunting of animals not as a heroic pursuit and mastery of dangerous wild beasts but as a rational method of preserving animals in "perpetual memory." Rather than emphasize bloody conquest of the hunt like the big game hunters do, Maxwell focuses on the end result of her hunting: the production and proliferation of natural history knowledge. This focus on scientific observation over killing ability is also reflected in a *New Century for Woman's* 1876 article, which first carefully points out that Maxwell is "simply and sincerely a naturalist, who shrinks from destroying life as sensitively as would the most delicately reared metropolitan woman," and later reiterates that "she is a naturalist, who studies the pose of her animals to a degree that drew from the most distinguished visitor at the Exposition an expression of admiration" ("The Colorado Naturalist"). Later on in *On the Plains, and Among the Peaks*, when Dartt recounts Maxwell successfully hunting a buffalo, Dartt (1879, 132) makes sure to note that shooting a large animal such as a buffalo was no stunning achievement: "Any *man* could have done what she did there. I have

FIGURE 0.1. Stereoview produced by the Centennial Photographic Company of Martha Maxwell's *Woman's Work* exhibit at the Philadelphia Centennial International Exposition

seen many a one who had, and considered it almost honor enough for a lifetime, and told of it with no end of flourishes. Well, it don't take much to satisfy some people. Now I'll tell you of something of which she had reason to be proud." Dartt goes on to recount how Maxwell discovered a new species of owl, concluding the chapter with the assertion that "a thousand years hence, when all people are mourning over the extinction of large animals from America, her name will live associated with a variety of the bird, that has been from time immemorial a symbol of wisdom" (133). What is important in Dartt's telling is not tales of hyperbolic and hyper-masculine struggles between man and beast but feats of perseverance, careful observation, and keen intellect—areas in which, as Dartt tell us, Maxwell excelled.

As mentioned previously, Maxwell sold images of herself and her animals at the Philadelphia Centennial International Exposition (figure 0.1). In *On the Plains, and Among the Peaks*, Dartt (1879, 211) explains that while Maxwell initially found "the idea of selling her own likeness" repulsive, she changed her mind as the public's demand for these images became apparent. The images draw attention to how Maxwell's female identity and body are intertwined

FIGURE 0.2. Photograph of Martha Maxwell in her hunting costume

with and shaped by the animal bodies she came into contact with in her work. Two particular photographs of Maxwell help illuminate the tension or dissonance in her public persona. The first one (figure 0.2) showcases Maxwell's hunting costume; the second one (figure 0.3) shows her "at work" in her studio. A rifle appears in the foreground of both photos, as well as a dead fox (clearly dead in the first image and "lifelike" in the second). These photographs emphasize Maxwell's "lady-like" poise while still gesturing to her work in killing and preserving her specimens. The images are not out in nature but in an indoor and controlled environment that gives the illusion of safety and feminine propriety; it does not reveal the reality of the strenuous physical exertion required in traversing the Rocky Mountains tracking, shooting, and retrieving specimens of all sizes.

For writer Helen Hunt Jackson, who wrote a review of Maxwell's Rocky Mountain Museum, the dissonance between gendered expectations and

FIGURE 0.3.
Photograph of
Martha Maxwell
posed at work
in her taxidermy
studio

Maxwell's work centered less on her shooting the animals and more on her skill as a taxidermist: "That a pioneer woman should shoot wild cats and grizzlies seemed not unnatural or improbable; but that the same woman who could fire a rifle so well could also stuff an animal with any sort of skill or artistic effect seemed very unlikely" (quoted in *Dartt 1879*, 11). Maxwell's hunting defied expectations for the average American woman but fit within expectations for a woman on the western frontier. But as a pioneer in taxidermy and natural history, Maxwell had truly broken new ground. Yet *On the Plains, and Among the Peaks* ends not with a reminder of Maxwell's trailblazing but with worry about Maxwell's daughter Mabel's education. The book's final chapter concludes with a paragraph calling attention to Maxwell's "ceaseless exertions and self-denials for her daughter's higher education" and reminds viewers that Maxwell's work in natural history does not "diminish the sweetness of true womanhood, or render the heart, once gentle and tender, harsh and cold" (216). The book allows Maxwell to be a trailblazing woman, but at its end she is safely returned to the role of caring mother, lest readers think she has strayed too far from prescribed gender roles.

Native Americans

Although *On the Plains, and Among the Peaks* presents readers with a progressive view of women's education, abilities, and accomplishments, its treatment of Native Americans is decidedly problematic. The indigenous peoples of the western United States occupy the periphery of Dartt's book, and their occasional presence reveals a troubling, although not atypical, depiction of white settlers' views of the American West.

On the Plains, and Among the Peaks takes place against an unacknowledged backdrop of excessive violence and the genocide of Native Americans, particularly the Sand Creek massacre of 1864, in which hundreds of Native Americans at a Cheyenne and Arapaho camp—many of whom were women and children—were brutally murdered and mutilated by members of Colorado troops led by Colonel John M. Chivington. Prior to the massacre, settlers in the West had increasingly encroached on Native lands, a problem exacerbated by Colorado's Gold Rush that brought the Maxwells to Boulder in 1859. Michael Shally-Jensen (2014, 99) writes that Native Americans presented the US government with a "quandary" of how to balance its goal of "the expansion of American power over the whole of the continent" while also upholding the American democracy's founding "principles of freedom and mutual respect." The United States frequently revised existing land treaties with Native tribes. For example, with the "massive influx of settlers" that resulted from the Gold Rush, the United States revised the 1851 Fort Laramie Treaty, "greatly reducing Native lands" and contributing to growing resentment from Native Americans (99). In addition, as Karen R. Jones and John Wills (2009, 176) observed, settlers essentialized Native Americans "as bloodthirsty and primitive, aberrant in their social practices and uniformly warlike," thus painting them as "hostile 'others' and enemies of the state deserving of eradication." In discussing the Sand Creek massacre, Jones and Wills emphasize how the negative perception of Native Americans by settlers was further exacerbated by John Evans, the governor of Colorado Territory, who in the months preceding the massacre "consistently spoke in threatening terms, warning of 'depredations' and imminent war. Such protestations fashioned a monolithic image of Indians as belligerent 'others' and asserted a concomitant imperative to armed action" (184). The initial public approval of the Sand Creek massacre soon gave way to horror and disapproval as details of the event began to emerge; yet despite a congressional investigation and recommendations for punishments, "no actions were taken against any of those responsible for the killing" (Shally-Jensen 2014, 109).

The prominence and significance of the Sand Creek massacre shaped and influenced how western writers wrote about both Native Americans and the West in general. In discussing another female-authored book on Colorado published the same year as *On the Plains, and Among the Peaks*, Anna Gordon's *Camping in Colorado, with Suggestions to Gold-Seekers, Tourists and Invalids* (1879), Baym (2012, 118) draws attention to "one of the earlier defensive references to the bitter fighting between Natives and settlers during the Civil War, which culminated in the Sand Creek massacre of 1864, where the wrong tribe—Cheyenne rather than Ute—paid the price in the brutal killing of noncombatants by soldiers under the command of Col. John Chivington." The Sand Creek massacre is never mentioned in *On the Plains, and Among the Peaks*; however, as the Maxwells moved to Boulder in 1859, they and Dartt would undoubtedly have been familiar with the event and its aftermath.

In *On the Plains, and Among the Peaks*, Dartt portrays Native Americans alternately as dangerous nuisances who impede white settlers from taking full advantage of the West's resources and as romanticized Others clearly equated with the region's large buffalo herds, noble and majestic but destined to vanish from the landscape. One particular scene demonstrates the perceived "threat" Native Americans posed for white settlers. At the start of a chapter describing one of Maxwell's hunting trips, Dartt (1879, 53) draws readers' attention to "a strip of valuable meadow land," which "white people had endeavored a number of times to occupy . . . long enough to cut and secure the grass, but had been driven away by the Indians and their work destroyed," as well as "an old adobe fort, formerly used as a government defence, but long since rendered—by the noble red men (?)—useless for such purpose." Dartt's reference to Native Americans driving away white settlers hints obliquely at the violence and tensions between the two groups, and her inclusion of the question mark immediately following "noble red men" at once challenges her stereotyping of Native Americans as "noble" and suggests, again somewhat indirectly, her true sentiments toward them.

On that hunting trip, Maxwell comes upon an apparently abandoned fort that actually holds two white frontiersmen; Maxwell and the men mistake each other for Native Americans. Maxwell believes the man she spies in the fort "from his clothing, or rather lack of it, was undoubtedly an Indian, and both he and the dog seemed furious with rage at her presence there, and came rushing toward her" (Dartt 1879, 55–56). Maxwell makes a calm, steady retreat back to her camp and warns the others in her party of the Native American. Her husband immediately insists that they leave the area, as he is certain that there must be more Native Americans nearby, and "they would be out soon to see what enemy or plunder was at hand; finding them alone, they would not hesitate to kill them and take what they had, for there would be no danger of the deed being reported and the terrible vengeance of the whites aroused" (56–57). Shortly thereafter, the two frontiersmen introduce themselves to Maxwell's group and relate their side of the encounter. They reveal that they initially believed Maxwell was a Native American. These men harbor more hostile attitudes toward Native Americans, referring to them as "ornery beasts" as they declare: "We've done sworn we'd shoot the first one of 'em that puts his condemned mug inside this valley, no matter what he's here for" (58). Their negative stereotypes and animosity toward Native Americans almost resulted in tragic violence. Furthermore, Dartt portrays Native Americans as innately hostile and combative, ignoring white settlers' role in creating such hostility and strained relations.

In a later section, Dartt describes Maxwell's efforts to acquire buffalo specimens. While approaching a herd of buffalo, Maxwell's party comes upon a Native American man pursuing a young female buffalo. Dartt (1879, 128) marvels at the skill of the hunter and his pony and contrasts it with the ignoble "atrocities" of white settlers shooting buffalo from the windows of a train. Dartt describes an innate sense of connectedness between the Native American man and his pony, noting that he "seemed instinct with his will, and, without being touched by his hands, which were busy sending arrows into the beast, at every turn it veered and tacked, duplicating every movement the buffalo made" (128). What might at first seem like a compliment about the man's skill, upon closer examination subtly dehumanizes the man, placing him closer to the "brutes" he hunts than to the white settler hunters in Maxwell's party. This animalization of Native Americans is made more explicit at another point in the book, in which Dartt lists Native Americans alongside other "herds" of animals: "vast herds of deer, buffalo, Indians, and other wild horses" (40). Dartt establishes a parallel between the "noble beasts" (the buffalo) and the Native Americans, both inextricably linked to the fantasy of the West and both under threat from its settlement by white people.

In another scene toward the end of the book, Dartt describes Maxwell's visit to and use of the Hot Sulphur Springs. As with the earlier scene with the two frontiersmen in the fort in which Maxwell is initially mistaken for a Native American, the scene begins with Dartt (1879, 198) recounting the story of how the footprints Maxwell left at the hot springs led to confusion from other visitors as to whether they were left by a Native American or a white woman, leading one trapper to note: "Squaws turn their toes in and white folks don't. The jaunt ain't a very likely one for 'em to take, I allow, and none of 'em ever took it afore, I know; but if you jest inquire 'round enough, you'll find out some white woman made it." While this little aside is not terribly relevant to the book's narrative, it does speak to Dartt's and Maxwell's preoccupation with Maxwell's image. With this scene, Dartt tells readers that even if her hunting expeditions might feature behavior and actions that run counter to the expected behavior of a white woman, Maxwell, as the trapper's assessment of her footprints attests, is definitely a white woman, effectively answering the questions from the start of the book "Is she a half-breed?" and "Is she an Indian?" (9) with a decided "no." Three paragraphs later, Dartt acknowledges that the Ute tribe previously enjoyed use of the hot springs but can no longer do so: "Alas for the poor Utes! They can no longer submerge their sick horses, pappooses, and puppies in its purifying waters! They were said to hold them in great reverence as possessing powers little less than miraculous. To judge from their appearance, they hold water, wherever found, as too sacred to be used except in a last extremity. It is useless to longer imagine that the picture memory holds of their utter ugliness and filth can ever be changed. Hot chemicals are no longer possible to them, and cold water would be powerless on a Ute" (198–199). The brief glimmer of sympathy for Native Americans' displacement ("Alas for the poor Utes!") is severely undercut in the scene by Dartt's denigration and mockery of the Utes with her insistence on "their utter ugliness and filth." Dartt's immediate return in the next paragraph to Maxwell's focus on searching for elk specimens abruptly ends the discussion of Native Americans, effectively signaling that they are of no real concern or consequence to her retelling of Maxwell's work. Yet the appearance of Native Americans in the periphery of *On the Plains, and Among the Peaks* provides a fuller picture of the context in which Maxwell completed her natural history work.

Animals

In contrast to her portrayal of Native Americans, Dartt offers a more nuanced and thoughtful look at the animals of the American West. She both showcases various animals as individual creatures with their own personalities and motivations and argues that their ultimate purpose is to serve as raw material for Maxwell's taxidermy. Dartt's depiction of animals as thinking, feeling creatures that, despite their sentience, must still be killed for the furtherance of scientific knowledge results in a curious and unsettling combination of feminized sentimentality and corporeal violence. Of particular note in her book are the descriptions of Maxwell's taxidermy work, her killing of specimens, the use of those specimens as commodities, and the juxtaposition of corporeal violence with feminized sentimentality. Dartt's (1879, 26) first extended discussion of Maxwell's taxidermy work is rendered in highly physical and visceral terms as she describes the "hours of careful, often intensely disagreeable work." For example, in working with a dead, rotting turkey buzzard specimen, Maxwell finds herself battling her own physical disgust and discomfort: "Too sick to endure its presence a moment longer, she would retreat for a while; but as soon as it was possible to summon the strength and resolution, go to work again. It was more than a week, however, before she recovered from the effects of such a disgusting task enough to be able to eat an ordinary meal; and it was many weeks before the mounted bird could be taken from the outer shed, that gave him shelter, and have a place among her other birds" (29–30). The physical presence of the dead buzzard and its putrefying corpse is powerful enough to disorder Maxwell's own body as a result of her close contact with it. Maxwell preferred to kill the animals herself, both so she had the opportunity to observe them alive first, which she felt gave her the ability to more accurately and truthfully present the animals after death (30), and because "it gave her the opportunity of studying the shape and disposition of prominent muscles, etc. She considered a knowledge of the anatomy of an animal as essential in taxidermy, as in sculpture, to the finest artistic effect" (109). Accurate, well-executed taxidermy, Dartt implies, requires intimate observation and contact with the animal bodies. This was in line with the increasingly professionalized field of taxidermy in the nineteenth century.

In discussing advancements in taxidermy in that century (but with no mention of Maxwell), Rachel Poliquin (2012, 72) notes that "the real poetry of taxidermy—was imparting the suggestions of life by capturing an animal's character. Ideally, taxidermy not only protected the carcasses of birds from decay, insects, and the ravages of time but preserved the elegance of life." Partly as a result of taxidermy's rising status, Maxwell's carefully prepared specimens became commodities that helped support her financially. On more than one occasion she sold her specimens, only to replenish her collection with new animals. Dartt (1879, 111) also notes that Maxwell always tried to collect "duplicate skins" when she went out hunting: "These, properly cured, could be sent to any part of the world, exchanged for skins from other lands, and were valuable for scientific institutions everywhere." Maxwell's attention to the financial potential of her work shows that she continued the practice of earlier (male) naturalists, including Hans Sloane, Mark Catesby, and John James Audubon, in recognizing the commercial potential and value of animals' bodies.

At multiple points in *On the Plains, and Among the Peaks*, Dartt emphasizes the scientific value of Maxwell's work in an effort to mitigate its inherent violence. "Ritualistically claiming the animal as a scientific specimen," Karen Jones (2015, 256) argues, "successfully neutralized questions of killing, violence, and species decline in the material environment; while the power of the taxidermy elevated the animal body to a higher status than other valuations of animal capital." Multiple scenes in the book, however, reveal that the situation was not quite as neutralized as Maxwell or Dartt might have wished. Along with the skunk scene discussed at the start of the introduction, two scenes in particular epitomize the unsettling combination of violence and sentimentality in Maxwell's work. In the first scene, Dartt (1879, 73) describes how Maxwell collects two baby birds to later kill and preserve them: "Both birds reached Boulder in safety the next day, where they were fed and cuddled, and made happy until their robes of snowy-white down were of the most desirable length, when a little chloroform induced them to stop growing. A nest, like the one they occupied in their native tree, was procured. They were stuffed, and placed in it, with their little mouths open and their necks stretched up toward their mother, which, with a rabbit in her talons, was suspended over them." The nurturing, maternal quality of this episode is quickly disturbed with the rather euphemistic description of the birds' deaths, only to have the maternal and nurturing image be re-created in the tableaux Maxwell constructs with the dead birds' bodies. The second scene concerns two bear cubs rescued by Maxwell:

> The mother of the [cubs] was killed at the same time as their capture. Ten days or more after her death, her skin being mounted, was placed in the museum. Mrs. Maxwell, to test her work and to see whether the cubs still remembered their mother, let them out into the room where she was. Selecting her from the other animals, they ran, whining, and jumped about her, licking her face, and seeming overjoyed at finding her again. But when conscious that she would not return their caresses, their grief was touching in the extreme. Standing up and stroking her face with their little paws in the most pleading manner, they licked her nose and cheeks, and moaned like two heartbroken children. It was more than Mrs. Maxwell could endure, and with tears of sympathy for their disappointment, she took them away. (178–179)

While Jones (2015, 257–258) briefly discusses this scene in her analysis of Maxwell's work, she curiously chooses to only emphasize the cubs' "affection and joy at the reunion" and makes no mention of the grief that quickly replaces the cubs' joy. An analysis of the scene in its entirety shows the changed physical, material, and maternal presence of the mother bear and how this change results in an increased visibility of the female body, both in the bear's taxidermied skin and in Maxwell's display of fellow feeling with her "tears of sympathy." It also highlights the tensions inherent in taxidermy between aesthetics and ethics, a tension theorized extensively by Poliquin.

Taxidermy, Poliquin (2012, 10) notes, "requires death of our closest compatriots—our fellow sentient creatures. Looking at dead animals necessarily engages our emotions." She argues that "by creating animal-things, taxidermy necessarily creates encounters. This is the strange, unsettling power of taxidermy; it offers—or forces—intimacies between you and an animal-thing that is no longer quite an animal but could not be mistaken for anything other than an animal" (39). Poliquin uses the term *visceral knowledge* to describe the "bodily knowing that occurs in contact with physical things, a knowing that blurs emotions with materiality and may even defy reason, logic, and explanatory language" (39). This concept of visceral knowledge ties in with post-human theories of shared double finitude and absolute materiality.

Such focus on flesh as a touchstone of shared corporeal vulnerability is common in animal studies theory. Cary Wolfe's (2012, 50) discussion of bio-politics in *Before the Law* emphasizes how beings, both human and animal, are reduced to flesh, which he labels a communal substrate that is manipulated and acted upon. This reduction of beings to flesh is also a key part of Reviel Netz's (2004, 39) theory about barbed wire, which he argues exploits the misfortune of our (humans' and animals') skin—a misfortune characterized by the fact that our skin, which contains pain-causing nerves, can be used against us as a form of control and exploitation. Barbed wire, Netz writes, reduces its victims to flesh, which becomes "a mere biological receptacle of pain and disease" (130). Shared corporeal vulnerability is also the cornerstone of Anat Pick's (2011) theory of creaturely poetics or creaturely ethics. Pick emphasizes the shared material, physical quality of humans and nonhuman animals as bodily creatures and, in doing so, tries to recast dehumanization as a potentially beneficial process (3–6). Pick advocates a creaturely poetics or ethics that aims to move beyond a kind of defensive humanism based on upholding "uniquely human" traits such as language, reason, empathy, and so on and instead moves toward a recognition of the experience of corporeal vulnerability shared by all creatures (193).

That experience of visceral knowledge "forces each viewer to confront the troubled relationship between the aesthetics and ethics of taxidermy: the compelling urge to look and the worry about what made that look-ing possible" (Poliquin 2012, 50). And while Poliquin rightly identifies the "painfully, powerfully beautiful" quality of taxidermy (50), there also exists a sense of imagination and play in which viewers must engage. To appreciate a taxidermy specimen in a museum, viewers must, according to Stephen T. Asma (2001, 38), "oscillate between knowing that it's a man-made construction and suspending [their] disbelief to enter into a play-along relationship with the display." Yet Poliquin and Asma are focused on the implications of human encounters with taxidermied specimens. The scene of the bear cubs that Dartt depicts introduces the prospect of ani-mals themselves as spectators of taxidermy. What do still-living animals make of taxidermied animal specimens, especially if those specimens were family members?

Because people can very easily recognize and identify with mother-child relationships in animals, they become a crucial bridge to understanding and appreciating the intelligence, sentience, and emotional richness of the non-human world—which, in turn, leads to greater awareness and consideration of humans' ethical responsibility to nonhuman animals. The perverse, disturbing image of dead stuffed mother and living inconsolable cubs combines the sympathetic identification of animals' familial relationships with the "visceral knowledge" of the taxidermied dead animal specimen. Human perception, emotion, and ethics become embodied and entangled with still-living animals' perception and bodies; at the root of that entanglement is the dead animal-object, the taxidermied animal, whose materiality has shifted and changed—not enough to be completely different but just enough to unsettle and dissolve the boundaries between human and animal, living and dead.

EPILOGUE AND CONCLUSION

After the centennial, Maxwell moved to Boston in 1878, where she enrolled in several science classes at the Women's Laboratory of the Massachusetts Institute of Technology; while there, she gave taxidermy lessons to help pay her tuition. Although she made two brief trips back to Boulder due to reports of her mother's failing health, Maxwell remained on the East Coast for the remainder of her life. In 1879, she moved to Brooklyn, New York, and leased land on Rockaway Beach, Long Island, to establish a seaside resort that would include a museum to house her collection. Her bathhouse/museum opened in 1880 but was not financially successful. During her time in New York, Maxwell's health began to fail. In addition, her marriage to James had been slowly deteriorating since the centennial; several factors contributed to their estrangement, including money issues, James's lack of support for Martha's work, and their long separation (James had remained in Colorado when Martha moved east). After Maxwell's death from an ovarian tumor in 1881, Mabel traveled to Rockaway Beach to try to turn her mother's business around; while she was able to pay off Maxwell's debts, she did not have enough money to move the collection. Mabel tried to find a museum or university willing to purchase the collection but found no takers (possibly because of its enormous size). By the time various scientific institutions realized the value of Maxwell's collection both to science and to history, it was too late.

There are a few competing narratives of what became of the collection. Henderson (1915) notes that her first collection, which was sold to Shaw's Garden in St. Louis, Missouri, in 1870, was not taken care of and had become degraded to the point of being unsalvageable (91) and that her *Woman's Work* collection eventually ended up in Saratoga Springs, New York, where a "large portion" of it was destroyed in a fire and the remainder "passed into the hands of a curio collector, who took no care of it" (90). Marcia Myers Bonta (1991, 44) notes that a few specimens remain at the Smithsonian's Arts and Industries Museum as part of an exhibit on the original 1876 centennial, but I have been unable to verify this, and it is the only reference to the existence of surviving specimens of Maxwell's taxidermy. Mary Dartt Thompson published a report titled "What Became of Mrs. Maxwell's Natural History Collection?" that was presented to the Colorado Historical Society in 1924 and was included in the epilogue of Benson's biography on Maxwell. Dartt Thompson began attempting to trace Maxwell's collection in 1893. She reports that Mabel had left it in the care of J. P. Haskins of Saratoga Springs in 1882. The collection, Dartt Thompson discovered, had been improperly stored and handled; attempts to salvage it were unsuccessful due to lack of interest from scientific institutions, unreasonable demands by Haskins, and the poor condition of specimens (which were either too expensive to repair or beyond repair). By the time there was enough serious interest from the State University of Colorado, around 1906, to acquire and preserve what remained of the collection, it was too far gone, and the matter was given up entirely by 1920. In her report, Dartt Thompson notes rather succinctly: "The story of Mrs. Maxwell's Collection is ended" (quoted in Benson 1986, 201).

Mary Dartt Thompson lived to be ninety-eight years old; she had three children, a son who died in infancy and two daughters; she "helped found the Laurel, Maryland, free public library, the woman's club in Laurel, and the Prince George's County Federation of Women's clubs" (Benson 1986, 202). Dartt Thompson died in 1940 in East Falls Church, Virginia.

On the Plains, and Among the Peaks tells the story of a woman whose lifelong passion and dedication to work and education made her a pioneer in more ways than one. It catalogs Maxwell's important scientific contributions and development of museum habitat groupings and lifelike taxidermy mounts, showcases engaging accounts of wilderness excursions on the frontier of the western United States in the 1860 and 1870s, and testifies to a woman's determination to show through her work that women were capable of succeeding in traditionally male-dominated fields.

NOTES

1. See Amato (2015), 202; Asma (2001), xii.

2. Notably, Poliquin's excellent comprehensive study of taxidermy, *The Breathless Zoo*, makes no mention of Maxwell.

3. Martha Maxwell to Marianne Dascomb, November 11, 1874. Martha Maxwell Collection (1821–1957), Hart Research Library, History Colorado Center, Denver (italics in the original).

4. Dartt includes excerpts of two reviews of the museum in *On the Plains, and Among the Peaks*. See chapter 2 and chapter 24.

5. As with Poliquin and Baym, Gianquitto does not mention Maxwell or Dartt in her book.

6. Newspaper clipping part of a scrapbook included in the Martha Maxwell Collection (1821–1957), Hart Research Library, History Colorado Center, Denver.

REFERENCES

Allen, Joel A. 1879. "A Woman's Work as a Naturalist." *Bulletin of the Nuttall Ornithological Club* 4, no. 2: 113–114.

Amato, Sarah. 2015. *Beastly Possessions: Animals in Victorian Culture*. Toronto: University of Toronto Press.

Asma, Stephen T. 2001. *Stuffed Animals and Pickled Heads: The Culture and Evolution of Natural History Museums*. Oxford: Oxford University Press.

Baym, Nina. 2012. *Women Writers of the American West, 1833–1927*. Urbana: University of Illinois Press.

Benson, Maxine. 1986. *Martha Maxwell: Rocky Mountain Naturalist*. Lincoln: University of Nebraska Press.

Bonta, Marcia Myers. 1991. *Women in the Field: America's Pioneering Women Naturalists*. College Station: Texas A&M University Press.

Brace, Mabel Maxwell. 1948. *Thanks to Abigail: A Family Chronicle*. Privately printed.

Browder, Laura. 2009. *Her Best Shot: Women and Guns in America*. Chapel Hill: University of North Carolina Press.

"The Colorado Naturalist." 1876. *The New Century for Woman* 8, July 1, n.p.

Coues, Elliott. 1879. "Notice of Mrs. Maxwell's Exhibit of Colorado Mammals."
1879. In *On the Plains, and Among the Peaks; or, How Mrs. Maxwell Made Her Natural*

History Collection, by Mary Dartt, 217–225. Philadelphia: Claxton, Remsen & Haffelfinger.

Dartt, Mary. 1879. *On the Plains, and Among the Peaks; or, How Mrs. Maxwell Made Her Natural History Collection*. Philadelphia: Claxton, Remsen & Haffelfinger.

Gianquitto, Tina. 2010. *"Good Observers of Nature": American Women and the Scientific Study of the Natural World, 1820–1885*. Athens: University of Georgia Press.

Henderson, Junius. 1915. "A Pioneer Venture in Habitat Grouping." *Proceedings of the American Association of Museums* 9: 87–91.

Jones, Karen R. 2015. *Epiphany in the Wilderness: Hunting Nature and Performance in the Nineteenth-Century American West*. Boulder: University Press of Colorado.

Jones, Karen R., and John Wills. 2009. *American West: Competing Visions*. Edinburgh: Edinburgh University Press.

Madsen-Brooks, Leslie. 2009. "Challenging Science as Usual: Women's Participation in American Natural History Museum Work, 1870–1950." *Journal of Women's History* 21, no. 2: 11–38.

Moring, John. 2005. *Early American Naturalists: Exploring the American West, 1804–1900*. Lanham, MD: Taylor Trade Publishing.

"Mrs. Maxwell's Rocky Mountain Museum." 1876. *Harper's Bazaar*, November 11, 730.

Netz, Reviel. 2004. *Barbed Wire: An Ecology of Modernity*. Middletown, CT: Wesleyan University Press.

Pick, Anat. 2011. *Creaturely Poetics: Animality and Vulnerability in Literature and Film*. New York: Columbia University Press.

Poliquin, Rachel. 2012. *The Breathless Zoo: Taxidermy and the Cultures of Longing*. University Park: Pennsylvania State University Press.

Ridgway, Robert. 1879. "Mrs. Maxwell's Colorado Museum. Catalogue of the Birds." In *On the Plains, and Among the Peaks; or, How Mrs. Maxwell Made Her Natural History Collection*, by Mary Dartt, 226–237. Philadelphia: Claxton, Remsen & Haffelfinger.

Ritvo, Harriet. 1987. *The Animal Estate: The English and Other Creatures in the Victorian Age*. Cambridge, MA: Harvard University Press.

Shally-Jensen, Michael. 2014. *American West (1836–1900)*. Ipswich, MA: Salem Press.

"A Suitable Book for Holiday Presents. Just Published. *On the Plains and Among the Peaks*." Claxton, Remsen, and Haffelfinger, Philadelphia. n.d.

Thompson, Mary Dartt. 1924. "What Became of Mrs. Maxwell's Natural History Collection?" November 28. Typeset copies at the History Colorado Center and in the Smithsonian archives.

Wolfe, Cary. 2012. *Before the Law: Humans and Other Animals in a Biopolitical Frame*. Chicago: University of Chicago Press.

Note on the Text

In its initial publication, *On the Plains, and Among the Peaks* went through two printings and one edition. There is no edition currently in print beyond on-demand printing of facsimile copies.

On the Plains, and Among the Peaks lacks formal chapter titles and numbers; instead, it is divided into chapter-like sections. The printers, the Philadelphia firm Claxton, Remsen and Haffelfinger, added descriptive subject headings at the top of each page. In this edition, these headings have been used to mark the start of each new section, which have been numbered. These two editorial decisions impart a sense of organization to the work that aids modern readers while not drastically departing from the format of its original publication.

The illustrations included in the text were in the original text and have been placed as close as possible to their original placement.

All spellings, punctuation, grammar, and typographical features, including italics and several instances of question and exclamation marks in parentheses (?) (!), are preserved from the original text. In some instances, clear grammatical errors are marked with square brackets.

On the Plains,
and
Among The Peaks.
Or,
How Mrs. Maxwell
Made Her
Natural History Collection

By
Mary Dartt.
Philadelphia:
Claxton, Remsen & Haffelfinger,
624, 626 & 628 Market. Street.
1879.

EXPOSITION COLLECTION.

FIGURE 0.4. Exposition collection

To
Spencer F. Baird,
The Sympathetic Friend of Nature's Friends,
as well as
Distinguished Naturalist,
This Sketch of an Amateur's Work
IS
RESPECTFULLY DEDICATED.[1]

---

1. Spencer Fullerton Baird (1823–1887) was an American naturalist and one of the foremost ornithologists of the late nineteenth century. He was the first curator of the Smithsonian Institution and served as assistant secretary of the Smithsonian from 1850 to 1878. He frequently corresponded with Martha Maxwell; Maxwell would send him bird specimens, and, in return, Baird would send her catalogs of birds and mammals to further aid her study of the natural sciences.

FIGURE 0.5. M. A. Maxwell

On the Plains,
and
Among the Peaks.

1

CURIOUS PEOPLE.

"'Woman's Work!' What does that mean? Can it be possible any one wishes us to believe a *woman* did all this?"[2]

"Couldn't say—I'm pretty sure I shan't stretch my credulity so much—it would ruin the article!"

"I should think so! Why one might think the ark just landed here!—buffaloes, bears, birds, wild-cats, mice, and who but Noah or Agassiz[3] could

---

2. Martha Maxwell's exhibit at the Philadelphia Centennial International Exposition of 1876 was titled *Woman's Work*. Included as part of Colorado's exhibit in the Kansas and Colorado Building, her taxidermy tableaux included 47 mammal species and 224 bird species arranged in natural groupings on an artificial landscape of mountain ledges, plains, and running water.

3. Louis Agassiz (1807–1873), a Swiss naturalist who emigrated to the United States in 1847, was one of the best-known naturalists in nineteenth-century America. He was instrumental in the establishment of the Lawrence Scientific School at Harvard University in 1847, where he was appointed professor of zoology and geology and later founded its Museum of Comparative Zoology in 1859. In addition to making extensive contributions to zoology and improvements to taxonomy and nomenclature, Agassiz was one of the leading critics against Darwinian evolution, favoring instead the

name what else! There must be hundreds of these creatures!" and the last speaker turned to me with the question:

"Does that placard really mean to tell us a woman mounted all these animals?" with an inclusive wave of a handsomely gloved hand.

"Yes," I replied.[4]

Instantly a dozen lips were parted and questions fell, "like leaves in Vallambrosa,"[5] upon my innocent ears.

"How could a woman do it?"

"What did she do it for?"

"Did she *kill* any of the animals?"

"Well, I never! Can a body see her?"

"What sort of a woman is she?"

"Are you the one?"

It was my first day at the Centennial, and I had volunteered to relieve Mrs. Maxwell by standing for an hour, and answering questions behind the iron paling that separated her "Natural History Collection" from the rest of the Kansas and Colorado Building, one side of a wing of which it occupied.[6]

Within the enclosure was a miniature landscape, representing a plain, and a mountainside, apparently formed of rocks and crowned with evergreens.

---

theory of special creation. He was also one of the major supporters of the theory of polygensim, a theory central to scientific racism in the nineteenth century that posits that the human races were created separately and did not have one common ancestor.

4. The speaker here is Mary Dartt, the author and Maxwell's half-sister. Mary Dartt graduated from the Baraboo Collegiate Institute in Wisconsin in 1865 and then taught at Catharine Beecher's Milwaukee Female College until she moved to Boulder to join the Maxwells in 1868. She frequently accompanied Maxwell and her husband on their excursions in the Rocky Mountains to collect specimens. Dartt married minister Nathan Thompson in 1870, and in 1875 they moved to Massachusetts. She lived to be ninety-eight years old, dying in 1940 in East Falls Church, Virginia. She had three children: a son who died in infancy and two daughters.

5. A reference to Vallombrosa, which Dartt spells as *Vallambrosa*, mentioned in Book I of John Milton's *Paradise Lost* (1667): "Thick as autumnal leaves that strew the brooks / In Vallombrosa, where th' Etruscan shades / High over-arch'd imbow'r." Vallombrosa is a Benedictine monastery founded in 1038 and located just outside Florence, Italy.

6. The Kansas and Colorado Building, located near the Women's Pavilion, was one of the buildings at the Centennial International Exposition of 1876 in Philadelphia. More than 200 buildings made up the exposition, including the Main Exhibition Building, Horticultural Hall, Memorial Hall, Agricultural Hall, the Women's Building, and additional buildings for individual states and foreign governments. Maxwell's exhibit took up one whole wall of the Kansas and Colorado Building.

Down the rugged descent leaped a little stream of sparkling water, which expanded at its base into a tiny lake, edged with pebbles and fringed, as was the brook-side, with growing grass and ferns. The water and the banks which confined it were peopled by aquatic creatures: fishes swimming in the lake—turtles sunning themselves on its half submerged rocks, while beavers, muskrats and water-fowl seemed at home upon its margin. Between the cascade and lakelet appeared the irregular vine-fringed mouth of a cave, its dark moss-grown recesses soon lost from sight in shadowy gloom. Above it and upon the upper heights of the mountain side—suggesting the altitudes at which they are found—were grouped those animals that frequent the Rocky Mountains; fierce bears, shy mountain sheep, savage mountain lions or pumas, and a multitude of smaller creatures, each in an attitude of life-like action. On the limited space allowed to represent the Plains that stretch eastward from that elevated chain were huge buffaloes, elk, antelope, and their native neighbors. The attitudes and surroundings of all were so artistic and unique as to form an attraction even among the many fascinations of the century's gathered productions.[7]

As the landscape was designed and made, the animals procured, stuffed and arranged upon it, by a woman, Mrs. M. A. Maxwell, the words *"Woman's Work"* were printed on a card suspended near the cave.[8] It was this which called forth the exclamation we first mentioned.

From the opening of the Exhibition gates in the morning until darkness made sight-seeing impossible, thousands of people pushed and crowded and jammed and jostled each other against the railing of that mimic landscape.

The idea of facing so many was at first not a little terrifying, but I fortified my courage with the thought of relieving Mrs. Maxwell, and that the American people are usually so polite, the task could not be a very unpleasant one. Alas! I had never measured their capacity for asking questions!

I had not finished assuring the large fat man in the white hat that I was by no means the person who had performed the work he saw before him, when the tall woman in the linen duster, and the short one in the white finger-puffs, and the young one in the idiot fringe,[9] and the old gentleman with the

---

7. Additional photographs of Maxwell's exhibit are included at the end of this book.
8. Maxwell's decision to title her centennial exhibit *Woman's Work* seems to reflect an awareness of how inextricably linked her gender was to her work.
9. An archaic slang term for a woman's hairstyle worn in a fringe.

gold-headed cane, and the man with the blue cotton umbrella, and the rough with the battered felt, and—I couldn't possibly begin to tell who else—all began at once to ask:

"Is she a young woman?"

"Is she married?"

"Where is she at?"

"Did she kill all these animals?"

"Did she kill them all?"

"How did she do it?"

"What did she do it with?"

"Where did she get them?"

"How did she stuff 'em?"

"Did she kill 'em *all?*"

"Did she kill them buf'lo" (I positively believe this question, with variations to suit linguistic attainments of different speakers, to have been asked, on average, every ten minutes through all the Exhibition!)?

"I don't believe them critters was shot; I've looked 'em all over and I can't see any holes. Did she pisen 'em?"

"Does she live in that cave?"

"Is all this (with a gesture) made to represent the place and the cave she lived in in Colorado?"

"Is game as thick as this all over the Rocky Mountains?"

"If she's married, why ain't it called *Mr.* Maxwell's collection?"

"How old is she?"

"Is she good-looking?"

"Has she any children?"

"Is she a half-breed?"

"Is she an Indian?" and as that crowd surged by, another wave continued the inundation of like questions![10]

---

10. In the mid- to late nineteenth century, it was not uncommon for women to be naturalists or proficient gun users. What seems to be unusual in Maxwell's case is the combination of a woman both engaging in big game hunting and skillfully preparing aesthetically pleasing and edifying scientific specimens. In addition to the questions Dartt recounts here, reviews of Maxwell's work repeatedly show a similar focus on her gender and appearance. See, for example, "Mrs. Maxwell's Rocky Mountain Museum," *Harper's Bazaar*, November 11, 1876, 730; Junius Henderson, "A Pioneer Venture in Habitat Grouping," *Proceedings of the American Association of Museums 9*

I kept hold of my departing senses with an effort, and leaned forward to catch the words of some dear old Quaker ladies. They were asking in soft, confiding voices:

"Will thee be so kind as to tell us something of the history of this collection?"

Blessings on their sweet, motherly faces! I would have attempted anything for them!

Gentlemen of scientific proclivities echoed the request—people of all kinds repeated it with an emphatic, "Do tell us who she is, and how she did it!"

The promise was made, and, though it is rather late, here is its fulfilment!

(1915): 87–91. For more on women and guns, see Laura Browder, *Her Best Shot: Women and Guns in America* (Chapel Hill: University of North Carolina Press, 2009). For more on women naturalists in the nineteenth century, see Tina Gianquitto, *"Good Observers of Nature": American Women and the Scientific Study of the Natural World, 1820–1885* (Athens: University of Georgia Press, 2010).

2

THE MOUNTAIN MUSEUM. DRAMATIC
TAXIDERMY. COMIC ART.

Mrs. Maxwell is the woman who made a collection of the animals of Colorado, procuring herself, either by shooting, poisoning, trapping, buying, or soliciting from her acquaintances, specimens of almost every kind of living creature found in that region, skinning, stuffing, or in other ways preserving them.

Colorado commissioned her to represent with this collection the fauna of its mountains and plains. She complied by arranging, singly, or in artistic groups, upon or near the miniature landscape we have described, over a hundred mammals and nearly four hundred birds. Before leaving Colorado she had these and many other objects of interest gathered in a museum,[11] an idea

---

11. The Rocky Mountain Museum opened in Boulder, Colorado, in June 1874 and charged twenty-five cents a ticket. Maxwell intended the museum to serve multiple functions, simultaneously contributing to scientific knowledge, educating the public (especially children and young women), and providing popular entertainment and curiosities. The centerpiece of the museum was Maxwell's taxidermy placed in her signature habitat groupings; however, the museum also featured other curiosities from human history. The museum was moved to the more populous and tourist-heavy Denver in 1875 in an effort to make it more profitable, but the museum was never financially successful.

of which can be obtained from the graceful pen of H.H., in "Bits of Travel at Home," in the *N. Y. Independent*:[12]

"On a corner of one of the streets in Boulder is a building with a narrow and somewhat rickety staircase leading up on the outside. At the top of the staircase is the sign, 'Museum.'

"'What a place to find a museum, to be sure!' and 'Museum of what?' are the instinctive comments of the traveller at the sight of this sign. The chances are a hundred to one that he will not go up the stairs and will never give the sign a second thought. Yet whosoever visits Boulder and goes away without seeing this museum loses one of the most interesting and character-istic things in Colorado. I smile to recollect how it was only an idle and not altogether good-natured curiosity which led me to visit it. Somebody said in my hearing that all the animals in the museum were shot and stuffed by Mrs. Maxwell herself, and the collection was nearly a complete one of the native animals of Colorado. That a pioneer woman should shoot wild cats and grizzlies seemed not unnatural or improbable; but that the same woman who could fire a rifle so well could also stuff an animal with any sort of skill or artistic effect seemed very unlikely. I went to the museum expecting to be much amused by a grotesque exhibition of stiff and ungainly corpses of beasts, only interesting as tokens of the prowess of a woman in a wilder-ness life.

"I stopped short on the threshold in utter amazement. The door opened into a little vestibule room, with a centre-table piled with books on natu-ral history; shelves containing minerals ranged on the walls, and a great deer standing by the table, in as easy and natural a position as if he had just walked in. This was Mrs. Maxwell's reading-room and study. On the right hand a door stood open into the museum. The first thing upon which my eyes fell was a black-and-tan terrier, lying on a mat. Not until after a second or two did the strange stillness of the creature suggest to me that it was not alive. Even after I had stood close by its side I could hardly believe it. As I moved about the room, I found myself looking back at it, from point after point, and wherever we went its eyes followed us, as the motionless eyes of a good portrait will always seem to follow one about. There was not a single

---

12. Helen Hunt, a poet and essayist who moved to Colorado Springs, Colorado, in 1873, married railroad promoter William S. Jackson in 1873. Her article "Mrs. Maxwell's Museum" was published in the *New York Independent* on September 23, 1875.

view in which he did not look as alive as a live dog can when he does not stir. This dog alone is enough to prove Mrs. Maxwell's claim to be called an artist.

"In the opposite corner was a huge bison, head down, forefeet planted wide apart and at a slant, eyes viciously glaring at the door—as distinct a charge as ever bison made. Next to him, on a high perch, was a huge eagle, flying with outstretched wings, carrying in his claws the limp body of a lamb. High about them a row of unblinking owls, labelled

"'THE NIGHT WATCH.'

In a cage on the floor were two tiny young owls, so gray and fluffy they looked like little more than owls' heads fastened on feather pincushions. Mrs. Maxwell opened the cage and let them out. One of them flew instantly up to its companions on the shelf, perched itself solemnly in the row, and sat there motionless, except for now and then lolling its head to right or left. The effect of this on the expression of the whole row of stuffed owls was something indescribable. It would have surprised nobody at any minute if one and all they had begun to loll their heads.

"The walls of the room were filled with the usual glass-doored cases of shelves, and, to our great surprise, there were curiosities from all parts of the world. Japanese, Chinese, Alaskan, Indian—the collection was wonderfully varied. Mrs. Maxwell has the insatiable passion of a born collector, and, having visited San Francisco, has had opportunities of gratifying it to a degree one would not have believed possible. The collection of minerals and ores of the territory is a very full and interesting one. There are also fine collections of shells from various countries. These and the other foreign curiosities she has obtained by exchange and by purchase.

"The distinctive feature of the museum, however, is a dramatic group of animals placed at the further end of the room.[13] Here are arranged mounds of earth, rocks, and pine trees, in a by no means bad imitation of a wild, rocky landscape. And among these rocks and trees are grouped the stuffed animals, in their families, in pairs, or singly, and every one in a most life-like and significant attitude. A doe is licking two exquisite little fawns, while the stag looks on with a proud expression. A bear is crawling out of the

---

13. Photographs of some of Maxwell's taxidermy from the Rocky Mountain Museum are included at the end of this book.

mouth of a cave. A fox is slyly prowling along, ready to spring on a rabbit. A mountain lion is springing literally through the branches of a tree on a deer, who is running for [its] life, with eyes bloodshot, tongue out, and every muscle tense and strained. Three mountain sheep—father, mother, and a little one—are climbing a rocky precipice. A group of ptarmigans shows the three colors—winter, spring, and summer. A mother grouse is clucking about with a brood of chickens in the most inimitably natural way. And last, not least, in an out-of-way corner is a touch of drollery for the children—a little wooden house, like a dog-kennel, and coming out of the door a very tiny squirrel, on his hind legs, with a very tiny, yellow duckling hanging on his arm. The conscious strut, the grotesque love-making of the pair is as positive and as ludicrous as anything ever seen in a German picture-book.[14] Only the most artistic arrangement of every fibre, every feather, every hair could have produced such a result. We laughed till we were glad to sit down on the railing, close to the grizzly bear, and rest.

"But a funnier thing still was on the left hand—a group of monkeys sitting round a small table playing poker. One scratching his head and scowling in perplexity and dismay at his bad cards, and another leaning back smirking with satisfaction over his certain triumph with his aces; one smoking with a nonchalant air; and all so absorbed in the game that they do not see the monkey on the floor, who is reaching up a cautious paw and drawing the stakes—a ten dollar bill—off the edge of the table.[15] Beard himself never painted a droller group of monkeys, nor [sic] one half so lifelike.[16] It will

---

14. Possibly referring to English translations of Goethe's retelling of *Reynard the Fox*, several editions of which were published in English with accompanying illustrations of anthropomorphic animals.

15. These two comic taxidermy tableaux bear a striking resemblance to two tableaux Maxwell saw at Woodward's Gardens in San Francisco during her trip to California in 1873. This type of taxidermy is a sub-genre known as anthropomorphic taxidermy, which became popular in the Victorian era and generally featured animals frequently dressed in human clothes and engaged in human activities. Two of the most famous British practitioners of the time were Walter Potter and Hermann Ploucquet. See Connor Creaney, "Paralytic Animation: The Anthropomorphic Taxidermy of Walter Potter," *Victorian Studies* 53, no. 1 (2010): 7–35; Michelle Henning, "Anthropomorphic Taxidermy and the Death of Nature: The Curious Art of Hermann Ploucquet, Walter Potter, and Charles Waterton," *Victorian Literature and Culture* 35 (2007): 663–678.

16. William Holbrook Beard (1824–1900) was an American painter known for satiric paintings of animals, including numerous ones featuring monkeys.

always be a mystery to me how to these dead, stiff faces Mrs. Maxwell suc-
ceeds in giving so live and keen and individual a look.

"The collection of birds is a beautiful one, nearly exhaustive of the
Colorado birds and containing many fine specimens from other countries."[17]

. . . .

Of course only the Colorado department of this museum was represented
at the Centennial, yet its groups of animals and birds were so numerous
and so instinct with something fresh and lifelike, that, weary as I became of
ceaseless questions, I could but sympathize with the desire to know what
circumstances could have enabled a woman to develop artistic power in such
a direction, and what motive could have inspired her, even with any amount
of skill, to undertake such a herculean enterprise.

---

17. The page break below is original to the published text and marks the end of the
     quoted section from Helen Hunt's review of the Rocky Mountain Museum.

3

THE LADY HERSELF. IN WISCONSIN. WISCONSIN
ACADEMY. SQUATTING. BREAKING A CONTRACT.
FIRST LESSONS. INGENIOUS SUCCESS.

In introducing Mrs. Maxwell to those who have never seen her, it may be well to premise that she is neither an Indian, nor half-breed, nor an Amazon, nor, despite the title of "Colorado Huntress," which many newspapers have given her, one who, thirsting for notoriety, seized deadly weapons and went out on a crusade against the animal kingdom.

On the contrary, she is a wee, modest, tender-hearted woman, lacking one inch of five feet in height, and "as shy as one of her own weasels!"

She simply has a passion, not unknown in the history of science, for all living creatures—an irresistible desire to study their habits and relations, together with a taste for the expression of beauty in form, that would have made her a sculptor had she been placed in circumstances to have cultivated it.

She began the practice of an art so unusual for a woman as taxidermy, then, in the following manner:

After a residence of three years in Colorado during its earliest settlement, she was recalled to Wisconsin by the serious illness of her mother.[18] She found her sisters,[19] whom she had left as little girls, young ladies in school. The institution they were attending was a new one, with little in its possession save unlimited hope for the future.[20] In this the girls owned large investments!

They were charmed with their studies, and enthusiastic admirers of their teachers, and Mrs. Maxwell was soon one with them in all their plans and interests.

Professor Hobart, the principal of their school, was very fond of the natural sciences, and was devoting no small amount of time and labor to the formation of a cabinet of natural history. He had the art of imparting his enthusiasm to his scholars, and many of them count as among the pleasantest recollections of their lives the memory of the long rambles over hills and beside streams, in which they were invited to join him for the study of nature from his stand-point of loving admiration.

It was in connection with the formation of this cabinet that Mrs. Maxwell made her *debut* as a taxidermist.

"We must have a Department of Zoology; can't some of you young ladies, who have more skillful fingers than I, assist me in putting up some birds?" asked the professor one day.

Her sisters declined the task, but recommended her as possessing the elements of touch and taste which they lacked. They recalled her account of an amusing attempt to learn taxidermy, which occurred just before her return

---

18. Maxwell's mother, Amy Sanford Dartt (1805–1901), married Spencer Dartt on June 25, 1830; Martha was their only child. Following Spencer's death from scarlet fever in 1833, Amy Sanford married Spencer's first cousin Josiah Dartt in 1841, and the couple had two daughters, Maxwell's half-sisters: Mary Emma (b. 1842) and Sarah Elizabeth (b. 1844). Maxwell's first stay in Boulder (1860–1862) was cut short in fall of 1862 when she received word of Dartt's illness. Maxwell stayed in Wisconsin for the next six years, returning to Colorado in 1868. Amy Dartt, along with her second husband, Josiah Dartt, eventually joined the Maxwells in Boulder in 1873.

19. Dartt switches from first person to third person here.

20. The Baraboo Collegiate Institute was a coed school founded in 1854 in Baraboo, Wisconsin. In 1861, Professor E. F. Hobart became its principal and pushed for more emphasis on natural science education and the need for a collection of mounted animal specimens, which would be Maxwell's first foray into the art of taxidermy. Maxwell's two half-sisters, Mary Dartt and Sarah Dartt, attended the Baraboo Collegiate Institute.

home.[21] During a temporary business visit of her husband to the East, she had purchased a ranch on the plains, a few miles below Denver. Need I explain that Coloradoans have appropriated a number of words from the Spanish which seem more appropriate to that country than their English synonyms. "Ranch" is one of them, and means any kind of a farm.[22] The one in question was a wholly unimproved portion of the plains; its only trace of human occupancy being a mud-and-pole cabin. It was before the days of any government organization of that region, and the way in which such property was obtained was by putting up something that, by common consent, could be called a house, and, in the expressive dialect of the frontier, "squatting!" The one that "squatted" first had the right to sell or to continue "squatting," and her purchase was of this right. Upon her husband's return they wished to leave the mines at Central, where they had been living, and cultivate her claim.

Meantime, finding the cabin before mentioned empty, a German had concluded to perform a feat then common at the West, *i.e.*, "jump" their claim. This meant to take and retain possession of it, unless forcibly removed.[23]

When they arrived they found him cozily ensconced under their shelter, surrounded by his camp equipage and a number of birds which he had mounted. They were the first unfinished specimens of taxidermy Mrs. Maxwell had ever seen, and she was fascinated with the idea of learning to preserve the strange creatures of that new land, and offered to pay almost any price if he would give her the necessary instruction.

After exacting a promise that she would not practise the art in Denver, then a thriving mining camp, he agreed to give her the needful lessons at ten dollars apiece, beginning the next day.

She came promptly at the appointed hour, full of the most enthusiastic anticipations, only to be told he had changed his mind "because she was a *woman!*"

As he expressed it:

---

21. Just before Maxwell moved from Boulder back to Baraboo, Wisconsin.

22. A borrowing from the Spanish word *rancho*; first appears in the United States in the early nineteenth century.

23. These kinds of informal rules of occupancy and land possession were upheld by Colorado's territorial legislature. There were actually three men "squatting" on the Maxwells' ranch. While the German taxidermist's name is unknown, the other two men, David Wood and Thomas Rease, were named in an arbitration hearing that ruled in 1861 in favor of the Maxwells' claim on the ranch.

"Vimin is besser as men mit den hands in shmall verks. Ven you know dis pisness you makes de pirds and peasts so quicker as I; you leave me no more verk at all! Es is besser fur me I keeps vat I knows mit mineself!"[24]

It was in vain she assured him she wished to learn only for her own gratification; he insisted it "vas besser" for him "to keep vat he knew mit" himself! Prophetic Teuton![25]

Two weeks after this—a court of squatters having in the meantime decided that he was an unwarranted intruder upon those premises; a verdict which he treated with sublime indifference—he had an occasion given him to remember his would-be-scholar by seeing his assertion of "vimins" superiority in some things verified.

Possession in those days was *ten* points in the law. Mrs. Maxwell had no idea of a surrender, and keeping watch of the disputed cabin from a neighboring ranch, made a raid upon it one day during his absence. Withdrawing the staple, which held his padlock, from the door-frame, she entered, and carefully gathering up his earthly effects, removed them to a convenient point on the plains, where she left them in a neat pile to await his further disposition, while she proceeded to adjust things to her own mind in the recovered domicile!

Among his possessions were not the birds she had seen—those he had already sold—but others in an early stage of preparation. Of them she felt at liberty to make a critical examination, and gather an idea of the materials he used in stuffing them, if nothing more.

Her sisters knew she would be only too glad to assist their teacher in his proposed experiment, so the collection was undertaken.

There was no taxidermist in the place, but a gentleman who was fond of field sports, and had learned something of the principles of "making skins," gave them the benefit of his knowledge, and they obtained what further

---

24. Dartt (1879, 20) seems to use the character of the German taxidermist as a foil for her broader argument "that capacity and ability, rather than birth, color, sex, or anything else, should determine where individuals belong, and what they shall do." By the late nineteenth century, taxidermy was both a skill that was difficult to master effectively and an occupation in which only a few could achieve enough success to make a living solely from their taxidermy work. For more on taxidermy as an occupation, see Sarah Amato, *Beastly Possessions: Animals in Victorian Culture* (Toronto: University of Toronto Press, 2015).

25. Teuton refers to a native of Germany or person of German origin.

information they could from the limited printed matter within their reach, Mrs. Maxwell's ingenuity supplying the rest.[26]

The professor procured the birds, and was to do the unpleasant work; she was to look on, suggest and give the finishing touches.

An amusing time they had mounting their first birds! After laboring long and faithfully over one which it was agreed they *must* save, in the vain endeavor to make its rumpled feather lay down, a brilliant idea suggested itself. "I'll tell you!" said Mrs. Maxwell; "we'll get a nest and put the bird up fighting! Of course, in that case, it would be all bristled up, and its feathers standing every way."

The nest was found, the bird perched on its edge, a few touches given it by her artistic fingers, and it had all the appearance of an enraged mother on the defensive! The next step was to procure a bird with which it could properly be fighting, and mount him in a suitable attitude. This done, the group was voted a complete success by the little circle interested in it.

It is needless to say the collection so begun never grew to be at all large.

The school did not receive pecuniary assistance that would allow of their going to any expense, and neither she nor the professor had a surplus of elegant leisure which they could donate to it. But the effort was successful in one thing—it showed to Mrs. Maxwell what a wonderful field for artistic effect taxidermy presented. Her mind, ever longing for methods of expression in forms of beauty, was captivated by it, and to be able to reproduce the characteristic grace and *abandon* of each animal's life became her dream as truly as it was ever Rosa Bonheur's.[27]

---

26. It is unclear which specific taxidermy guides Maxwell might have consulted. Based on their publication dates, possibilities include Sarah Lee, *Taxidermy, or the Art of Collecting, Preparing, and Mounting Objects of Natural History for the Use of Museums and Travellers* (London: Longman, Hurst, Rees, Orme, and Brown, 1821); William Swainson, *Taxidermy, Bibliography and Biography* (London: Longman, Hurst, Rees, Orme, and Brown, 1840); Charles Waterton, *Essays on Natural History* (London: Longman, Brown, Green, Longmans, and Roberts, 1858).

27. Rosa Bonheur (1822–1899) was a French painter and sculptor famous for her realistic paintings of animals. Similar to Maxwell, Bonheur had a childhood fascination with animals that influenced her artistic endeavors, and she engaged in scientific study of animals as part of her artistic process.

4

━ ━ ━

PEEWITT'S NEST.

A field for the exercise of her new enthusiasm was not long wanting.[28] About this time her father's family removed from the village of Baraboo to their old homestead at the "Peewitt's Nest," three miles distant.[29]

---

28. Maxwell returned to Baraboo in 1862 after she received word that her mother was seriously ill. While there, Maxwell was reunited with her daughter, Mabel, but her husband, James, remained in Boulder, only making occasional visits to Baraboo. She also began her work as a taxidermist during this time. Maxwell's health declined while she was in Wisconsin. She entered a sanitarium, the Western Health Reform Institute in Battle Creek, Michigan, in the fall of 1866 and remained there until spring 1867. Although it is unclear what specific ailments, physical or psychological, led to Maxwell's poor health, Maxine Benson speculates on possible causes, including "an unhappy marriage, resentment over the burdens of her stepchildren, [and] growing frustration about the lack of opportunity for self-fulfillment" (Maxine Benson, *Martha Maxwell: Rocky Mountain Naturalist* [Lincoln: University of Nebraska Press, 1986], 72).

29. Pewit's Nest (which Dartt spells as *Peewitt's Nest*), in the Devil's Lake area approximately 3 miles southwest of Baraboo, Wisconsin, was the location of the Dartt family home, purchased in 1853.

The house there was old, its rooms bare and unattractive; but taste rather than wealth has ever been the sceptre beauty obeys. Her mother, with an ardent love of flowers, had every sunny window filled with plants, while a beautiful English ivy was trained up the walls, over doors, windows, book-case, and cabinet.

With only these plants, in addition to ordinary furniture, Mrs. Maxwell, with the aid of her newly-acquired art, soon had it transformed into one of the loveliest of places.

In the parlor the plant-pots were arranged upon the flower-stand as com-pactly as possible, and completely hidden by moss. Bright birds were then placed among the foliage and vines in such lifelike attitudes, one could hardly believe they would not fly.

Over the top of her father's cabinet of fossils and mineralogical specimens were placed grasses and heavy heads of millet. From under the latter peeped timidly a little red squirrel, while farther along its mate sat eating a butternut. The fact that the nut had a large hole gnawed in one side, and that the little fellow was apparently on the *qui vive*[30] for intruders, made the illusion of life seem perfect.

On the lower shelf of the cabinet, just above the floor, she arranged some of the larger specimens, so as to represent a ledge of rocks just over a stream. On it was a group of young ducks, in the attitude those little creatures take when enjoying a tranquil sunning—all save one, who was a picture of terror, having caught sight of a sly weasel creeping around the corner of the rock.

Other rooms were enlivened in a similar manner, until each was in itself a study.

---

30. On the alert; on the lookout.

5

COLORADO FAUNA. LEARNING TO SHOOT. WISCONSIN
EXPERIENCES. HER MOUNTAIN HOME. DISAGREEABLE
WORK. TURKEY BUZZARDS. SICKENING WORK.
THAT CHICKEN. DEFORMED, TRANSFORMED. NOT
MY SPHERE. GUN IN HAND. ANIMAL CONGRESS.
A "GOPHER GOD." "WINKS OUT." THE COYOTE.

In the spring of 1868, Mrs. Maxwell found herself a second time in Colorado.[31]
Having comparative leisure, she was inspired with a desire to make a collection of its fauna as being the most useful and practical way in which she could embody her new enthusiasm.[32] It seemed especially desirable this work should be done, from the fact that the strange and curious animals peculiar to its plains and mountains were rapidly disappearing.

At first she depended upon her husband and the boys in the neighborhood, who were soon her enthusiastic allies, to shoot her specimens. She soon found, however, that in order not to lose the rarer and more desirable ones,

---

31. Maxwell returned to Colorado, with both Mabel and Mary Dartt, in February 1868.

32. "Comparative leisure" could refer either to Maxwell's first stay in Boulder or to the immediately preceding six years in Wisconsin. During her first stay in Boulder, Maxwell worked a number of jobs including selling pies, doing laundry, and running a boardinghouse. Following her return to Wisconsin, Maxwell found herself in charge of running the Maxwell household, which included her father-in-law and her three youngest stepchildren from James Maxwell's first marriage, as well as her own daughter.

she must kill them herself. Her husband's business took him from home much of the time, and was there ever a boy that could be depended upon to be in sight at a critical moment![33]

Those boys' homes were from a quarter of a mile to five times that distance from the grove in which she lived, and the coincidence of their presence, and that of the visit of a desirable bird to the spot, was as little to be hoped for as a special conjunction of the planets! She must either abandon her project, or use the gun herself.

Why not? She wasn't afraid, and had the skill.

I'm not sure—but did I hear somebody suggest, "because she was a woman?" Pshaw! Go talk to the pre-Adamites![34]

Did you ever go to a Fourth of July celebration, and hear them read that venerable document that talks about "liberty and the pursuit of happiness?"

Well, in the new States at least, they have grown to believe it, and to think it includes everybody, and can't see why a woman shouldn't do as she pleases, provided she can, as well as a man!

She was very sure she could shoot, for she'd tried it.

I think it has been growing on the human mind ever since that little drama at the gate of Eden, that *capacity* and *ability*, rather than birth, color, sex, or anything else, should determine where individuals belong, and what they shall do. If they can use a gun, and are so inclined, what is to hinder their doing it?[35]

She had had occasion to handle one years before, when a girl in Wisconsin. Her parents removed to that State when she was about thirteen years of age. Two years later found them in an unfinished house, on a woodland farm quite a distance from any neighbors.

---

33. Following his first arrival in Colorado in 1860, James Maxwell spent most of his time prospecting for gold, although he never achieved success. He went on to have numerous business ventures in Boulder and the surrounding areas, including starting sawmills, shipping lumber, and leading construction of a wagon road up Boulder Canyon. Maxwell was not successful in his business ventures and frequently found himself in dire financial straits, often as the result of his tendency to be too trusting of people and to make bad investments.

34. Pre-Adamites believed humans existed before Adam; pre-Adamism was often used in support of polygenist theories that aimed to back up beliefs about white supremacy and innate inequality among humans.

35. Dartt capitalizes on Maxwell's gun usage, turning it into an opportunity to make a broader claim about women's abilities and their right to pursue their own interests.

Her father Josiah Dartt,[36] was a surveyor, and in following his vocation was usually from home. During one of his absences, she and her mother were startled one morning by an unusual noise, seeming to come from the corner of the unfinished part of the house. Their horror can be imagined when, upon reaching the door, they discovered on the timbers of an unfinished part of the house a huge rattlesnake coiled up, his neck arched as though preparing to spring, and his rattles in rapid motion, while her little sister,[37] hardly four years of age, was playing within a few feet of him.

Quick as thought she sprang and caught the child, gave it to her mother, and seizing her father's ever-ready gun, placed it across some rails not far from the reptile, aimed and fired, sending it mangled and dying into the cellar![38]

Realizing, from the child's narrow escape, the danger of leaving his family wholly unprotected, Mr. Dartt taught the brave girl how to load and manage a gun, without danger to herself.

Although years of life with very different surroundings had intervened, she felt sure her steadiness of nerve and firmness of purpose had not diminished. A gun was now procured, and she became mistress of the situation!

To be sure, her husband always laughed at her for aiming with her left eye; but when was a woman ever defeated in gaining an end her heart was fixed upon, because she couldn't reach it by doing exactly as everybody else did! He was free to confess her shot was as effective as his, aimed with the approved orb of vision.

A low shelf, in a convenient room of the little house in which they lived, served as a work-table, and beside it, between the demands of household duties, she spent many hours of patient absorbing labor.

No matter how beautiful the form or coloring of an animal, between the time her fingers first stroked it in admiring interest, and the time when they gave it its finishing touch, a mounted specimen, lay hours of careful, often intensely disagreeable work.

---

36. Martha Maxwell's stepfather, Josiah Dartt, was educated as a surveyor and civil engineer; he became one of Maxwell's strongest encouragers of her pursuit of knowledge and education.

37. Mary Dartt, referring to herself in third person.

38. Such use of a gun for self-defense was not uncommon for women at the time, especially in the West. See Laura Browder, *Her Best Shot: Women and Guns in America* (Chapel Hill: University of North Carolina Press, 2009).

To remove the skin of a bird, without rumpling or soiling its plumage requires a very skilful use of both instruments and fingers. A still more delicate task, in young birds, is the removal of the flesh from the bones that should be preserved, especially where they are exceedingly thin and liable to injury, as in the case of the skull.

In ordinary birds, when dressed as soon as killed, the task is not offensive; but many specimens which she bought, or received as contributions to her scheme, did not reach her before decomposition had begun, and occasionally one was found by nature so depraved, that only a lover-like devotion to science could have tempted any one to prepare it for mounting.

To this latter class emphatically belongs the Turkey Buzzard. He is undoubtedly a useful bird, for do we not read of his supplying the place, and doing the work of entire Boards of Health, in many Southern villages?

He is not wholly unattractive—when viewed from a distance!

It's true, his coat usually seems to need re-dyeing; but then that is suggestive of long hours spent in the scorching sun, in the discharge of his official duties. One has no right to complain if the glossy black of a public servant's coat does get a little rusty. It is to be expected. His is black enough when it is new.

His manners, also, when not disturbed, are very dignified and sedate. A little too heavy, though, to be interesting after dinner, they say.

He has a fashion of not wearing a thing on his head and neck, which makes his appearance quite singular and striking. One might think he was an immense raven, if it wasn't for that, and associate him with memories of the "Bust of Pallas" and "that rare and radiant maiden whom the angels named Lenore!"[39]

The idea of a turkey buzzard being in such company even in one's thought!

As it is, some people call him a bald eagle, which is almost complimentary! They are not ornithologists, however.

He really has illustrious relatives. There are the South American condors, who are his own cousins, and whom he must resemble in one point at least—his lofty and long-continued flight, for he is truly graceful on the wing.

To come down to his solid merits, he has one virtue, which it would be well for the world if his brethren, the social scavengers, possessed—he almost never uses his voice!

---

39. From Edgar Allan Poe's poem "The Raven" (1845).

It is true, naturalists say, it is because he hasn't any, or at least any to speak of; but how can they distinguish between incapacity and good sense, when they would both have the same effect!

Be this as it may, one thing is certain: the much-abused quotation, "distance lends enchantment,"[40] etc. never was more appropriately applied than to him.

I think no one of the four persons, who constituted Mrs. Maxwell's family at the time of which we write, will ever forget her experience in putting up one of this brotherhood.

Of course, when any such specimen appeared, her work-table was abandoned for a plank on the bank of the creek, under the trees.

Even at that distance from the house, her daughter and sister[41] protested that the odor was unendurable!

When they saw her half-averted, sick, white face, its every muscle speaking of determined effort to endure, they stood afar off, and counselled a hasty burial of the vile bird, even though its name and race perished forever from the memory of man.

But they counselled in vain. Too sick to endure its presence a moment longer, she would retreat for a while; but as soon as it was possible to summon the strength and resolution, go to work again. It was more than a week, however, before she recovered from the effects of such a disgusting task enough to be able to eat an ordinary meal; and it was many weeks before the mounted bird could be taken from the outer shed, that gave him shelter, and have a place among her other birds.

But such unpleasant specimens are, fortunately, exceptional. With the majority the removal of the skin is only an insignificant part of the work to be done.

When it again contains a body, the special field of the artist is but fairly entered. To make the stiff, distorted-looking object seem instinct with nervous life, requires a touch of no ordinary genius. I know, for I've tried it![42]

It was a chicken, of tender age and downy aspect, that I aspired to resurrect to an eternal youth.

<hr />

40. A line from Thomas Campbell's poem "The Pleasures of Hope" (1799).

41. Maxwell's daughter, Mabel, and Mary Dartt had both joined Maxwell when she returned to Colorado in 1868.

42. Dartt switches back to first person.

I did the mechanics of the thing perfectly. Not a cat could have eaten it and lived—not a moth could have touched it and escaped dyspepsia![43]

The measurements were all right. No one could have mistrusted the down hadn't grown on the body I gave it. Its eyes were the best in the market. Mrs. Maxell looked it over, and said, "Well done. All it wants now is a graceful attitude and pleasant expression."

I was aware of the fact!

It had all the appearance of having died in a frightful fit!

I worked over it an hour longer. The idea of death from cold and stony neglect took the place of any suggestion of a more active form of disease.

I continued my labors, holding it at intervals at arm's length and looking at it with my head on one side, after the manner of great artists.

In half an hour the cause of its death could not have been guessed by the most skilful coroner, but the *fact* of it stood out in every line of its form, and penetrated each particle of its down. It glared at me from eyes that would be glass, and reproached me from claws that would look rigid.

Its presence became unendurable, and I was about to put it suddenly beyond the reach of mortal ken when Mrs. Maxwell asked:

"Why! what's the matter with you? You look the picture of disgust!"

"Humph! I shouldn't think you'd ask! Look at that chicken!"

There was a poorly suppressed laugh in her eyes as she took it from me, with the remark:

"Oh! can't you make it come to life?"

The idea of her asking such a question! after watching all my efforts in that direction!

"'Come to life!' I'm ready to affirm it never had any to come to—that even the egg it came from was a china one! Look at the horrid thing!"

She was looking at it—and giving it a little twist here, and a pinch there, and a touch somewhere else, sticking a needle first in one eye and then in the other, when she said, "Pshaw! I don't see that anything is the matter with it!"

---

43. The taxidermy process included treating the skins of the animal to prevent insect consumption. Chemicals used included arsenic, lime, and corrosive sublimate (now known as mercuric chloride).

Well—I didn't either! I thought it would peep! Its own mother would have clucked to it. How had she done it? Was it possible the trouble had all been in me?

As I gazed upon it the conviction was borne in upon me that taxidermy wasn't my "sphere." I'm very particular about spheres myself; I'm of the opinion that the artist in this line, like the poet, has to be born, not manufactured out of second-hand material! But a close and accurate study of each animal is an indispensable foundation for the exercise of even his skill.[44]

To give the staid and dignified owl the expression and position proper to the lively little tomtit, would obviously be as truly a mistake as to sculpture one of the prophets in the *posé* of a ballet-dancer!

Truthfulness in this department can only be secured by careful study of animals in their native haunts, where, without knowing that they are observed, their movements are free and unrestrained.

Mrs. Maxwell's natural tastes were of invaluable service to her here, for from her childhood an irresistible love of all living creatures had led her to study them with artist eyes. She had never been satisfied with anything less than a personal acquaintance with each creature she saw; so now, when they became the subjects for the exercise of her skill, her memory of their peculiar attitudes and graces served her in selecting the most desirable ones—as does an intimate acquaintance with the tastes and disposition of his subject serve the artist who is painting the face of a friend.

Her acquaintance with those which she had had no previous opportunity to study was obtained by stealing, gun in hand, through underbrush, among rocks or bogs, over mountains and by brook-sides, pausing sometimes an hour or more, almost as motionless as the earth beneath her, to watch the "family jars," conjugal or parental expressions of tenderness of birds, prairie-dogs, or shy creatures like the otter and beaver, or other equally timid.

"Why! wasn't she afraid?" I hear some one inquire.

---

44. Dartt takes pains to note that excellent taxidermy involved not just scientific knowledge and skill but artistic skill as well. To succeed in her work, Dartt implies, Maxwell had to be both an excellent naturalist and an excellent artist. Dartt's repeated mentions of the skill and art of Maxwell's work attempt to minimize the inherent violence and gore involved in killing and preparing taxidermy specimens.

No, indeed! What should she be afraid of? Really, human beings are about the only dangerous animals left on our continent to fear!

But the opportunities for living studies of specimens were not always to be obtained; but when she killed them herself she had a chance, which she considered almost invaluable, of seeing them a few moments, at least, alive and in action.

So both her love of natural history, and her desire for truthfulness in art, impelled her to the capture of her own subjects when practicable.

As soon as a specimen was completed it was placed either alone or as a member of some tableau in her parlor.

This room was fitted up with its usual furniture, *plus* a low tree with numerous branches, standing upon a mossy rock-work in one corner, and it soon assumed the appearance of a general council hall, to which were gathering delegates from every part of the animal kingdom!

Birds looked down in listening attitudes into the music-book upon the organ; scolded each other from the corners of neighboring picture-frames, while they occupied every conceivable attitude of action or repose upon the tree which was their special property. The smaller mammals of the neighborhood were represented among the rocks at its foot, and the whole formed a picture not less interesting than novel.

At every important addition a group, composed of the family, and, usually, some one or more of the lads before alluded to, would gather around the collection to express admiration and discuss its further needs.

One day when a fox just mounted was to be put with the other specimens, the outside member of the circle, a genuine frontier lad, nearly six feet in height and sixteen years of age, decided—

"You'd be all right now, Mrs. Maxwell, if you only had a gopher-god."

"A 'gopher-god!' and pray what may that be?" she inquired, settling the fox, which had a bird in its mouth, on the rock-work.

"Wall, now! Don't *you* know what gopher-gods are?" and his hands settled an inch deeper into his pantaloons' pockets and a merry light beamed in his honest, gray eyes, as he exclaimed, "Why they're *coyotes!*"*[45]

"Oh! are they?" she said.

---

45. Dartt's note: "*Pronounced ki-oats."

"Well," remarked her sister,[46] "if you please, will you bring your information down to the level of common understandings; *I'd* like to know what coyotes are?"

"Why," he answered, with a look of no small amount of incredulity, "I didn't know as there was anybody but what knew coyotes. They are them small wolves you can hear barking almost any night off on the plains."

"Oh, thank you!—are they—what do you want to call them such heathenish names for?"

"Don't you think you're *rather* particular?" and his face put on a quizzing look. "You just see one after a gopher once, and you'd know where the name came from. You bet! the little fellow *winks out* pretty quick!"

Her face assumed a vacant, despairing look, as she slowly repeated "winks out!" but brightened as she asked, "Are you ever accompanied by an interpreter?"

"Why, don't you know what winking out means? It passes in its checks! Goes up the flume! The gopher-god comes the dead-wood on him, you know!"

"Oh, you barbarian! I know *you* have a gift for slang; I wish I could compliment Colorado by saying it is a rare one, and confined to you!"

"Wall, now! Do you know you'll die an old maid if you don't get married—you're so nice and notional about the way folks talk!"

Here Mrs. Maxwell interrupted their badinage by inquiring where he supposed she could get a coyote.

"Oh," she added, in answer to her sister's look of disgust, which said more plainly than words, "Can it be possible you have gone over to the enemy!" "that name is proper! It's just as correct to use it as *ranch*, or *cañon*, or any of our Spanish-American words! I will say nothing about the other title, master—if you will tell me where a *coyote* is to be found!"

"Oh," he replied, arching his eyebrows, "pretty much anywhere they are! I saw one the other night when I was out for the cows, over toward the Coal-banks a ways. You just take your gun, most any time, and creep around the point of that bluff off there, and it's ten to one you'll see one."

Mrs. Maxwell did not fail to try this experiment, but several trips were made without the prophesied success. At length one day, while riding across the country, one was discovered. Mrs. Maxwell, gun in hand, was on the ground in a moment.

---

46. Mary Dartt returns to third person here.

The coyote was running leisurely along, his handsome, bushy tail just curved enough to avoid touching the ground, his ears erect, his head and nose down, as though tracking his way by smell toward some point or object. He was at some distance from the road and had not perceived her. Stealthily but rapidly she approached him; but suddenly, as though impressed with a sense of unexpected danger, he paused, with foot suspended, raised his head and looked with keen eyes about him. It was Mrs. Maxwell's opportunity; a sharp click, a ringing report, and she was in possession of the means to supply the deficiency that had called forth her young friend's criticism.

When he was mounted her great desire became to obtain those animals which frequent the wilder regions, and some of her attempts to accomplish this end will be given in the next section.

6

COLORADO TOPOGRAPHY. COLORADO MOUNTAINS. IRRIGATION. BOULDER. CHEYENNE. GYMNASTIC SUIT. PLAYING DOG. MUD-WADING. SHY BIRDS.

Colorado is composed of two regions, as different from each other as we can imagine two worlds may be.

The one region has thousands of square miles where hardly a tree or a large rock can be found; the other similar areas where it would be hard to find anything else. The one gives the eye only endless monotony; the other affords almost limitless variety, both in surface, productions, and climate.

The plains, which cover about half the State, are not at all like anything in New England, or any of the Eastern States. They are very different from the great prairies of Illinois and southern Wisconsin. In fact, they have a strong individuality, which cannot be put in words.

Though they are far from being level, they sweep with a broad, clean look, as though they had been rolled and prepared for lawns, up to the very foot of the mountains.

In Colorado there are shown no such hesitating attempts at making elevation as are manifested in the formation of Eastern mountains, where whole states are wrinkled up and spoiled for all level purposes, and nothing so vastly imposing produced after all!

When Nature got as far west as the Mississippi river she grew decided, and when she made plains, she made plains, and when she made mountains, they were mountains which no one could possibly mistake for hills!

Eastern mountains will do very well to prepare one's mind for them—that's about all!

Really, Mount Washington and the famous peaks of the Appalachian system would, beside Pike's, Grey's and Long's peaks, be only nice little hills—entitled to a passing glance if they put on no arrogant airs!

I[47] mean no disrespect to them—am only suggesting that as mountains among mountains they are rather small. I know with what historic interests they are associated—what poets and writers have hallowed them in story and song. In these they have a charm no newer scenes, it matters not how majestic, can possess.

(Aside to Coloradoans.) This must be conceded now, but just wait until the centuries shall have thrown over your peaks—upon which Nature rests her brow when she weeps, and from whose broad shoulders her snowy hand is never wholly withdrawn—a human history commensurate with their grandeur, a poetry as beautiful and sublime as their fir-fringed gorges, and a romance as varied as their changing hues in light and shade—and then![48]

The plains of Colorado now form one of the finest wheat-growing sections in the world, but for years after the State's first settlement it can hardly be said to have had any agricultural resources. Its soil, except in the mountains, although wonderfully fertile when irrigated, is productive of nothing except buffalo-grass, cactus and a few varieties of other plants, without this artificial application of water. And this, while no very laborious task on the low lands bordering streams, requires long canals to render possible the irrigation of any considerable area of upland. Their construction has taken capital and labor, and has progressed extensively only within a few years.

---

47. Dartt returns to first person.

48. Dartt's prediction that poetry would eventually acknowledge the beauty and grandeur of the Rocky Mountains was realized with Katherine Lee Bates's poem "Pikes Peak," originally published in 1895, which later became the lyrics to "America the Beautiful."

Its first settlers were attracted to it by its mineral wealth only, and supposed its plains to belong as the old geographies said they did to the "great American Desert," over which as the boys used to recite, "roamed vast herds of deer, buffalo, Indians, and other wild horses!"

The mining population naturally centred in towns and mining camps, and was confined to the mountains and the few places near their base, which served as harbors for the emigrant and freight craft that came westward over the ocean of land which stretches between them and the older States.

Boulder, Mr. Maxwell's chosen home, was one of these latter places. Its location is beautiful.

To the average tourist Colorado means Denver, and I am afraid there is a chance to imagine something of a jealous spirit between it and Boulder, inasmuch as Denver does not see much more that is attractive about it than New York sees in Boston, and therefore tourists have not visited it so much as some other spots; but, notwithstanding such an unfortunate lack of appreciation, its scenery is magnificent.

Twenty-five miles northwest of Denver, Boulder lies at the base of the mountains whose foothills there rise abruptly from eleven hundred to two thousand feet above the plain, and hold between their precipitous sides some of the wildest and grandest of gorges.

It is true, its inhabitants cannot see the storms gather and break upon the mountains' snowy peaks, nor [sic] watch the play of forked lightning about their cloud-capped summits, so far away that not an echo of their deep-voiced thunders reach[es] the ear, though they must jar the rocks among which they vibrate. The village is too near their base for that, but it is not too near to have the clouds rest like a cowl on the tops of its guardian cliffs—to have them, as they grow heavy with their treasured rain or snow, settle slowly down until all trace of mountains is lost, and the town seems but a point beneath a cloud-built arch upon a boundless plain. It *is* too near to watch the snowy peaks grow rosy with the hues of coming day, or blaze like brazen battlements at night against a sea of sunset glory; but it is not too near to catch the first reflected flash of sunlight that falls on their grand foundation walls, and have the cool arms of their lengthening afternoon shadows enfold it every sunny summer's day—not too near to have their swift streams, cool and sparkling from their parent snowdrifts, with their cascades and magnificent gorges, within easy walk or ride for all who love nature in her wildest moods.

FIGURE 6.1.
Mrs. Maxwell's hunting costume

In 1868 it was a village of only about three hundred inhabitants—the centre for supplies of a gold, silver and coal mining region, since found to be very rich, but then only worked at a few points, and of an agricultural section but just beginning to be developed.

Cheyenne was then the terminus of the Union Pacific Railroad, and it and the towns beyond it along the unfinished road afforded a fine market for lumber, and the like products of the timber-growing region, in which Mr. Maxwell had an interest.

He often made journeys to these points, travelling distances of from eighty five to one hundred and fifty miles, over the then almost unbroken plains.

As the road was inhabited at only a few points, he took his food with him, camped at night, built a fire and cooked it, and then retired to the privacy of his own blanket spread under his wagon, to enjoy the luxury of sleep!

That new specimens might be added to her collection, Mrs. Maxwell resolved to accompany him and share these novelties of travel.

All superfluous graces and ornaments of costume were dispensed with, and their place was supplied by a gymnastic suit of neutral tint and firm texture. Substantial shoes and stockings, a simple shade hat, a game bag, ammunition and gun completed her personal "out-fit."

When she had prepared as much food as they could eat while it would remain fresh and sweet, she was ready to take a seat on the top of the loaded lumber wagon beside her husband, or occasionally to occupy the saddle of a restless little "broncho" that was taken along to do duty whenever occasion demanded.[49]

Many were the exciting adventures through which they passed; and many more the hardships. The latter were soon forgotten when the specimens were obtained for which they were endured.

Such success, however, was not always attained.

At one time they camped upon the banks of a lonely little lake in the Laramie valley. A ranch which had once served as a stage station on the overland route to California, occupied at this time by a single man, bore the only trace of humanity for miles around.

The borders of the lake were deeply edged with tall reeds and rushes, which had grown up year after year, and fallen undisturbed each winter about their submerged roots. On and around the water were large numbers of beautiful water fowl; how to obtain some of them was soon Mrs. Maxwell's absorbing thought.

They had no dog. The moment the water was rippled by the rude little skiff belonging to the ranch, the birds would retreat to the rushes and remain hidden while it was in sight.

It was soon apparent that there was no way to secure them but for either herself or [her] husband to play dog, and by wading around among the reeds, frighten them out on to the lake where the other could shoot them.

Mr. Maxwell had hardly recovered from an attack of rheumatic fever, and such exposure was not to be thought of for him. He could, however, lend his boots and an extra pair of his lower garments.

Equipped in these, surmounted by her loose dress, Mrs. Maxwell waded boldly out into the half-submerged, tangled mass of decayed and growing

---

49. A bronco is an untrained horse that bucks frequently. Derived from the Spanish word *bronco*, meaning rough.

vegetation. At every step, she sank, with a shiver, sometimes a few inches, sometimes to her waist in the cold water. She was soon compelled to make a disorderly retreat.

The boots were at the bottom of it! They tangled themselves in the rushes. They filled with water. They seemed determined to remain fixtures in the mud! It was only by an exertion that greatly endangered her equilibrium that they could be drawn up for the steps necessary to reach the shore. Once there, they were left in disgrace, while she returned in her stocking-feet.

This made the experiment a matter of far more ease, and secured her the tantalizing success of seeing numbers of the birds start up before her only to dodge into the covert in another place!

For nearly two hours she waded about among the slimy vegetation, curbing her fancy when it pictured snakes and leeches about her limbs, resolutely beating about to drive some fowl within range of her husband's gun, which he, in the skiff upon the lake, held ready to discharge.

Then darkness interfered, and compelled her to go into camp with nothing but her "clinging drapery" and benumbed limbs to reward her for her exertion!

The next day, approaching another pond, she met with better success.

Leaving the wagon as soon as they came within its neighborhood, she stole carefully between two knolls until within a couple hundred yards of the water.

The pond was a naked one; that is, a little sheet of water held in a depression of a treeless, rockless plain, with no vegetation upon its border except short grass.

Plover, avocet and other waders frequented it; but the difficulty was to get within range of them unobserved. They are very shy, having learned that man is the most dreadful of all their enemies. Their long, stilt-like legs and swift wings—such good security against four-footed foes are of little avail where man is concerned; so, if he would approach them, he must lay aside his superior dignity and put himself at least on a level with the beasts of the field.

There was not an object—not even a clump of grass—to shield her from view; so, gun in hand, she cautiously crept toward the water upon her hands and knees.

Tall avocets were standing in the shallows, occasionally thrusting their long, recurved bills into the mud for worms and tiny muscles, or flying up to try their success in other spots. A few plover and an occasional snipe were running or flying about on the slimy soil left by the gradual evaporation of the water. Whenever they showed any signs of disturbance from her presence, she would lie perfectly still, close to the ground, for a time, and then creep forward.

When within good range, she waited until one shot would cover two or more of the birds; then, still reclining, fired one barrel of her gun, and, as the birds rose, discharged the other.

Two plover and an avocet were killed. The plover victims of her last shot, had fallen not far apart, a few feet from the water; but the avocet had not been so accommodating. It had fluttered forward, and lay floating several feet beyond the reach of her ramrod.

It was too desirable a specimen to be lost. Her experience of the night before had not invested wading with any new charm; still, that avocet *must* be obtained. He was!

7

A PORCUPINE. SINGULAR PET. PORCUPINE
WEAPONS. PORCUPINE MOODS. LITTLE
ATTENTIONS. DEATH OF YOCKCO.

One evening, just as they were preparing to camp on the side of one of the mountains that lie between Laramie valley and the eastern plains, a porcupine was discovered.

Seeing them, he made all haste to get out of their way; and an exciting chase ensued. Gun in hand, they followed him over the steep, uneven ground, catching him, one moment under a blackened log, the next just disappearing between huge boulders. Each, at different points in the chase, gave him a wound. At last a shot, it is not remembered from whose gun, proved fatal; and with a cry, not unlike a human being in mortal agony, he died.

When first seen by them, he was descending a tree, upon whose twigs and bark he had been feeding.

Permit me here to dispel some popular illusions regarding this curious and interesting animal.

Some time before the Centennial,[50] Mrs. Maxwell bought a live one of [sic] an enterprising boy in Boulder, and kept it six months or more, in order to study its tastes and habits.

---

50. The Philadelphia Centennial International Exposition in 1876.

Instead of a repulsive, fiery creature, ready to throw a shower of stinging spines at anything which might come near it, she found it a most affectionate and intelligent being—really quite companionable!

Her pet rejoiced in the name of Yockco, a fact he was not long in discovering and to which he was seldom indifferent, being nearly always ready to respond when it was spoken.

With the rest of his family—the rodents—he resembled in his tastes and many of his habits a mammoth, clumsy squirrel. He would run all about the house, climbing up on the chairs and tables and all kinds of furniture, careful of only one thing—to be able to come down tail first.

This method of retreat was not so absurd as it appears. He possessed a remarkably fine nervous organization, and was susceptible of feeling the faintest touch given his longest hair. He would slide down anything a little distance, and then begin to feel around, with the end of his tail, for a landing-place; the first hint of which, the long, sensitive hairs in that appendage always brought. Then, too, there was another reason: if an enemy was encountered, his tail was his defensive weapon, and it was but prudent to present it first. When vexed or threatened with danger he would whirl around as rapidly as his clumsy body would permit, and deal his offender swift blows with the back of that appendage, one stroke of which, few animals would care to have repeated.

As the spines, with which it and his body generally were so well armed, came out very easily and were barbed at the end, so that wherever they struck there they stuck, it is not at all surprising that careless and terrified observers should have supposed he was capable of throwing them.

Mrs. Maxwell found he had but one spot upon which she could administer discipline. That was the end of his broad, peculiarly-shaped nose.

A few snaps of the finger on that was sufficient punishment to make him retreat in good order from any mischief in which he might be found.

As he had a most inquisitive mind, it was not seldom, by any means, that such correction was needed.

Not a particle of flour or any of its compounds, or any kind of fruit, could be left within the power of his discovery by smell (which sense was very acute), without his making a most thorough and persistent search therefor.

Like many geniuses, he was much subject to moods and tenses! Sometimes, for hours together, he would roll himself up, so that he resembled nothing in the world but a ball of hair and spines, from the centre of which would come the most piteous little moans, almost human in their touching accents. As he seemed perfectly well in every way, it became the opinion of unsympathetic observers, that they were his rendering of "The Girl I left behind me," or "Home, Sweet Home."[51]

Mrs. Maxwell was far from making light of his heart-aches, and used to assure him of her deepest sympathy, and try to draw away his attention from himself by sweetmeats and other dainties, tending to sooth wounded spirits.

At times he was very playful, balancing himself on his hind feet and tail, and with extended paws and open mouth, pretending he was about to pounce upon and bite his friends.

He was quite fond of climbing up into Mrs. Maxwell's lap for dainties and caresses. These latter had to be given with a good degree of caution, as it was a serious matter to stroke him the wrong way—not on his account at all!

She found it no small art to show her regard for him without injury to herself!

His spines stood on his back so nearly perpendicular, and came out so easily, it was necessary, if one would not exchange a caress for a wound, to begin the petting stroke as near the nose, where the spines were neither hard nor long, as possible, and continue it with sufficient pressure to keep them close to his skin. Then, it was quite important to know when to stop.

His back had a most unusual arch, and if one's hand went too far, the spines came out and were carried away in its skin.

Such trouble, to pet a porcupine! But, then, he was so fond of a little attention!

His feet, and the underside of his body and of his tail, were free from spines. This caudal[52] appendage served him for a kind of balancing-pole when he wished to walk upright, as well as for a weapon of defence.

He had a most unmistakable way of informing the family when he considered refreshments in order.

---

51. "The Girl I Left Behind Me" was an English folk song dating back to the Elizabethan era that became popular during the American Civil War. "Home, Sweet Home" was a popular song from the 1823 opera *Clari, or the Maid of Milan* (Henry Bishop, composer; John Howard Payne, lyricist).

52. Of, at, or near the tail or the posterior end of the body.

He would come sniffing up to one of them, and when near enough to touch them, would stand up and beg as little dogs are sometimes taught to do. If no immediate attention was given him, he gave a teasing little whine, varied with most expressive movements of the muscles of his nose and face.

When food was given him, he grasped it in one of his paws—he used these as a monkey does its hands—settled back on his haunches and tail, and ate it as squirrels do nuts.

Poor Yocko! He died on the way to the Centennial; and this fragment of his biography is given here to do justice to his family, which, by the reputation usually given it, is shamefully maligned.

8

MORNING WORK. LONELY LOVELINESS.
SAY'S STRIPED SQUIRREL. STRATEGY. VISITORS.
NOT SCALPERS. SAFETY IN COURAGE.

By experience Mrs. Maxwell learned that the best time for securing animals and observing their habits was the early morning, when they first appear in search of food. So it was her custom to rise as soon as it was light enough to see, and make a careful inspection of the neighborhood in which they camped. Upon one of their trips they stopped, late in the evening, upon the bank of a small stream, some distance from any frequented route.

The creek was bordered, as such streams in Colorado usually are, by a growth of low bushes, but between them and the high ground lay a strip of valuable meadow land.

White people had endeavored a number of times to occupy it long enough to cut and secure the grass, but had been driven away by the Indians and their work destroyed.

A few rods back from the creek stood the remains of an old adobe fort, formerly used as a government defence, but long since rendered—by the noble red men (?)—useless for such a purpose. Mr. and Mrs. Maxwell made their camp upon the creek below and just out of sight of it.

With the coming of the dawn Mrs. Maxwell, as usual, was out with her gun. There was no dew on the low, gray-green grass that clothes the foot-hills. The air was cool and bracing, and the silence was broken only by the far-off waking song of the meadow lark, or the occasional twitter of some nearer bird.

Slowly the rocky heights beyond her grew rosy, then suddenly flashed back the sunlight as its first beams touched them. How sternly grand they looked in that all-revealing sunlight! their shadows dispelled, not a film of mist, not even a slender, blue curl of smoke from a prospector's camp to divert the mind from their sharp, gray granite outlines. The human hopes that, like lichens, might some time find a home upon their sides, were yet unborn. Even the grace of verdure which the yellow pines, springing from every crevice, strove to throw around them, in that undimmed light, showed a thankless, unappreciated task. They could not, struggle as they might, grow leaves enough to hide their gnarled and knotted trunks and limbs. Many of them had ceased to try, and their bare, gaunt arms stretched above the gray waste seemed to emphasize the solitude. Some keen-eyed eagle might make those forbidding heights a tower from which to watch the little valley she had left; but for other life, the lower grass-grown slopes would form a more inviting home, and over them she wandered.

An occasional point of rocks, where one low swell suddenly ceased, as though unable to reach the height of the preceding wave, that had washed up and petrified upon that stern, rock-edged coast of a former seas, afforded her a hiding-place from which to watch the ways of the shy occupants of the land.

After a brief study, for the morning hours of these creatures are very busy ones, and none of them stayed long at a time in one spot, she would climb on over the crest of one wavelike hill to the high shallow depression between it and the next more lofty one.

The sunlight had just crept around into the valley of the stream where lay their camp, when, after a somewhat lengthy ramble, her ear again caught the musical gurgle of its waters. She was nearly opposite the old fort, and thinking, as she saw its broken, crumbling walls, how rapidly nature was removing all trace of man and redeeming to her lesser children what he had vainly tried to claim, when she caught sight of one of Say's striped squirrels.[53]

---

53. Gold-mantled ground squirrel (*spermophilus lateralis* or *Callospermophilus lateralis*), native to western North America.

She had no specimen of its family, and it was to be studied and secured.

In and out among the rocks and bushes it scampered, stopping occasionally to raise up on its hind feet and look about it, or to give a touch to its dress where some meddlesome twig had disarranged a hair or two. It seemed intent upon a call on some neighbor down the bank of the stream, and she followed it unperceived until she feared she should lose it; then she fired and stepped from her ambush to secure it.

Almost at the same moment she was transfixed with astonishment by an unearthly howl or shout from the supposed deserted fort, and the appearance from among its ruins of a man and a dog!

The man, from his clothing, or rather lack of it, was undoubtedly an Indian, and both he and the dog seemed furious with rage at her presence there, and came rushing toward her. After advancing a few feet, the man paused and raised his gun and aimed it at her. Her time to die seemed to have come, but with that desperate coolness that is sometimes given to the human soul when it feels that only perfect presence of mind can avert instant death, she reasoned, "He can't suppose I'm alone, and he will not run the risk of being shot by my companions, unless he thinks I have something he very much wants. My safest way is to let him see I am *not afraid*, and am going off about my affairs, and have only an old shot-gun about me," and she picked up her squirrel and turned down the creek toward camp as coolly, to all appearances, as though an infuriated dog and loaded rifle were not approaching her, taking pains only to walk so far out from the brush, that she could be well seen.

Three times she was aware the man paused and took aim at her, but for some reason changed his purpose and did not fire; then he turned and recalled his dog.

Trembling, but collected, she reached camp and recited her adventure. Her escape seemed hardly less miraculous. Mr. Maxwell deemed their safety demanded immediate flight. There were doubtless other Indians in the fort, and they would be out soon to see what enemy or plunder was at hand; finding them alone, they would not hesitate to kill them and take what they had, for there would be no danger of the deed being reported and the terrible vengeance of the whites aroused; the nearest settlement alone could afford them protection. With all haste they both began to harness the horses.

Their fears and preparations, however, were soon ended by the appearance of the dog from whose teeth she had so recently escaped, and two men, considerably excited in their appearance, but still, unmistakably, not savages! The harnessing was suspended, and they were conscious of but two sensations: a relief from fear, and curiosity with regard to their approaching visitors.

Mrs. Maxwell advanced toward the dog, and with many motions tending to show her good-will and win his, asked if he was the same fellow she had excited so a few minutes before.

The men, two rough, honest-looking young frontiersmen, replied that he was; the taller, an odd-looking genius, adding:

"He wasn't the only one you scared—not by fifty horse-power! When I heard that gun I thought the Injuns was on us, dead sure! I tell you I didn't waste no time foolin', dressin' an' fixin' up and the like, afore I was out, ready to give the cusses what they all need!"

"But how did you come to be in the fort?" Mr. Maxwell inquired. "We didn't dream of being near any one here."

"There aint nobody else here but us. We come up to cut that grass.[54] You see there's a good bit of it, and it's worth something, and Bill here," with a nod to his companion, "and I jest made up our minds we'd have it. Whites have tried to get it a good many times afore, but the Injuns never'd let 'em be. By gorry! there's been enough of that, and we allow if they get our scalps it won't be till there's a few less of the ornery pests in the world than there is now! We've done sworn we'd shoot the first one of 'em that puts his condemned mug inside this valley, no matter what he's here for. You bet high, we keep ready for 'em!"

"Did you take me for one of them?" Mrs. Maxwell asked. "I didn't know that I looked like an Indian!"

"Wal, you see, as for that," he replied, looking rather embarrassed, "we weren't thinkin' of nobody but Injuns. *Gewhillikens!* when a feller expects to be scalped he don't mind nothin'! I was out before I was awake enough to look particular at anything. You see it's dev'lish sorter lonesome here of an evenin', and so Bill and I play cards jest to pass the time, and last night we got

---

54. Native Colorado grasses were valued as livestock feed that helped produce heavier animals.

to playin' and it was nigh on to two o'clock when we turned in. Je-rusalem! the next thing we know'd that gun went off right in our ears! I was out and takin' aim, at what I s'posed, in couse, was an Injun, before my eyes was squarly open."

"Why didn't you shoot?" asked Mrs. Maxwell.

"Wal, durn my cats if I can tell! I got all ready, then I thought you acted kinder queer for an Injun, and I'd jest take a look at you; but I was so riled up I couldn't make out nothin', and allowed I was a fool to think of white folks, for there aint [*sic*] none lives hereabouts, and I couldn't have believed any could git so near us and we not have know'd it. So I aimed agin—but I know'd you see me—still you didn't skulk nor [*sic*] run. Great Peter! If you had it'd been a bad job for us all!" and he shook his head solemnly, while, to hide his emotion, he looked intently at the hole in the smouldering ashes of the camp-fire that he was making with the toe of his boot.

"That's so!" added his companion, impressively, "for Jim never misses what he draws a bead on."

"Injuns—blarst their shadders!—allers run when a feller comes out on 'em the way Bose and me did on you," the first speaker continued, "but I couldn't make you out—I didn't see no men's clothes, and it wasn't till I aimed the third time that it come to me you might be a woman! I hope you'll pardon a feller, marm. You see, it's gospel truth, we don't see women often enough to know 'em even when they're right afore our eyes!"

9

NEW EXPEDITION. COOL AND DARK. DIFFICULT PASSAGE.
ROARING WATERS. MINIATURE NIAGARA.
ICE-RIMMED SOURCE. PRAIRIE DOGS. THE PROFESSOR.
DISSIMILAR TASTES. HAWK'S NEST. A PUZZLE.
WOMAN'S WILL. DIFFICULT DESCENT. YOUNG HAWK.

After making several trips to the North, Mr. Maxwell's business called him across a portion of the country, then hardly more thickly settled than that of which we have formerly spoken, although lying in an opposite direction, viz., the section between the Platte river and the Boulder creek. Mrs. Maxwell, as usual, accompanied him.

The Boulder is a swift, rock-embedded stream, rising in little snow-rimmed lakes, far up among the peaks on the Snowy Range, and finding its way to the plains through one of the grandest cañons in America.[55]

I suppose just here I ought to stop and tell every one who does not already know what cañon is. The word is pronounced kan-yun. I would suggest the dictionary as a means of getting further information concerning it, only no one would get any idea of what I have in my mind, when I use the word, from what that says: "A deep gorge, ravine, or gulch, between high, steep

---

55. Canyon; derived from the Spanish word referring to a tube, pipe, conduit, barrel, or cannon.

banks, worn by water;" that will do very well for a cañon in a dictionary, but I'd like to have you see one in the Rocky Mountains!

Get into a carriage at Boulder, and we will drive up its creek for ten miles.[56] Imagine a summer morning, faultlessly cool and clear. We are just a mile from the mouth of the defile[57] we would explore when we start. You can see it perfectly, though, right up the main street, just where the purple shadows take for a little way the place of the glaring rocks of the mountain sides. We do not care for houses so we will not notice mills and reduction works. This hill at our left, as we enter the cañon, is eleven hundred feet high, but that is nothing to what we shall come to by-and-by! How cool and dark the evergreens look up among the precipices upon its side! I do not know the height of those sandstone cliffs at the right. But see! Our road is occupying all the space between two streams of water! This one, on a level with the track, is the Farmer's Ditch. It winds around the base of the foot-hills and out on to the plains to irrigate the land. That embankment you see, fifty feet or more above it, is the edge of the ditch that feeds the reservoir for the town. This water, eight or ten feet down the embankment at our left, is the creek proper. See how swift it is, and how its waters are dashed into foam against its rocks! It is so all its way.

You wonder what would happen if we should meet some one? We must look out for that, and when a team is seen approaching, stop in some place where the road is widened to allow them to pass us.

Once before the road was perfect as now, a lady and I were driving up here, and just as we were approaching a sharp curve around a lofty point of rocks, a four-horse stage-coach, loaded with passengers, came dashing into view! The horses attached to the two vehicles were stopped while they were still a few feet apart, but for either party to turn out was impossible, for the roaring stream was not two feet from one side of our wheels, and piles of rocks were on the other side. Some gentlemen dismounted from the coach; we got out of the carriage, and they, backing it to where the rocks would permit, lifted it up on to them, and held it there until the stage could pass.

I believe all those curves are provided with passing places at present; still it isn't advisable for drivers to go to sleep on the road even now!

---

56. Boulder Creek is located west of Boulder and runs through Boulder Canyon.

57. A narrow pass or gorge between mountains.

Here is where the upper ditch we saw leaves the stream. We have hardly seemed to be coming up hill, yet in less than two miles we have risen more than two hundred feet. The rise in the heights about us has not been so imperceptible. How they shut in around us! How they tower up, and up, and up! The pines on their summits seem only shrubs. Surely one's hand could touch the blue from those high cliffs! How far beyond the power of words to paint the awful grandeur of these riven rocks!

They are too vast and stern to awaken poetic inspiration. What is the fiercest human passion to the throes that rent earth's bosom when these cliffs were formed!

Ages of human history must clothe their deep recesses with memories of heroic deeds, of bitter griefs, and tender loves, before the heart can find, like the pine and lichen, soil in which to fasten itself and cling about them in poetic familiarity.

Into what endless variety the cañon shapes itself! The rocky walls receding with a sudden curve one moment, until a garden spot might lie between them and one bank of the stream, then as suddenly approaching each other, until the water alone has room and the road is built almost wholly above it. Now we are on one bank, now on the other, but always with its deafening thunder in our ears. There the granite rocks rise, bare and stern, hundreds of feet without a spray of foliage—here they are broken into wild, irregular masses, above and among which evergreens and the lighter leaves of rock-maples and aspens sigh and quiver. There the stream is half hidden from our sight by a fringe of clematis and alders—here its spray is in our faces and its dashing green-tinted waters hold our gaze with a fascination which towering cliffs and shadowed caverns cannot rival. Here a chasm opens in the granite wall upon our right, and another foam-white stream comes dashing down to mingle its roaring flood with that beside us. The low thunder of a waterfall is in our ears, and a few rods up the new cañon a miniature Niagara is pouring its rainbow-touched waters into a rocky basin.

A few minutes' clamber over the sharp stones, and we stand where the moss is always green, drenched by its ever-falling spray.

How the cool air and pine-scented shadows invite us to rest! Who could imagine a shower of literal pearls and diamonds would look half so beautiful as the myriad drops into which that sheet of water is breaking as it falls! Into what fine mist the particles are shattered as they strike the rock in the stream below! How, as the angry waves shake off the falling hail of brilliants, this spray rises, and, catching the sunbeams, holds that bit of rainbow in its midst! It is exquisite! With such a scene of the mountain Genii's enchanted play before our eyes, what care we for miles more of frowning precipices and ever-varying green-wreathed cliffs! When the twilight peoples with mysterious shadows every cavern, right and fir-fringed dell among the rocks, we will retrace our steps, and hope to hear in dreams, through all the coming years, the sublime music to which the wind among the dusky pines plays soft accompaniment—to hear the deep-voiced roar of these ever-rushing waters—to have the memory of the touch of their spray upon our cheeks, be like the recollection of a caress, and the vision of their majestic guardian walls, symbols of those eternal heights whereon the soul may find repose.

This is only a hint of all the word cañon may suggest; but in giving it, I have made quite a digression. I was speaking of Boulder creek itself, and telling how it slips from the keeping of its ice-rimmed parent lakes, down through green mosses and grasses to darkle under heavy fir shadows no human foot has ever disturbed. It is not long that its waters are suffered to play with useless rocks and hide in secluded chasms.

Their aid is needed to gain possession of their gold and silver in the many rich veins in their imprisoning mountains; and they are never suffered to be idle long through their whole journey to the plains. Having reached them, instead of propelling mills alone, during the hot, dry months of summer, they are called upon to visit the roots of every plant and tree in all their valley, and only reach the Platte[58] after doing an amount of service that, to hear recounted, would make even a New England manufacturing stream blush at its own uselessness!

At the time of which we write, the facilities for doing much of this work—namely, numerous irrigating canals—had not been given them; and after Mr. and Mrs. Maxwell left their house, they were not long in passing all traces of human occupation, and finding themselves amid the native haunts of coyotes and prairie dogs.

The odd little villages and comical manners of these latter animals are a never-failing source of interest to passers-by.

---

58. Boulder Creek drains into the South Platte River, which merges with the North Platte River in Nebraska to become the Platte River.

Their residences are said to be quite extensive and complicated; but as they are wholly under ground, people with ordinary eyes see only their turrets or observatories—round little mounds, from six inches to a foot high, and at varying distances from each other. To these the whole family are in the habit of resorting on a pleasant day to take the air and gossip with their neighbors.

These families are not formed on the plan adopted by animals in general—that of choosing their table-mates from those of their own species—and so they have been the subject of no small amount of criticism and remark.

As it is purely a matter of taste, however, whether they find owls and rat-tlesnakes agreeable enough to live with, or not, I shall do no more than state that they do all live together, and all *seem* to have a good time.

I confess, were I disposed to pry into what is none of my affairs, I should wonder what such lively little creatures as the prairie dogs are, can find attractive in those stupid-looking owls! They sit on the edge of the little mound, with their eyes half-closed, and their wings folded together; so they look, for all the world, like rusty, snuff-colored, swallow-tailed coats; and one can only think of weazen[ed], near-sighted professors of some abstruse science, who are out for an airing, and look instinctively for the end of the well-worn umbrella that ought to appear at their side!

They seem to be forever meditating upon that vexed problem, whether the owl had the precedence of the egg, or the egg the precedence of the owl, and to be as far from its satisfactory solution as our modern scientists are! When their cogitations are interrupted, they have the most absurd way of blinking their eyes, stretching out their heads and drawing them back again, and then shuffling down into the obscurity of those holes they never lifted a claw to dig!

They seem to be quite too far removed from this world to know enough to get out of danger were it not for their bright-eyed, lively little companions. They—the cunning little dogs—are all curiosity about everything, and not at all given to speculation. They pop up on their hind feet when they hear a noise, and, with a quick turn or two of their heads, have taken in the whole situation, and give out their verdict in a few decisive, sharp little barks, accompanying each with a very emphatic jerky gesture of the tail; and then, before one has thought of firing, if they have malicious designs upon them, are gone.

Nothing could be more unlike than the tastes, habit, everything about them, and the owls; and Dr. Coues[59] and some other naturalists, who are always prying into such matters do assert that the relations between them are not such as should exist in a family.

They hint darkly of the most terrible things, such as dinners made of baby dogs, by both snakes and owls, and of tragedies I can't think of repeating here! However, I never lived in the family, and really have no right to speak of their private affairs. I do know Mrs. Maxwell shot one of the owls, and, what was more to her purpose, secured it before it was lost in one of the holes into which they are always ready to drop; and that she mounted him, looking, as one of her friends said, "as though what he didn't know, was not worth knowing."

Aside from the owls and prairie dogs, they saw no object of interest until afternoon, when they came to one of the small streams that flow into the Platte. These streams are bordered at intervals by cotton-wood trees of great age and size; and far up above one of them they saw a hawk, circling. After watching its motions for some time, she became convinced its nest was secreted in one of the largest of the trees, and upon examination, discovered it, hidden among the aspen-like foliage of its highest branches.

Science has at present more interest in the eggs and young of animals than in those that are mature, and young hawks of that variety were not to be left to try their new-fledged wings upon the Colorado air, if she could get possession of them before those wings were grown.[60]

But how to get possession—that was a problem!

The lower limbs of the tree were at quite a distance from the ground, and its trunk was large and comparatively smooth.

---

59. Elliott Coues (1842–1899) was a prominent ornithologist and the author of *Key to North American Birds* (1872). At Maxwell's request, he wrote the catalog of mammals "Notice of Mrs. Maxwell's Exhibit of Colorado Mammals," completed in May 1877 and included as an appendix in *On the Plains, and Among the Peaks*. Coues had been particularly interested in Maxwell's work, as she had been able to acquire specimens of the black-footed ferret, a task he had been unable to complete successfully.

60. In later years, Maxwell would receive specific requests from naturalists to obtain egg specimens from various bird species. She kept up regular correspondence with naturalists at the Smithsonian Institution, including Robert Ridgway, who contributed the catalog of bird species included at the end of *On the Plains*, and Spencer Baird, to whom *On the Plains* is dedicated.

Mr. Maxwell was consulted. He coolly affirmed "that, under the circum-stances, in the absence of ladders, balloons or other means of ascension, he didn't consider it an open question. There was only one way, and that was, to climb for them. He used to be expert in that business in the days before he was too old to be whipped for robbing birds' nests; and if she wished him to return to that reprehensible practice, he would make the attempt!"

She did wish it, very decidedly. So, his boots were drawn off, and—well—the tree was large, and it was a long way up to any branches, and he was out of practice in that business—so—

"Oh, dear! must I give up that nest?" Mrs. Maxwell laughed as her husband brushed himself, after his failure, which at least was not without a comic side.

"I don't want to, if it can possibly be helped."

"Oh! I have an idea!" she exclaimed, giving the tree another searching glance. "If I were upon your shoulders I believe I could reach that lowest limb, and then I'm *sure* I could climb to the nest."

"You'd better not risk breaking your neck for it," Mr. Maxwell replied; "besides, how do you know but you'd have to fight the old hawk? I should judge from her size she was capable of having something to say as to whether you could have her family or not. She could half kill you, for all you could do toward defending yourself against her beak and talons."

"Oh, pshaw! I don't believe she'd dare touch me! besides, you can shoot her. It would be cruel to leave her to grieve over the loss of her children; and then, I ought to preserve her any way, for she is different from any hawk I have. Come; you take care of her, and let me get the little ones," she added, coaxingly.

"Oh,

> " 'Where a woman wills, she will,
> You may depend on't—
> Where she won't, she won't,
> And there's the end on't' "[61]

He quoted, with a laugh. "Come on! but first tell me where to look for a stepmother for your family of beasts, birds and creeping things? There are few who would accept even me with such encumbrances."

---

61. A variation of a common proverb at the time.

"Nonsense! In place of that, I'll take off my shoes," she said, unfastening them, in high spirits. "There, now; I'm ready."

Mr. Maxwell, by the way, is six feet high and well-proportioned; so, it was no difficult feat for him, while standing by the tree, to put such a little thing as his wife upon his shoulders.

"There, how is that?" he asked, picking her up.

"All right, thanks; only I wish you were a little taller," she replied, "I can only just touch the limb. Could you possibly stand on tip-toe? That's it! Hold you neck stiff, now!" and putting one foot on his head, she braced the other against the inequalities of the bark and drew herself up among the branches.

"Oh! this is splendid!" she called down from among the leaves. "Now, you'll be sure to take care of the old bird! I want her, you know."

"Don't you worry about her," he replied advancing to the wagon and taking up the gun.

Alarmed for the safety of her nest, the hawk was not long in giving him an opportunity to quiet all apprehension of danger from her beak and talons, thus leaving Mrs. Maxwell free to realize her lofty aspirations without other concern than to preserve her own bones unbroken.

The ascent was in every way successful. It is true, the limbs of the tree were not all arranged to the best advantage for the accommodation of aspiring bodies; but then, she remembered having heard that upward progress is always attended with difficulties that seem insurmountable. Contrary to approved ideas, the descent was not without them either, in this case.

Where it had been an almost impossible feat to draw one's body up to a branch just within one's reach over-head, in coming down, it was not pleasant to hang suspended by one's hands. Suppose one's feet should miss the limb by no means exactly below them. If, as the Irishman asserted, "the fall didn't hurt any," the stopping most assuredly would! By great exertion and skill, she managed to avoid trying the experiment, however, and with nothing more serious than a few narrow escapes and some scratches, succeeded in slipping safely into Mr. Maxwell's arms again, with one downy hawklet and an unhatched egg in her bosom!

Upon reaching their destination—a ranch on the Platte—the egg was given to the kindly care of a setting hen, which had the dubious satisfaction of ending happily the incubation of one of her worst enemies.

The one already hatched Mrs. Maxwell dared not trust to her keeping, lest she should recognize in its voice, or in some other way, its lineage, and kill it as it slept. So she took upon herself the maternal responsibility of supplying its slumbers with needed warmth and covering.

Both birds reached Boulder in safety the next day, where they were fed and cuddled, and made happy until their robes of snowy-white down were of the most desirable length, when a little chloroform induced them to stop growing. A nest, like the one they occupied in their native tree, was procured. They were stuffed, and placed in it, with their little mouths open and their necks stretched up toward their mother, which, with a rabbit in her talons, was suspended over them.[62]

---

62. This is the first of four such mother-child scenes that underscore how Dartt presents Maxwell's taxidermy work in a way that evokes both feminized sentimentality and violence. The other examples are the scenes when Maxwell shoots a mother skunk and her kit (chapter 19), when she kills and stuffs a mother bear and lets her living cubs interact with it (chapter 24), and when she is angry because she cannot kill a buffalo calf after killing its mother (chapter 26).

10

PLEASURE PARTY. OUTFITTINGS. PRIMITIVE STYLE. FEASTS
IN THE FOREST. HIGH ALTITUDES. CAMPING ALONE.
CHIPMUNKS. TUFTED-EARED SQUIRRELS.
THUNDER-STORMS. RETURN HOME. "BUCKING."
CHILD IN TROUBLE. DIFFICULTIES INCREASE.
LIGHTNING AND DARKNESS. INTREPID COURAGE.
FLOOD AND THUNDER. RESCUED.

During the latter part of this summer, excursion parties for pleasure were often formed to visit various points of interest.

Don't let any one innocently imagine these were basket picnics, where everybody rode out in fresh dresses and blue ribbons at nine in the morning, partook of sandwiches, cold chicken, champagne and ice-cream, on rustic seats in a grove, and returned in good order to their usual domiciles at night. If any one has such an idea lingering around that word, excursion, I advise its banishment as soon as possible.

The Colorado variety is no such affair. The parties, in the first place, expect to be out of doors not less than three days, sometimes three times that number of weeks. They expect to eat bacon and beans, with fish and game of their own killing; to sleep on the ground, in tents or out of them, as circumstances dictate. The ladies to dress after a fashion similar to the one Mrs. Maxwell had adopted for such trips; one short suit, a warm wrapper, a shade hat or a sun-bonnet, and some outside wraps, are all that any sensible lady excursionist sanctions; anything more is a weariness and a vexation.

For long trips an "outfit" must be provided which shall include all necessaries and no superfluities—and its first requisite, a determination to reduce the sum of one's physical wants to the lowest possible figure; its next a pleasant party—one that shall contain not more than one *shirk* or grumbler. An individual of this kind, if the company is to be large, is rather desirable. Should there prove to be no other point of common interest, the sentiment of disgust for him or her will be a magnetic cord of the best quality, warranted to wear, to bind the others together. I assure you if there seems to be not a single subject upon which they agree, let his or her name be mentioned, and they are one in a moment.

This matter and the question of costume disposed of, food, shelter and the means of conveying the same from one point of interest to another, remain. Unless pack-animals are to be used to carry the baggage, a large mess-box, in which to put food and dishes, is convenient. For these latter, iron and tin are found to be far more desirable than silver, glass and china. If a large wagon is used, a second box is usually carried, into which a camp-kettle, bake-kettle or dutch-oven, tin dipper, coffee-pot, and frying-pan are placed. When pack animals are used, these articles are suspended from any point on the pack where they can be conveniently fastened. In addition to these culinary contrivances, a small kit of tools is necessary to repair broken harness and wagons.

For bedding, rubber blankets or buffalo robes to lay next [to] the ground, and a good supply of warm woolen blankets, are indispensable.

Colorado nights are always cool, and even if one cares for but little covering, beginners at least will not object, before they have tried that resting-place a few hours, to even half a dozen thicknesses of something between them and the breast of mother earth.

Pillows, in dark-colored calico cases, are among permissible luxuries; though I believe veterans in this kind of life prefer a pair of good, hob-nailed, cow-hide boots! For Sundays and rainy days, some books and magazines are quite essential. Some standard medicines, too, are usually carried; and sporting parties, of course, provide for securing game. When a tent of some kind (or, if the party is large, more than one) is added, and everything packed, either in a large covered wagon or on the backs of donkeys or horses and each person is provided with a pony, the party is ready to face life in its primitive conditions! Every one is expected to endure all hardships without a murmur, and to assist in all necessary work without being asked. As for enjoyment—these conditions being complied with—the amount to be had, in anticipation at least, is perfectly limitless!

Of one kind the realization is almost certain. No one can help being happy, blessed with an excursionist's appetite—which is usually keen enough to put him in sympathy with a bear that has just arisen from a six months' fast—when a nice oil-cloth is spread before him on the ground, its centre filled with tin pans of savory bean-soup, boiled or fried potatoes, tin plates of crispy mountain trout or delicious venison, and biscuit hot from the bake kettle, bottles of pickles and cans of fruit, while its circumference is edged with bright tin plates, cups, spoons, and steel knives and forks.

He needs no second invitation to help himself to a set on an inverted pail, folded blanket, camp-stool or stone—whichever is most convenient—and assist in disposing of the tempting repast. If he has eyes for anything beside the food, the dining-room in its size and magnificent appointments—its ceiling, Colorado's matchless sky—its walls, a succession of landscapes, which Bierstadt[63] can never equal—is all that could be desired, to gratify the most aesthetic taste.

Among the excursions of that season was one to the Hot Sulphur Springs, in Middle Park.[64] Mr. and Mrs. Maxwell and their child, Mabel, a girl of nine years, joined it.

They were provided with a pack-horse, carrying a small tent and outfit—as above described—of their own, which they expected, as usual in such cases, to share with the company. But, after going some ten miles into the mountains, they were overtaken by a messenger, and Mr. Maxwell was called back to appear as a witness in court. The rest of the party must go on. He hoped to return and overtake them.

---

63. Albert Bierstadt (1830–1902) was an American painter known for his landscapes of the American West, including the Rocky Mountains. His dramatic landscape paintings highlight the romantic or sublime. Bierstadt is considered part of the Rocky Mountain School of painters along with Thomas Moran and William Keith.

64. Middle Park is a basin in the Rocky Mountains about 50 miles west of Boulder on the west side of the Continental Divide. Originally a Ute campground where Native Americans used the hot springs for medicinal purposes, Hot Sulphur Springs is a town in Middle Park along the Colorado River, established in 1860. The trip described in this chapter took place in August 1868.

They were in the midst of an abundance of mountain raspberries; and Mrs. Maxwell decided to camp, gather some, and collect specimens of the animals of that altitude, till Mr. Maxwell came back.

This matter of altitude seems very strange to one who has never thought about it. It modifies everything, even the rocks. Though they had travelled but ten miles from home, they had risen at least two thousand feet, and were in a climate materially changed by its proximity to the clouds. Boulder and its vicinity are over five thousand five hundred feet above the sea, almost as high as the top of Mount Washington; still it is so much farther south, that beautiful wheat, corn, and almost all kinds of grains and vegetables, raised in any of the Northern States, mature there. But, two thousand feet above it, a different state of things exists. There, only potatoes, oats and vegetables that will either mature in a few weeks, or that will bear frosts, can be raised. Each foot added to the altitude shortens the season for growth, until, upon the Snowy Range—that succession of peaks rising above timber line which forms the watershed between the streams flowing into the Gulf of Mexico and those emptying into the Pacific ocean—discouraged vegetation gives up altogether, and winter and snow have their own way the year round.

The effect of the change in altitude upon the animal world makes mountain regions among the most favorable of all fields for the study of the variation of species, and, therefore, especially interesting to the naturalist.

Although Mr. Maxwell hoped to return so soon, it was two weeks before he was again at liberty. Mrs. Maxwell and her little girl spent the time clambering over the rocks in quest of berries, in pursuit of the shy birds and squirrels, who were the only companions, and in preserving the varied fruits of their rambles. The berries were taken into camp, and, by a process of which Mrs. Maxwell was perfect mistress, made into delicious jam, while the care of her other trophies so fully occupied her remaining time, that, even had she been disposed, she had no leisure to be oppressed by loneliness.

"To him who, in the love of nature, holds communion with her visible forms, she speaks a varied language,"[65] leaving no more occasion for that kind of oppression, if one be a good listener, than would be felt in the

---

65. Opening lines from the poem "Thanatopsis" (1821) by the American romantic poet William Cullen Bryant (1794–1878).

company of many friends. In no place is her voice more audible than amid the mountains, and Mrs. Maxwell had no more thought of loneliness, than had Thoreau in his hermitage, or Audubon in his wanderings.[66]

Mountains, like the sea, satisfy one's deepest cravings for what is grand and sublime, and, like it, shadow forth all one's changing moods. They never look twice alike: each variation in the density of the atmosphere, each increase of light or shade, changes their aspect. The eye never tires of watching their variety, nor [sic] ceases, when it has learned to love them and has parted from them, to hunger for their smiles and frowns.

But Mrs. Maxwell's time did not pass without its small excitements. The rocks and trees were frequented by a variety of different kinds of squirrels. One kind—four-striped chipmunks—were very numerous and cunning. They resemble the Eastern chipmunks, only they are much smaller and more sprightly. As an old miner remarked, "Them critters are just lightnin' on legs. You can't look at one on [sic] 'em afore it's gone, and while you're trying to sense the fact, what d'ye see, but the same critter a cuttin' round on another rock right afore your eyes, but a heap further off."

A few days after they went into camp, these little neighbors seemed to assemble for a picnic, council, or something of the kind, on a level spot among the rocks. They didn't invite Mrs. Maxwell to be present; but, having her share of feminine curiosity, she crept near to see what they were about. They were simply scampering around, so she concluded to call them to order by firing a signal-gun. One discharge furnished her five of the little fellows ready for taxidermic honors.

At another time she shot some tufted-eared squirrels, a species peculiar to the Rocky Mountains. Their ears are the most marked peculiarity, being ornamented in a grotesque fashion by tufts of long hair. Colorado seems to be particularly favorable to the growth of ears. Please don't think I mean any

---

66. Dartt places Maxwell alongside two of the most influential nature writers of the nineteenth century: Henry David Thoreau (1817–1862) and John James Audubon (1785–1851). She draws parallels between the two men's largely solitary experiences in nature with Maxwell's experiences in the Rocky Mountains. Dartt refers to Thoreau's hermitage at Walden Pond that forms the basis of his book *Walden* (1854) and Audubon's many excursions through North America in pursuit of specimens for the eventual publication of *Birds of America* (1827–1839). Maxwell's frugal, practical, and economical way of living also seems in line with Thoreau's goal to live simply.

disrespect to the new-fledged State.[67] I only state a fact. Donkeys flourish there; so do mules. People have always supposed that rabbits everywhere had one feature sufficiently developed, but there their ears grow so much longer than at the East, that the bunnies of our childhood had none worth speaking of in comparison. And those squirrel's ears, aside from the tufts of hair that finished them off, were a third longer than those of their Eastern brothers.

Mrs. Maxwell also captured here rare birds of several kinds; and, what might be of scientific value, could it be estimated, and any one was curious as to the amount a woman can endure when interested in her work, she was captured by a great number of thunder-storms, and wet through and through time and again. It was during the latter part of August, a time of the year when every cloud of any size that sails over the mountains is liable to get its equilibrium sufficiently disturbed to capsize it before it gets away from among the peaks. The getting wet was not so bad as the getting dry again. Of course, as soon as there was any sign of a shower, they would start for the tent; but, if they were any distance away, could only reach it in time to change their drenched clothing, and if possible warm their chilled and shivering bodies. If they were out in two showers in one day and had both suits wet, they were obliged to go to bed. A fire was frequently impossible upon these damp occasions, as the same shower that drenched them wet their fuel also.

The getting up in the morning after such an adventure is what tests one's amount of "clear grit." Clothes damp, boots hard and stiff, frost a quarter of an inch thick on everything outside the tent, and no hope of warmth and breakfast, till, from under sheltering rocks and logs, enough fuel can be gathered for a fire.

Late one evening they were startled by a deep growl coming from behind a tree close to the tent. The child shuddered and turned pale; but Mrs. Maxwell, with her characteristic coolness and determination, grasped her gun and prepared to secure a new specimen, or at least defend herself and [her] child from harm. The growl was repeated. The California or mountain lion was not uncommon in the neighborhood. One must be in or behind the tree, and she put her gun—one barrel of which was always kept in readiness for such

---

67. Colorado became a state in 1876, which was three years before the publication of *On the Plains* and one year before Dartt began writing the book.

large creatures—in position to fire as soon as she could discover it; when a familiar voice exclaimed, *"Hold on! Don't shoot!"* and Mr. Maxwell emerged, laughing, and protesting, *"You don't scare worth a cent!"*

Of course, the party they had hoped to regain was on its way home by that time, and there was nothing for them to do except return. They did not wish to remain over Sunday, but were unable to start until late Saturday afternoon. Mr. Maxwell had brought his son's wife and family to the nearest house, a mile or so distant from the camp, and it was arranged that in returning he should take them back in the carriage in which they came up; Mrs. Maxwell and Mabel should ride their ponies, and the baggage be packed upon the third horse, which the former should lead.

Mr. Maxwell, feeling sure they would meet with no difficulty his wife was not competent to manage, took the lead, and, anxious to reach his son's as soon as possible on account of the little children, was soon out of sight. The pony Mabel rode proved a vicious little beast, of the breed familiarly known at the West as broncho—a cross between the Mexican and Indian ponies, possessing all the vices and few of the virtues of both ancestral lines. The art of "bucking" is one of its birthrights. It will be necessary to explain to Eastern intellects that this accomplishment consists in arching the back somewhat after the manner of an angry cat, and jumping up, coming down stiff-legged on the fore-feet while throwing up the hind ones.

No matter how scientific and "Rareyfied"[68] (!) the treatment he may have received, it is impossible ever to be certain, that a horse of this lineage is so broken or so thoroughly trained, that a week's rest and liberty will not render him next to unmanageable.

Mabel's pony had had quite a taste of freedom, and had no idea of tamely submitting to subjection again. She had ridden only a little way before he began a series of antics, annoying not only to his rider, but to both of the horses compelled to be in his company. If near them, he kept them in commotion by viciously biting whatever portion of their bodies came within his reach. If prevented from indulging in this pastime he would "buck," in a mild manner to be sure, but still in a way calculated to shake the constitution as well as the courage of his little rider.

---

68. Refers to training or taming a horse using the Rarey technique, named after John Solomon Rarey (1827–1866), known for his ability to train violent or abused horses.

To obviate this difficulty, Mrs. Maxwell tried putting Mabel behind her on her horse and leading the brute, while the child led the pack-animal.

"Now you must be sure and keep hold of him, May," was her injunction, as she placed the halter in her hands. "You see it is growing dark; if you should let go, it will be so much trouble to get him again, and take so much time."

The poor little girl quite appreciated the importance of the command, and clung desperately with one small hand to her mother, and still more desperately to the halter with the other. Mrs. Maxwell's attention was fully occupied with her new charge, which by no means proposed to reform under the change. Presently there was a scream. The child lay on her back in a rut between the bank and a stone, clinging to the halter of the pack-horse, which was looking down into her face.

That animal had concluded to stop a few minutes, and, not having communicated the fact to the horse Mabel was on, the distance between the horses became greater than the length of the halter and the child, with Casabiancan[69] determination, had to take the consequences!

To add to the comfort of this situation, one of those energetic thunderstorms, with which they had made such familiar acquaintance during their camping experience, gave notice that it was about to commence operations. They were just at the summit of Carl's Hill, above the now famous Magnolia mining-camp.[70] However populous that mountain side may be at present, there was then not a human being living near it. The road, for the next four miles, descended constantly, in many places as rapidly as was practicable and permit teams to pass over it. The only way it was possible for a road to be there at all, was by having its bed dug into the mountain side and carried back and forth zigzag fashion, running a short distance in one direction, then turning abruptly and running back again, each turn being on a lower plane. The lower side was prevented from being washed away by logs and rocks, which formed, with the steep slopes, a nearly perpendicular precipice; while on the upper side was in most places a high wall of earth. The whole affair,

---

69. Casabiancan refers to the poem "Casabianca" (1826) by the British poet Felicia Dorothea Hemans (1793–1835), which tells the story of Giocante, the adolescent son of an eighteenth-century French naval officer, who refused to abandon the post his father directed he keep during the Battle of the Nile (1798).

70. Southwest of Boulder, near present-day Breckenridge, Colorado.

like all mountain and cañon roads, was no wider than was necessary to make a safe track for one vehicle, except in occasional places where, for the length of a team, it was widened for a "turn-out."

With great difficulty the three horses were led to a point where the child could resume her lost seat, and then, amid pelting rain-drops—for the storm had begun—and gathering gloom, Mrs. Maxwell attempted to guide them all three abreast down the steep and slippery road. As the pack-animal required for its bulky load double space, and the broncho was so vicious, the experiment was both difficult and dangerous. She was soon obliged to give it up, as her horse, in defending itself from its malicious neighbor, was continually jerking its head and bringing the pack-horse in front of them, and in the consequent confusion, one or more of them was in imminent danger of going over the bank to certain death.

One other way remained to be tried. Mrs. Maxwell, with her horse between the other two, drew the horses' heads as close together as was possible and leave them room to walk—took a rein from the bridle of the pack-horse with a rein from the bridle of the beast she was riding in one hand, and a rein from the hateful broncho's bit with the remaining one from her bridle in her other hand, and holding her horse so firmly it could not turn its head, hoped she had solved the problem.

Not at all! Exasperated at not being able to defend itself with its teeth, her horse began kicking vigorously, and she and her child barely escaped being thrown over its head and killed. To remain on its back under such circumstances was impossible. There were still fully five miles between them and any shelter. They were drenched through, and shivering with the cold. The darkness was perfect; their narrow ledge of road only visible when some flash of vivid lightning lit up the awful depths beneath them, and the terrific thunder, crash on crash, jarred the earth on which they stood. To stay there was impossible, to go forward was perilous.

Mrs. Maxwell dismounted, and placed the child in her saddle, resolved to walk the remaining distance and lead the unridden horses. Putting herself between them, she slowly and cautiously felt her way down the steep and winding road over which the water was rushing in a flood. She often found herself slipping and falling under their feet; and in her continual fear of going over the lower bank, was coming in collision with the upper one. But bracing herself against the storm and all manifestation of weakness and fear that should further alarm her child, she resolutely kept on her way, although it seemed at times as though both strength and courage were almost gone. Nor need it seem strange; aside from the discomfort of being drenched by icy rain, there are few things in nature that inspire the human soul with a more perfect sense of awe, not un-mixed with fear, than a thunder-storm in the mountains at night. The darkness, the wild rush of winds among the pines and down the gorges, the heavy beating of the rain, the awful picture of abysmal depths and frowning heights which the lightning reveals, the heavy thunder meeting peal on peal, the echo and re-echo, forming for many minutes one continuous roar, ceasing only to bring out in stronger relief the beginning of another cannonade so deafening, it seems, as though the solid heavens had fallen in awful ruins on the granite rocks beneath—all combine in grandeur that is terrible.

What, amid such an awful passion-burst of nature, is a tiny human form?

That winding ledge, upon the mountain's storm-swept side, seemed fearfully narrow. With desperation they clung to it as the wind gathered the falling rain in sheets and dashed it against them. Between the gusts, drearily, step by step, they advanced as the lightning showed them their pathway. Ere long, between the thunder-peals, was heard the roar of threatening waters, and they knew the stream was booming among the rocks at their side. They had reached the Boulder cañon. Its creek, swollen to its brim and rushing a resistless flood, made them tremble for the safety of each bridge that crossed its tortuous course. Once the lightning revealed a scene that thrilled the terrified mother cold with horror.

Mabel's horse had mistaken the road, and, ignorant of this, she was urging it with all her energy into the boiling, seething flood. One moment more and they would be swept under a bridge and be dashed against the dark, pitiless rocks. Mrs. Maxwell's whole being seemed voiced in the scream that reached her child just as she discovered her danger and turned from the threatened grasp of inevitable death.

Sobbing with fright, exhausted with cold and fatigue, she regained the road, but was too much overcome to have retained her hold upon the saddle much longer; nor could Mrs. Maxwell, with the added anxiety for her, have borne up to complete the journey, had not assistance reached them. Just as the last point of endurance seemed to be reached, a light was visible before them, and Mr. Maxwell's son appeared for their rescue.

11

———

ANTELOPE FAWN. NIBBLING HOUSE-
PLANTS. GOES TO SUNDAY-SCHOOL.

During the autumn of this year,[71] an antelope fawn was caught and given to Mabel. When first taken, he was about the size of a young lamb; and though he could eat some grass he was taught to drink milk and feed upon a variety of other things. He grew rapidly, and was soon so tame, he would follow his young mistress, or any member of the family, about like a dog.

The antelope is a pretty, graceful creature, but very singularly marked. Its body stands about three feet high, is of a uniform brownish red, except upon the underside and rump, which are pure white. The hairs upon the latter are of greater length than elsewhere upon its body; and when angry, or excited in any way, it elevates them and spreads them apart, which gives it, upon such occasions, a very comical appearance.

Dick, as the pet was called, was one of the many wild creatures with which Mrs. Maxwell became acquainted, and in which she found much that would interest any person whose sympathies are not strictly confined to our own

———

71. 1868.

species. She avers that all the animals she has thus intimately known have much more than is ordinarily supposed in common with humanity. Among them have been, aside from domestic creatures, raccoons, rabbits, squirrels, porcupines, ferrets, owls, antelopes, bears, prairie dogs, snakes, and wild-cats. All except the latter, which she had but a few weeks, showed appreciation of kindness, and a pleasure in her sympathy. Even her rattlesnakes, after being in the care of strangers a few days, would raise their heads with a look of interest, at the sound of her voice—a sign of recognition they never gave any one else.

Dick not only manifested affection, but a great amount of curiosity. When at home there was no end to his inquisitiveness about household affairs. No sooner was an outside door open, than his beautiful bright eyes were seen looking through it. Nor was he content with that. If no one prevented him, there was not a room on the lower floor he would not enter and examine. It was in vain the girls boxed his ears and lectured him on the impropriety of such conduct, and at times even applied a small willow switch to his slender legs. He would make a hasty retreat to the street or back yard, whichever was the nearer; and, as soon as he could do so without being observed, return to take another nibble of house-plants, or examine a little more closely the contents of some pan or pail in the kitchen. The hired man pronounced him a "perfect hen-hussy," and the "help" in-doors approved of the appellation; for, if the pantry door was open, he was sure to go in and either taste or smell everything within his reach. He tried to go upstairs one day, and, had not the steps been winding, would probably have astonished passers in the street, by looking down upon them from the windows of "my lady's chamber."[72]

Nor was his curiosity confined to the limits of his home. He would visit the principal streets of the village, and look into the business places and grew to be quite familiar with a number of shop-keepers. His special favorites were grocers; but I regret to say, he was not above entering a low saloon occasionally!

I think he must have been enticed into such places though, as a little incident will show that his tastes sometimes ran in quite an opposite direction:

One Sunday morning he strolled around to the Congregational church. It was just Sunday-school time. That service was held in the vestry; its doors stood open, and he saw no impropriety in entering and attending the

---

72. Possibly a reference to *Hamlet*, act 5, scene 1.

exercises. He seemed much pleased to find his young mistress there, as well as several others with whom he was acquainted. As no one offered to drive him out, he, not appreciating the fact that it was because the opening prayer was being offered, proceeded to make himself at home. After looking about a few moments and smelling of things, he discovered the superintendent kneeling, his bald head resting on one hand as he prayed.

Without any hesitation, he advanced to him and nearly convulsed the less devout who were looking on, by proceeding to examine his exposed phrenological developments[73] with his nose; in the meantime that gentleman, in solemn unconsciousness, was passing his hand over his head, as if trying to brush off flies!

---

73. Phrenology (developed by Franz Joseph Gall in 1796), a pseudoscientific discipline that rose to prominence in the nineteenth century, held that people's mental characteristics were located in discrete sections of the brain and that an external study of the shape of people's craniums could indicate or predict those mental traits.

12

SOUTH PARK TRIP. WEIRD SCENERY.
SAD ACCIDENT. SURGERY. A SOLDIER SAVED.

Mrs. Maxwell had a great desire to visit southern Colorado; and in July of 1869, an opportunity presented itself which promised to give her this pleasure. Her husband and his business partner, Mr. S. M—, wished to go to Pueblo and South Park,[74] in the execution of some of their plans, and offered to make the journey with a wagon and camping outfit, if she and her sister[75] would accompany them. The invitation was gladly accepted; and at dawn one morning a "ship of the plains"—as Coloradoans used to call their large covered wagons—freighted and provisioned, moved from their door, to carry them on this excursion.

In the vehicle, above the other baggage, lay the bedding and a gun; on the former, Mrs. Maxwell's sister, unused to such early hours, lay down and

---

74. The town of Pueblo is 112 miles south of Denver. El Pueblo or Fort Pueblo, a trading post, was constructed in 1842 but was abandoned following the Fort Pueblo massacre in 1854. The town of Pueblo was incorporated in 1870. South Park is a grassland flat about 60 miles southwest of Denver and was a center of the 1859 Colorado Gold Rush.
75. Mary Dartt switches back to third person here.

was soon asleep. Mr. S. M— and Mrs. Maxwell—Mr. Maxwell was already in Denver, where they expected to meet him—occupied the seat in front, which commanded a view of all they were passing.

The day promised to be a warm one. They had hardly crossed the Boulder creek before the sun was pouring a flood of heated light down through an atmosphere that seemed never to have known a film of haze or held the vestige of a cloud.

Slowly they climbed to the first plateau stretching southward from the steep bank overlooking the stream.[76] From that point, away toward the east, its silver thread can be traced for miles, flashing in and out between groves and cultivated farms. Then a single isolated pile of rocks, rising abruptly two hundred and fifty feet from the valley, intervenes and shuts it from sight. As though to compensate for its absence from the landscape, a little beyond and to the south of the butte (so the rocky point is called), two little lakes lie sparkling in the morning sun. To the westward, only a mile away, but in that peculiarly transparent atmosphere seeming far nearer, rise in abrupt grandeur the Rocky Mountains, one peak of their snowy range gleaming, cool and white, above the deep shadows of the Boulder cañon. Its presence, in such contrast to the summer light on the nearer landscape makes it the point to which the eye is constantly returning. How weird and spirit-like it looks! Just to the left, the majestic granite cliffs look down in endless vigils on the village dead; but the still, white faces to their keeping given, never wore a look of more unbroken silence and far-off calm, than rests upon that mountain's pale, unshadowed brow. Through all the summer's fitful heat, it knows no change. Above, beyond all other heights, against the western sky, it rests, an object from another clime, above the world of man!

Behind our excursionists lay the waking village and its background of limitless plains. Little did they dream, as they remarked the exquisite beauty of the scene, that before seven years should pass, the State University of Colorado would occupy that very spot. Yet there it stands to-day.[77]

Things move rapidly at the West—so did they.

------

76. Greenbelt Plateau and Coal Creek.
77. Dartt refers to the University of Colorado Boulder, which was founded in 1876.

The fields and houses were all passed, and they were climbing the hills that form the watershed between Boulder and Coal creeks, when Mr. S. M— descried a large bird.

It was hopping along the ground at some distance from them, and passed so quickly behind a knoll, that he could not determine what it was.

Tossing Mrs. Maxwell the reins, with the injunction to "drive on," he sprang down to see if he could find out what it might be. The horses were slowly toiling up the hill. Mrs. Maxwell's attention was riveted to the hiding-place of the missing bird. She did not notice that after leaving the road for a few moments, Mr. S. M— had returned to the back of the wagon for the gun. Suddenly she was startled by its report immediately behind her. Turning her head, she saw him reeling to the ground, and heard him exclaim—

"I've shot myself!"

Her sister was springing up with startled face, and hands pressed to her ears. Quick as thought the horses were stopped, and both women sprang to the ground and rushed to the wounded man. In the dusty road he lay writhing with pain, his clothes covered with blood which was gushing from his right arm. Quicker than it can be told, Mrs. Maxwell was knotting her handkerchief around the limb above the wound, he, in the meantime, averring between his groans, "that it was good enough for him! He had always said a man who is fool enough to draw a loaded gun toward him by the muzzle, ought to be shot!"

When this first surgical operation was finished, he rose up and staggered to the roadside in an attempt to get into the wagon. Too faint from loss of blood, he again sank down on the ground.

"Oh, if I had some water!" he moaned; "I might have strength to get in."

The heat was already aggravating the terrible thirst that accompanies a gun-shot wound.

They had passed a ditch a quarter of a mile or more back. Blocking the wheels and unfastening a tug, that the horses might not move off with the wagon, Mrs. Maxwell seized a pail and ran back for water.

Her sister, with handkerchief pressed to the wound to staunch its bleeding, knelt by the old soldier, who was in a measure repeating a battlefield experience. As she fanned him with his hat—the only thing within reach to give shade or air to either of them—he told her, in broken sentences, how he had caught sight of the bird again, and hurried to the wagon for the gun.

Not wishing to disturb any one, he had seized it by its muzzle and drawn it toward him. The trigger had caught on something, and the charge had passed within a few inches of her head, and lodged in the fleshy part of his arm near the chest.

It seemed very long, under that scorching sun, before Mrs. Maxwell returned; but at last she reached them, panting with her rapid exertion and the heat; and, handing her sister the water, sat down in utter exhaustion. The ditch proved to be nearly dry, and she had gone still farther back, to try a well near a deserted cabin. She found it dry, and was compelled to bring him what she could of the warm, muddy contents of the ditch.

Bad as it was, the wounded man drank it eagerly; then came the question of returning home. The vehicle was turned about, and, through the combined strength and ingenuity of them all, he at length reached the bed and was made as comfortable as possible for the painful ride. His wound proved a dangerous one, and for many weeks Mrs. Maxwell's whole time and attention were absorbed in his care. To her friends in sickness she is ever a most skillful and devoted nurse; and though her trip to southern Colorado was lost, she was happy at last in seeing her charge again able to be about and still in the possession of two arms.

13

THE BLACK HILLS. TREELESS LAND-OCEAN.
A GALE. CAMPING. SHAWL PARTITION. "BLISTERING
BLAZES!" GALE-SWEPT BEDS. BRIGHTER MORNING.
SABBATH CAMP. GAME DISCOVERED. OCTOBER
SNOW. NEARLY FROZEN. SHOT ON THE WING.

A few months later Mr. and Mrs. Maxwell and her sister found themselves
at Cheyenne.[78] Their boarding-place was with the family of a professional
hunter, and many and marvelous were the accounts he gave of game among
the Black Hills. At length it was proposed that both families unite and form
a camping party to that happy hunting-ground! Mr. Maxwell was to take
his camp equipage and team, Mrs. Maxwell and her sister; Mr. C—, simi-
larly provided, his wife and their two boys; and together proceed a couple of
days' journey into the hills. They were to take provisions for ten days, but to
return sooner if game enough to load both wagons should be found before
the expiration of that time.

The weather had been beautiful; the exquisite Indian summer of the
Rocky Mountains, so mild as to make out-door life a delight, so clear that
the far-off hills seemed only a pleasant walk away, the delicate veil of most
transparent purple haze resting upon all distant objects, softening but not
obscuring their outlines.

---

78. Cheyenne, Wyoming. Fall of 1869.

To memory, the Cheyenne of this date is like a point at sea: "One could look the farthest there and see nothing of any spot in the world!"[79] Land, land everywhere, but not a tree, not a rock, not a stream in sight! save at the west. There the long, petrified billows of America's great inland ocean seemed to break against something, and a dark, surflike outline of low, dusky hills lay against the sky. Toward them they journeyed.

For the first few hours their road lay parallel with the track of the Union Pacific Railroad. Its grade here is so even that the ascent is hardly perceptible to the eye, yet so great as to frequently necessitate a double force of engines from Cheyenne to Sherman. Every little way a spark from some passing locomotive had set fire to the grass along the roadside, and the irregular patch burned over showed in black and striking contrast to the even brown of the unnumbered acres of natural pasture they were traversing.

Just afternoon, the sky which had before shut down, a perfect dome of faultless blue, showed a little drift of pure white clouds where its western rim was serrated by the outline of the hills. Clouds of this kind are peculiar. Their frayed edges seem blown toward one as though a strong current of air was forcing itself between them and the mountain tops; otherwise, more ordinary, innocent-looking mist banks never showed themselves to mortal eyes. They may lie for days not a handbreadth above the western horizon, but, notwithstanding their harmless aspect, every old frontiersman—which means any one who has lived in sight of the mountains [for] two years!— begins to fasten down all moveable articles and to hold on to his hat for a "blow!" He has learned to recognize in that dainty-looking pile of vapor the untied mouth of the leathern sack wherein old Æolus[80] keeps his fiercest blasts!

And blasts indeed they are! If nothing else can be said in favor of the climate of Colorado and her sister States, it must be admitted that at times they enjoy a free circulation of air!

Sometimes for three days together all the windows of heaven seem to be thrown open for ventilating purposes; and if any corner escapes having its atmosphere changed a few thousand times, those who live in its vicinity would like to know how it is done!

---

79. This quotation cannot be sourced. But the succeeding sentence plays with the wording and imagery of Samuel Taylor Coleridge's *The Rime of the Ancient Mariner* (1798).

80. Æolus, in Classical mythology, was the ruler of the winds.

Premonitory gusts were making the possession of wraps and loose property exceedingly precarious when our excursionists camped for the night. The horses were *lariatted* out (which means, they were prevented from running away by being tied by ropes from fifty to a hundred feet long, fastened to iron pins driven into the ground) to feed on the brown grass, hay-cured standing!—which is the glory of the plains in winter—and the party proceeded to discuss the prospects for the night.

"You can't make a tent stand in such a wind as this! and such ground, too, to hold the pins! There's no use in trying," decided Mr. C—, after several ineffectual attempts to pitch it had been made.

"There isn't a rock nor [*sic*] a bank of earth near here, and just the only thing we can do is to make our beds and get into them before they are taken off," he continued.

Some lunch was eaten, and then they proceeded to follow his suggestion. When "the bosom of our common mother"[81] is to serve one as bedstead and mattress both, one discovers before morning that it is policy to select as smooth and soft a spot upon it as possible! A little gentle persuasion with the head of a hatchet given to over-ambitious grass roots is conducive to repose. One can maintain the same position so much longer when the ridge between one's seventeenth and eighteenth vertebra[e] is only an inch high, than they can when it is three!

The removal of small stones and the substitution of a few leaves and slender twigs also has a soothing effect. Excursion parties usually sleep in tents. Where the company is not very large, and one of those portable hotels answers for all, as soon as it is pitched a part of the number assume the duties of chambermaids and proceed to pick up the stones, smooth off the ground, and, where they are to be found, cover it thickly with boughs of evergreens, willows or aspens. A partition is made of shawls, or anything which will answer the purpose. One side is the gentlemen's, the other the ladies' sleeping apartment.

When the tent is small, the extremities of the sleepers are sometimes brought very near the dividing partition, but, ordinarily, this doesn't matter. I[82] never was with a party but once when it was other than a subject of

---

81. Jean-Jacques Rousseau, *Reveries of a Solitary Walker* (1782).

82. Dartt returns to first person.

indifference. Then the curtain dividing the tent was put parallel with the door, before which was a blazing fire. The ladies of the party—there were four of us—had the back room, while the husbands and fathers lay with their heads from the fire, and of course in close proximity to the partition, which was at the foot of our couch. The nights were frosty—it was high up in the mountains—and our feet had previously failed to get warm for some time after retiring.

"Let's heat some large stones while we are getting supper and put them on the ground at the foot of our bed," suggested Mrs. K—. "They will get it nice and warm by bedtime, and no one but ourselves need know anything about our being so fussy!"

The idea pleased us, and, while the men were busy caring for the horses and getting wood, a hot stone wall was laid through the tent snugly hidden under the blankets, and in due time we retired in silence and comfort.

Just as we were courting our first dreams, a voice from the other side of the partition was heard softly saying:

"Captain, what in thunder do you suppose ails this tent to-night? It's as hot as an oven!"

"Do *you* think so? *I* was just wondering if we had camped over the crater of a volcano; my head is half-baked!"

"So is mine!" whispered another voice, "and—by the great fire in London! *this ground is positively hot under my pillow!*"

There was a sound, as of men moving to an investigation, while any one might have heard a pin drop on the other side of that curtain, for four females were holding their breath, and trembling with suppressed laughter and fear of discovery. Not one of us had thought of the effect of our comfortable little arrangement upon any one beside [sic] ourselves.

"Blistering blazes! if here isn't a stone just sizzling hot!"

"Good heavens! here's another!"

The atmosphere of intense excitement was rent, just at that moment, by a burst of illy suppressed laughter from within the veil.

Explanations follow; earth safe; gentlemen relieved; final tableau: moonlight on a tent full of tranquil slumber!

As to our present wind-swept company, neither the comfort of a tent, the consolation of a fire, nor the luxury of boughs was possible, they were forced to be content to make their beds by spreading one blanket on the ground and

standing on it until another could be got the right way of the wind to lie parallel with it. By adroitly backing off to the windward until its edge could be
brought to the level of their feet, they were then ready to repeat the process
until the supply of bedding was exhausted, when their duties in that direction ceased, and nothing remained but to keep possession.

I have no doubt myself that the man who declared he picked up a dozen
of Brigham Young's hats in the streets of Cheyenne the morning after a wind
exaggerated.[83] Had he said they were that gentleman's wives' hats, it would
have seemed more probable. Be that as it may, it was certain that where
bedding or anything else would stop, when out from under one's weight, it
would be impossible to determine; so they retired! Undressing was a very
simple process—simply the removing of a few refractory hair-pins; nothing that required the privacy of a dressing-room or the modest veiling of
the moon.

But such a night as it was to sleep! The very thought of it was impossible
from the cold. Though their supply of blankets was ample, wrap themselves
as they might, each gust seemed to penetrate every fibre of their bodies
and to chill the very marrow in their bones. The moon and stars looked
pale and troubled, as, numb and shivering, they watched them through the
interminable hours of that fearful night. But at last, with a cold, exhausted
look, the sun arose and succeeded in quieting the wind to such an extent
that a fire was possible. Some breakfast was eaten; and they started from
their dreary camp. Their road—if a scarcely perceptible trail could be called
one—lay over rolling hills. At first these were quite destitute of trees; but
before nightfall clumps of yellow pine appeared, disposed in such a way as to
remind one of a country gentleman's park. Here and there, too, were passed
strange, wind-worn rocks, from eight to twenty feet high, and from two to
twelve feet in thickness. The rich, brown grass was much taller and more
abundant than on the plains, and gave the landscape a more inviting aspect.
During most of the day the wind kept blowing furiously at times; and every
one but Mr. Maxwell grew nervous from its exhausting effects. His vigor of
body and equanimity of mind were seldom disturbed. If the weather was
disagreeable and the roads almost impassable, he was jolly and smiling. If

---

83. Brigham Young (1801–1877) became the second president of the Church of Jesus Christ
    of Latter-Day Saints in 1847, founded in Salt Lake City that year, and was the first
    governor of Utah Territory from 1851 to 1858. He had fifty-five wives.

the team grew fractious and the harness broke—no uncommon event—he whistled, talked to the beasts, and "tinkered the gearing." If the weather, roads, team, and everything went wrong, he both whistled and sung, until Mrs. Maxwell began to fear that, unless excursions were given up, he would become a second Mr. Chick, and she, when in society, like that gentleman's wife, the far-from-fascinating relative of "Dombey and Son," would have to smother "Annie Laurie," or recall him "From Jordan's stormy banks" every few minutes, to preserve his decorum.[84] He was proverbial for driving over the most breakneck places without breaking any one's neck.

At night fortunately the wind grew calm, and they camped on the banks of a lovely, bush-fringed brook. Behind them lay the beautiful, park-like country. Before them, over broken, rocky hills, rose exquisitely tinted snow-capped mountain peaks. Here they passed Sunday. Their tent was pitched and luxuriantly carpeted with evergreens. Their literary supplies were brought out—a Bible, copies of the *Northwestern Christian Advocate*, "Captain Riley's Life and Adventures in Africa," some *Atlantics*, and works on geology and natural history.[85] Each lounged, or read, as fancy dictated. The C—s were clever people—Mrs. C—, like Mr. Maxwell, blessed with the memory of many beautiful hymns; so the day closed, as Sunday always should, with music.

The next morning they started for a small lake not many miles distant, and the pursuit of game, or rather the discovery of some to pursue, became the absorbing subject of interest. Noon came and the water was reached before anything worthy of a charge of powder was seen. Then, while the others were busy with the tent, horses, and preparations for dinner, Mrs. Maxwell and the two boys stole cautiously around a low, rocky hill, lying between the camp and lake, to see if any game could be discerned on its border. One of the boys soon appeared at the brow of the elevation, telling by excited signals that a discovery had been made. The men seized their guns, and all made their way swiftly, but silently, to a spot where they could see the surface of

---

84. Charles Dickens's serial novel *Dombey and Son* (1846–1848).

85. The *Northwestern Christian Advocate* was a weekly newspaper published by the Methodist Episcopal Church. "Captain Riley's Life and Adventures in Africa" most likely refers to the 1817 memoir *Authentic Narrative of the Loss of the American Brig Commerce* by the "Late Master and Supercargo" James Riley (1777–1840), later re-titled *Sufferings in Africa*. It recounts Riley and his crew's enslavement after an 1815 shipwreck in the western Sahara. The *Atlantic Monthly* magazine was founded in 1857 in Boston, Massachusetts.

the lake. On its opposite side a herd of antelope were feeding. Mrs. Maxwell was already halfway along the right bank, creeping unobserved toward them. Something soon gave them a premonition of evil. They raised their heads and looked toward her. Those who were watching held their breath, lest they should turn and disappear before she could get near enough for a shot. It must be they saw her. Still they did not run. The secret was soon discovered. Upon the end of her ramrod fluttered a piece of bright red cloth. This was held above her as she crept forward, to excite their curiosity. In their efforts to determine what it could be, danger was forgotten; and she was within easy range when the report of her fire rang out, and a fine buck fell struggling in the grass. The afternoon was passed by Mrs. Maxwell in skinning her trophy and in taking measurements of it, to assist her in building up the artificial body over which the skin was to be placed.

Of these measurements, in large animals, from fifteen to twenty were needed, and, aside from the length and the height, it was desirable to take them from the body after the removal of the skin. This work, together with the cleaning of such bones as it was important to preserve, was neither easy nor agreeable, but she always preferred doing it herself, as it gave her the opportunity of studying the shape and disposition of prominent muscles, etc. She considered a knowledge of the anatomy of an animal as essential in taxidermy, as in sculpture, to the finest artistic effect.

The next morning the wind rose, and snow began to fall. It was late in October, and their altitude was not less than 8,000 feet above the level of the sea; so that what would have been a mild autumnal rain in a lower region, there was snow and sleet. Not the snow that poets rhapsodize, that comes floating earthward through the shadowed air,

"Like down from angel wings cast off,

As plumed for joyous flight."[86]

Not a bit of it!

If in any way it suggested poetry, it was by making them wonder that Milton[87] had not stretched his infernal heroes upon such a plain to be pelted with the sharp, cutting crystals, and to be pierced through and through by the pitiless wind which accompanied it.

---

86. Lines of verse appear to be of Dartt's creation.
87. John Milton (1608–1674), English poet and author of the epic poem *Paradise Lost* (1667).

Theirs was only an "A" tent, but all were obliged to take refuge in it. A fire was an impossible luxury. The two boys and three women wrapped themselves in the bedding to keep from freezing.

It was anything but droll then, though it does make a picture that one can smile at now—the way in which that wretched day was passed: how they took turns in reading Captain Riley's adventures in the burning sands of the Sahara, to keep their imaginations warm; how, as they looked in each other's [sic] blue faces, just peering out of the gray blankets, they envied him some of the superfluous heat from which he so nearly perished. The delineations of scenes that would have filled their eyes with tears—read on a July day—called forth nothing more tender than a compassionate wish that they could change places with him for a few hours.

The storm continued until the afternoon of the following day, although it softened enough so that in the morning Mrs. Maxwell and the men, impatient of the close confinement, went out in search of game around a second lake, a mile or more distant.

As most western lakes are, it was the haunt of great numbers of waterfowl. But they are very shy, and their capture by no means easy or certain. After trying in vain to get a shot at some, Mrs. Maxwell climbed a rocky point to look for other game; when a shot from her husband's gun, aimed at a flock of wild geese, sent them flying over her head, and this enabled her to shoot one of them on the wing. It was a beautiful bird, and she felt abundantly paid for her disagreeable walk.

Although game was not so plentiful as they had hoped, the remainder of their stay was in pleasant weather and very enjoyable.

During the trip just described, and on all previous occasions, the collection of duplicate skins was an object never forgotten. These, properly cured, could be sent to any part of the world, exchanged for skins from other lands, and were valuable for scientific institutions everywhere.

14

SALE OF SPECIMENS.

Before the summer of 1870 was over, her collection had grown to such pro-
portions as to have attracted the attention of the leading men in the Territory,
and she received an offer of a pass to St. Louis and return, with transportation for it thither if she wished, if she would consent to arrange it in Denver
for the Territorial Fair.[88] This she felt obliged to accept, as it became apparent that she must make a disposal of all her mounted specimens. Through
adverse business fortunes, the finances of the family were in a straitened
condition. Her utmost sacrifices, with those of her husband, were needed
to rescue some fragments from the wreck. Yet, so great was her attachment
to her specimens, so enthusiastic had been her desire that each one should
be of permanent good to natural history, that it was with the bitterest pain
she thought of their disposal. She had given them all an artist's love for his
work, and his patient care and labor; aside from that, many had cost her

---

88. In the fall of 1870, Maxwell displayed her specimens at the Colorado Agricultural
Society fair in Denver. She had first exhibited her specimens there in 1868.

great exposure and suffering, and many, from other associations, were very dear to her. But there was no alternative, and after vexations and anxieties at St. Louis, which we will not recount,[89] they became, for a sum insignificant compared with their cost to her, the property of Shaw's Garden, in that city.[90]

However, with this timely assistance, a home at least was made sure to herself and family, and her untiring will and energy left less fettered. With the many duplicate skins which she had, unmounted, she resolved to begin again, and at least replace the specimens with which she had parted.

89. James's business failures necessitated selling Maxwell's collection, despite her strong attachment to her specimens.

90. Shaw's Garden, now known as the Missouri Botanical Garden, paid $600 for the collection, which included over 600 specimens. The specimens were displayed until 1889, when, badly damaged by insects, they were put into storage. In 1906, when the University of Colorado Museum inquired about the specimens, it was told the condition of the collection was beyond repair.

15

NATURALIST'S HOME. SACRIFICE A PLEASURE. SUCCESSFUL
SHOT. SNOW ON FLOWERS. EATING (?) STUFFED BIRDS.
MRS. MAXWELL'S DEN. THE DOG "PILLS." DOM PEDRO'S
VERDICT. WHISTLE SOFTLY. UNCONTROLLABLE LAUGHTER.

The place purchased for their new home was on the right bank of the Boulder creek, just at the mouth of its cañon.

Before the house, as far as the eye could reach, stretched the village-and-tree-dotted valley of the stream; behind it rose the first abrupt elevation of the mountains, eleven hundred feet in height, its precipitous sides green and tree-crowned.

The situation was an admirable one for a naturalist, as it was visited by animals from both the mountain ranges and the plains. Here, while varying the monotony of house-keeping (?) by assisting her husband in planting hundreds of fruit and forest trees and cultivating small fruits, she kept her gun at hand, and her eyes and ears open to the arrival of any living creature that could be appropriate to her enterprise. Her old friends, the boys, farmers and miners, remembered her still, and it was a "bad day" that did not see some specimen added to the new collection. She was up early and late, and to say that her time was "more than occupied," does not express it! Society was ignored, all superfluous articles of food and dress were dispensed with, and the large margin of time which such things demand was used, with the closest and most rigid economy in the furtherance of her plan.

The inside of the house was soon a fit study for an artist, to say nothing of its interest for one devoted to natural history. But little time could be given to house-plants, though a few grew in the windows; but native grasses, mosses, ferns, and a lovely little evergreen vine with red berries, under the magic of her fingers more than supplied their place. However it was not in the graceful evergreen sprays, forming lambrequins[91] more dainty than could have been made from any woven fabric, over the mist-like curtains; nor [sic] in the lovely landscapes, and sweet, noble faces, that looked out from frames shadowed by feathery grasses and glossy ivy leaves, that the charm of the rooms lay. They were instinct with life! One could not feel alone in the presence of the owl that looked down in absent-minded benignity from above the door; nor [sic] with the squirrels, which were playing with each other on the picture-frame. Then the humming-bird! Had it just come in through the open window and thrust its beak into the heart of the flower in the hanging-basket? Its tiny feet were drawn up. Had its open wings just ceased to vibrate for a moment that one might catch a better glimpse of their imperial purple, green and gold? And the Bohemian wax-wings, too—exquisite little beauties! Did the murmur of the stream, flowing just below the window, alone prevent their voices being heard?

To those who knew the history of those perched within that room, they were interesting, not only from their beauty and associations with Arctic storms, but also as reminders of an unusually fortunate shot. I cannot tell how it happened—only it did—a flock of them came into Mr. Maxwell's garden one day, and Mrs. Maxwell killed thirteen of them with one discharge of her gun!

It was in May, but it had been snowing for nearly twenty-four hours, a light, feathery snow, that would have been rain had Boulder been two or three thousand feet lower in altitude. Elevated positions have, as all who occupy them testify, their peculiar disadvantages. One of those attendant upon living so near heaven is, that its clouds are manufactured just over your chimney-top, and you have their contents first-hand, which is very likely to be in some kind of frozen condition. Flowers appear in Colorado, on sheltered, sunny

---

91. A short curtain or piece of drapery suspended as an ornament from a mantel shelf.

slopes, in February, but that is no sign the visits of snow-storms are over. By no means!

One needn't be surprised to look out and see their white mantles wrapping the green hill-tops the 9th day of June! Of course, a few hours of sunshine translates them into spirit-like clouds that strand themselves among the mountain-tops, until those greedy wreckers, the dry breezes, drink them up and they disappear. The fact that this snow fell on flowers and budding trees did not prevent its being fifteen or sixteen inches deep, but those birds like perpetual cold weather, rarely leaving the Arctic regions or the tops of high mountains, except when snow goes with them; and to this storm Mrs. Maxwell was indebted for their presence.

Successful as she was with her gun in her new surroundings, she was not always dependent upon it, as she captured several specimens without its aid. One of them, a beautiful, fierce goshawk, she caught with her naked hands!

His presence was announced by a wild outcry from the poultry. Hastening to the barn she discovered him trying to bury his talons in the back of the very king of the roost! Shutting the doors, she interfered in behalf of his black-Spanish majesty, by seizing his foe from behind by the pegs, and pinioning his head under her arm before he had time to use his savage beak! He was a beautiful bird—one of the very handsomest of the predatory family—a dark slate color, with richly penciled light and dark breast. He had such a fearless face, and such keen, flashing eyes, Mrs. Maxwell did not like to kill him, so she took him into the bird-house, and, as they would say on the plains, "lariatted" him to the antler of an elk. For two days he hopped about in a restless, discontented fashion, spending his energies in pulling on his string. Then he tried another plan. He seemed to have reasoned it all out, just as anybody would have done: he began and very persistently picked it to pieces. As soon as he was at liberty, he attempted to gratify his instinct for preying upon other birds, by capturing and devouring a few that were perched in his prison. As they were stuffed, the first part of the task was not difficult, but the latter part—Mrs. Maxwell would have given something for his verdict upon the quality and flavor of her dressing, though it didn't seem to agree with him. He must have been capable of an opinion, for if he didn't reason about that string, what did he do? Why did it take instinct two days to tell him it could be picked to pieces?

His prison, the bird-house, was not such an uninteresting affair as places of confinement are usually supposed to be. Mrs. Maxwell's family called it her "den." It was a small building a little distance from the house, made expressly for her work-room, and what a curiosity-shop it soon became! Wire, hemp, cotton, and hay; clay, salt, plaster, and alum; mosses, grasses, and branches of trees; bars of iron, and blocks of wood; palette brushes, putty, and paints; nests and eggs of birds, and fresh-water shells; bottles of insects, and reptiles, glass eyes, and tools; fossils, minerals, and bones of beasts; heads and horns of buffalo, antelope, and mountain sheep; birds' skins, heads, and antlers of deer and elk; guns and ammunition; in fact, something of almost every created thing she could get in all stages of transformation and preservation!

To this castle of miscellanies all candidates for taxidermic immortality were brought, and before a year had passed its walls were picturesque with rows of various kinds of owls, looking down in unblinking solemnity on multitudinous perches filled with all manner of feathered neighbors, while the centre of the room was occupied with incomplete groups of beasts of all kinds and sizes, from a grizzly bear to a jumping mouse.

"You fearful woman! how can you have the heart to take so many lives?" was a frequent exclamation of Mrs. Maxwell's lady friends, upon entering it.

"Oh," she would laughingly reply, "I suppose you think me very cruel, but I doubt if I am as much so as you! There isn't a day you don't tacitly consent to have some creature killed that you may eat it. I never take life for such carnivorous purposes! All must die some time; I only shorten the period of consciousness that I may give their forms a perpetual memory; and, I leave it to you, which is the more cruel? to kill to eat, or kill to *immortalize?*"[92]

All the candidates for her skill in this direction were not specimens of scientific value. Occasionally a fine owl or other bird would be shot by some one who wished it mounted for themselves or friends, and would bring it to her. Sometimes a pet would come to an untimely end, and the grief in its circle of human admirers would demand its preservation. This was the case with *"Pills."*

Those who have never seen her collection may be pleased to know that "Pills" is the dog of which H.H.[93] speaks—a black-and-tan terrier, about whose condition there is still no end of dispute.

---

92. This passage marks Dartt's most direct response to questions about the ethics of Maxwell's taxidermy. In her dialogue, Maxwell shifts the narrative of her killing of animals from cruel blood sport to thoughtful preservation, arguing that the animals she kills serve a greater purpose than do animals killed for food.

93. Helen Hunt, see note 12.

"Is that air dog alive, or not?" was a common Centennial form of the question. Here are a few of its variations:

"Do see that little dog! He lies so still there among those stuffed animals, I almost thought he was stuffed too!"

"Maybe he is," and a parasol handle is carefully applied to his body. "As true as you live! He is as dead as a door-nail!"

"Well, I never!"

"What'll you bet that dog ain't stuffed?"

"Bet? I'll bet you a 'V' you won't think so when he tears your clothes. You'd better let him alone!" The end of a cane settles the question for them.

Even Dom Pedro,[94] after inspecting him with his royal eyes, said:

"Very good! Very good! Like live!" and he emphasized his verdict by a cordial shake of Mrs. Maxwell's hand, in token of his appreciation of her success. Certainly, when first mounted, his appearance was natural enough to deceive any one.

There was no one in Mrs. Maxwell's sitting-room when I came into her house one day and saw him lying in a large rocking-chair, the very one in which I wished to sit.

"What does this mean?" I thought. "Mrs. Maxwell is not a lover of small dogs, and has none of her own. For some one else's dog to be taking such liberties was a piece of impudence.

"Get down, sir!" and my hand came down on him in anything but a caress.

Whatever may be general opinion concerning my face, it must have been expressive then—that dog was as hard as a brick!

Had there been a wild cat in that chair, with glaring eyes and ferocious jaws, just ready to spring at me, I should have smiled and said, "Well done!" Had there been a rattlesnake coiled, with head erect, and black tongue darting in and out, I should have taken hold of it, and asked "how she got the motion?" There wasn't a *wild* beast existing, so dangerous or so rare, that I shouldn't have *known* it was stuffed if I had seen it there; but a dog, just an ordinary black-and-tan dog, I wasn't prepared for that! Nor were my friends, when afterward it lay under the hat-rack in my hall. There had been an

---

94. Emperor Dom Pedro II of Brazil (1831–1889) and President Ulysses S. Grant (1822–1885) opened the Philadelphia Centennial International Exposition together on May 10, 1876. Dom Pedro was one of many visitors to Maxwell's *Woman's Work* exhibit at the centennial.

entertainment, and "Pills" had made a successful debut on the stage. After the performance he sojourned with me for a while, and occupied the position indicated. It was summer, and the door usually stood open. There was no end to the amusement afforded the family over callers, for the majority of them took care, before announcing themselves, to whistle softly and soothingly to that canine, patting themselves meantime in a manner most ludicrous to those who knew the secret.

Mrs. Maxwell designated "Pills" "a monument to man's inconstancy." His master, a druggist, was deeply affected by his death, and ordered his preservation with emotion in his voice, but before his pet was ready to leave her care, he had recovered from his grief and failed to call for him. So poor "Pills" laid about almost anywhere, but he attracted so much attention that he gradually became a feature among her possessions; and, during the Centennial, as we have said, was the subject of continual discussion.

One thing more—it's quite shocking, but it's too funny not to tell.

Soon after "Pills" was mounted, Mrs. Maxwell had a call from an editor in the place, whose habits of sobriety were decidedly dubious. No sooner did his eyes rest on the dog than he began to laugh in the most uncalled-for manner.

"Is there anything the matter with the dog?" asked Mrs. Maxwell.

"No! ha! ha! ha!"

"Isn't he natural?"

"Oh, yes!" and he held his sides and continued to laugh.

"Do tell me if there is anything that is absurd about that dog?"

"Oh, there isn't a thing! He's perfectly natural!" and off he went again into another spasm of laughter.

Mrs. Maxwell was puzzled. The next time she saw the druggist she remarks, "Mr. S— seems to find 'Pills' exceedingly amusing. I don't know what he sees about him so funny."

"It's the recollection of a joke on himself, I guess," was the reply. "One day, when he was in a very unsettled condition, while leaning his head against the corner of the house to relieve his stomach of the abuses he had heaped upon it, 'Pills' appeared under his nose, whereupon he soliloquized:

"I—I 'member where I ate the sardines, I know who gave 'em oysters, but be hanged if I can tell when I ate that dog."

16

Every day Mrs. Maxwell occupied her new home she was better pleased with
its location. Though it was only a mile from the village, many of the shyest
animals visited it. A herd of deer frequented the mountain, and several times
were seen upon the heights above the house. A number of them were shot
by members of the family, but I need not go into the detail of their capture.
It is no great feat, for one who is used to climbing, to clamber up among the
rocks, and hide or creep about in ambush until within range, and then fire.
I could do it myself if I wasn't a coward, and didn't want both hands at my
ears, and my eyes shut, too, when the gun goes off! More men than I can
count have done it, and not a few pioneer women. It's a fact well known
among those who have given zoology any thought, that neither the beauty,
size, or [sic] ferocity of an animal gives it value to the student of natural history. With most such creatures naturalists are already familiar. Although representatives of their kind are necessary to a complete museum, the interest
of the student does not centre in them. To those seeking merely the profit or
excitement of the chase, size and danger are important factors; but to those

who are intent upon knowing the secrets of the animal world, the capture of the smallest bird or insect, before unknown to naturalists, affords more pleasure than to have outwitted and slain the fiercest grizzly of the mountains, or the largest buffalo of the plains.

While Mrs. Maxwell made it a rule to shrink from nothing that the success of her undertaking demanded, she felt far more interest in obtaining facts about the "flicker"—an unobtrusive little bird—than in taking the largest pair of antlers the country afforded. About the bird, naturalists differ; and only close search and observation can decide the disputed point; but about animals that interest every sportsman from their size, there is no particular question. Many times, to shoot a buffalo is only an act of barbarism that any unthinking person might perform. However, I suppose some people would always feel that I had not done my duty by Mrs. Maxwell and them, if I do not tell them she did, at one time, shoot one of those huge beasts.

I confess that during the Centennial I grew a little out of patience with a good many people of our dear republic. Nothing but physical courage seemed to them of any account. They never saw those tiny humming-birds, with heads no bigger than small peas, that were stuffed and lay in their little nest, looking just as they did when they were alive—the very triumph of a difficult art. They never asked for the person who designed that landscape, and gave the numerous animals upon it their life-like pose and expression; but there was no end of inquiry for "the woman that killed *all those animals!*" and of questions as to *how* Mrs. Maxwell killed the great buffalo and elk, that one *couldn't* miss if they were near enough to them, any more than they could miss an ox!

I'm a little cross yet, I guess; I confess I don't tell the story with a very good grace. But, to begin:

"Once upon a time"—there's nothing like having a narrative commence with a ring of originality—Mr. and Mrs. Maxwell, and a small party, were camping on the plains, when a herd of buffalo were seen in the distance, on the opposite side of the Platte. This stream is broad and shallow, and its channel ever changing about among its shifting sands; but, in order to reach them, they must ford it. Now, this was not such a simple thing as might be imagined, where the bed of the stream was unexplored. Only a trial could determine where the dangerous quicksands and deep holes lay. They had driven their wagon in but a little distance before it began to sink, and an exciting time followed getting it back to the shore, by means of ropes tied to its rear, saddle-horses and men being made to assist the regular team.

"Let's leave it, and have some sport while there's a chance," suggested Miss —. "We can all go on horseback, and live on crackers and buffalo steak!"

"Agreed! That's the idea!" was the general response. There was but one dissenting voice, and that was General E—'s, who said aside to Mr. Maxwell:

"You wife *isn't* insane enough to think of going on, is she? Of course Miss — won't go without her. Why, they might as well commit suicide, and done with it, as to attempt this stream on horseback! They had better stay here—I'll stay with them, if they are afraid to remain alone."

There was a twinkle in Mr. Maxwell's eyes, as he replied:

"I know my wife a little too well to propose such a thing to *her*. She is constitutionally opposed to turning back, and would sooner swim now, than lose a chance of getting among those beasts!"

So the team was unharnessed; all the horses saddled; those before unmounted soon had riders on their backs, and the party plunged into the stream.

"I must say, I think this is a foolhardy adventure," protested the General, as his horse splashed and floundered after the rest. It did look a little like it. They couldn't keep their feet out of the water, except by holding them on a line with their animals' necks, and those beasts were in constant danger of sinking in the quicksands where it was shallow, or of being obliged to swim where it was deep. However, they all happened to land, with at least a semblance of being dry, except for the General. Whether it was because he was so sure that was a proper place to be drowned, or for some other reason, it is certain he reached the land only by clinging to his horse's neck, and came out dripping and shaking himself like a huge Newfoundland, to the no small amusement of the others.

"I told you that was a dangerous venture!" he began, as soon as he could speak. "Zounds! I'd like to know what a fellow's to do here!"

"Never mind your clothes, General! Colorado has a dry climate! Bridget takes her washing out in the yard, and by the time the last of her basketful is on the line, the first are ready to come in. Hurrah for the buffalo! Just keep in motion, and in half an hour you won't know you've ever seen a drop of water!"

"Bridget and the buffalo be—"

No one heard the last of that sentence; but as the General was a lawyer and an ex-Congressman, it is to be presumed it closed with an appropriate ending.

The party was in full gallop for the herd, which, though it had looked so near, was fully four miles away.

As they approached it, an Indian was seen pursuing a fine young cow he had separated from the rest. Like other animals when pursued by creatures of greater speed, it was dodging and doubling, in fierce desperation; but, so well was the savage's pony trained, it seemed instinct with his will, and, without being touched by his hands, which were busy sending arrows into the beast, at every turn it veered and tacked, duplicating every movement the buffalo made.

How long it took to kill the brute was a problem they did not stop to solve. The immense herd—there must have been thousands in it—was moving toward them at a rapid pace. To get in their pathway was to be trodden to death; for, when travelling in such numbers, they are orthodox, and believe man to be only "a worm of the dust," quite too insignificant to turn aside for. Even whole trains of cars are sometimes obliged to wait for them to pass over the track; and until there were strict laws forbidding it, the people, who, at the Centennial, were so anxious to know if Mrs. Maxwell killed that buffalo, used to shoot the noble beasts from the car windows. Did you suggest that I am mistaken about the persons who committed those atrocities? Possibly I am. Of course, I cannot *prove* I am not. I only know I saw the dead creatures lying at short distances from the track, every little way, the first time I went over the Kansas Pacific road, and that I saw one man fire a pistol at a live one, from the window of the car I was in. Wasn't I glad that he missed it!

If the people who, at the Centennial, were so anxious about the answer to the buffalo question, were not the ones who shot them, simply for the sake of saying they had done so, it is safe to presume they were killed by people very like them.

There is one thing quite certain—both parties had one idea in common: that to kill so *big* a thing was a very notable feat! But you say, "You will see how absurd it is, even to suppose the two parties the same, when you remember many of those inquisitive Centennial people were women."

Oh, that does not prove anything. One of the judges of award, when those worthies were inspecting Mrs. Maxwell's collection at the Centennial, said his daughter, while on a trip across this continent, shot two buffalo. I know a young lady, a fashionable Eastern city belle, who fired a pistol at a stone post and hit it. I myself once pulled the trigger of a gun that was aimed at a barn-door and hit it! I really did! Now, it is quite certain a buffalo is larger than a post. There is more to a full-grown one than there is to a barn-door; and if those women were out on the plains, and if the buffalo were as thick as they sometimes are, it wouldn't have taken any more skill to have hit one of them than it did to hit the barn-door!

Now, with your permission, I will finish my story about Mrs. Maxwell's buffalo-hunt.

The party did not see any sport in firing haphazard[ly] into the herd; the probabilities were too great of simply wounding one they would have no opportunity of finally killing; even buffalo have "rights, white people" should be "bound to respect." The herd were going south. They used to migrate like birds before their pastures were invaded by railroads and civilization. When they were not disturbed, they marched one behind another in a very sedate manner, forming a number of nearly parallel trails, fording streams at particular points where the banks were worn by them almost to the level of the water. They were disturbed then, for their human enemies were among them, and their usually orderly proceedings were broken up. They were divided into groups of ten, twenty, a hundred or more of all ages and sizes, all keeping the same general direction, but constantly changing places.

There was a strange excitement about the scene which thrilled both horses and riders. The cloud of dust, the continuous thud of their heavy tread, the rocking motion of their huge, ungainly forms as they plunged forward to escape their pursuers. Mrs. Maxwell was mounted on the General's horse, a blooded mare of mettle and spirit, and for the time both it and its rider forgot they were not a part of the vast rushing herd about them. With flashing eyes and quickened breath they dashed among the groups, escaping the horns of one huge brute, only to be jostled against another—heedless of the shouts of the party, "They will gore your horse!" "They will kill you!" They might as well have called to the wind! On they rushed.

At length the peril of her situation seeming to dawn upon her, she wheeled her foaming horse and made her way to the outer edge of the herd. Here a single beast, a few rods from any of the others, engaged her attention, and the resolve to secure him was hers in a moment. A shot, aimed a little below and just behind his shoulder, made the securing of steaks an easy matter. As in their haste the crackers were forgotten, and their return was delayed until moonlight, the demand for the article, even without salt, was good!

Any *man* could have done what she did there. I have seen many a one who had, and considered it almost honor enough for a lifetime, and told of it with no end of flourishes. Well, it don't take much to satisfy some people. Now I'll tell you of something of which she had reason to be proud.[95]

One day a child called her attention to what it supposed was a "baby-owl." It sat winking and blinking after the manner of that family when out in the sunlight. The little fellow was a small, gray fluffy individual, not much bigger than a lump of salt. He certainly was never guilty of robbing a hen-roost. A spring-chicken by June could have completely overpowered him. A charge of fine shot soon convinced him that the surrender of his body to the cause of science was the final act of his life. The inspection of said *corpus* not only brought Mrs. Maxwell to the same conclusion, but also persuaded her that he was a new variety of Minerva's chosen bird.

Could it be possible! She dared not trust her own judgment. He was submitted to the inspection of the ornithologists of the Smithsonian Institute,[96] and they pronounced him indeed a specimen of a *new* variety, and christened him Scops Maxwellæ.

There! I call that something to be proud of! A thousand years hence, when all people are mourning over the extinction of large animals from America, her name will live associated with a variety of the bird, that has been from time immemorial a symbol of wisdom!

---

95. Dartt draws a stark contrast between her book's discussion of Maxwell's hunting expeditions and the kinds of hunting narratives popular among big game hunters at the time. Dartt de-emphasizes the violent conquest of animals in favor of the advancement of scientific knowledge epitomized by Maxwell's discovery of a new owl species, Scops Maxwellæ.

96. Robert Ridgway (1850–1929), an ornithologist at the Smithsonian Institution (which Dartt refers to as *Smithsonian Institute*), named the owl after Maxwell.

17

DROWNED OUT. ECONOMICAL BIRD.

Scops Maxwellæ is not the only specimen about which Mrs. Maxwell has especial reason to be pleased. A long, slim creature, with keen eyes, and, except for his black feet, reminding one of an overgrown weasel, has attracted with surprise, the attention of naturalists. It is very rare, and is said to be the only specimen, except those in the Smithsonian Institute, which is known.[97]

Years ago that distinguished naturalist, Audubon, described one of this species—the black-footed ferret—but as no specimen of it was found by other naturalists, it became the received opinion that its existence was a fancy of his vivid and graceful imagination. Alas! for the faith of mankind in man! It is so much easier for us of this age to believe some one has been the unfortunate subject of an optical illusion, or has tried to deceive us, than to think that our experience has not compassed the universe! Fortunately for

---

97. The black-footed ferret (*Mustela nigripes*) was first described by John James Audubon in 1851, but no specimens of the animal had been obtained until Maxwell acquired three specimens.

the memory of Audubon, within the past few years a number of those interesting animals have been found. The world has seen: therefore it has believed!

Mrs. Maxwell obtained three specimens. One was drowned out of a prairie-dog hole near Boulder by some boys and captured alive. How he came to be in somebody else's home is an open question. Perhaps he was trying to ferret out the secret of the strange domestic relations existing in said house. It's true he has a taste for infant owls and dogs, but then who would say, of one since so distinguished, that he was there for such a carnal purpose?

Be that as it may, he did not fancy the house-cleaning those boys instituted for its legitimate owners, and astonished them by appearing in a half-dead condition at the opening they were watching for dogs.

They did not recognize him, and so took him to Mrs. Maxwell. She kept him several months, long enough to get pretty well acquainted with him.

In the catalogue Dr. Coues[98] has mentioned most of his leading characteristics, though I believe he has failed to state that he was exceedingly economical—a virtue so highly commended nowadays, that, for his credit, I would not omit saying that he possessed it in a remarkable degree. As he was captured without baggage, the matter of food gave him the only opportunity for its display. About that he was very particular, not eating more than he needed, and burying carefully in his bedding, for the next meal, every mouthful he left.

Dr. Coues has also failed to speak of his passion for mice. I think they were his dream by day and his search by night. He not only saw and seized them when put within his reach, but imagined he saw them when he did not. Mr. Maxwell had a practical illustration of this. One day, when he put a single finger into his cage in such a way that his hand was hidden, the ferret instantly had a vision of a "Wee, sleekit, cow'rin, tim'rous beastie,"[99] and as instantly his teeth closed on the finger. It was not until Mr. Maxwell, with his other hand, choked him almost to death, that he was convinced he had made a mistake. Any person's finger might have been put into the cage with impunity, had only the hand been visible.

---

98. Elliott Coues, see note 59.

99. Opening line from "To a Mouse, on Turning up in Her Nest with the Plough, November, 1785" (1785) by the Scottish poet Robert Burns (1759–1796).

18

A MUSEUM. HIGHER EDUCATION. VALUABLE AIDS.

Before this time, the spring of 1873, Mrs. Maxwell had succeeded in replacing most of the specimens sold at St. Louis, and had added so many more, they were far too numerous to be even properly stored in ordinary private rooms.

Her friends advised placing them before the public, insisting that, if arranged with her usual taste in some large hall, by charging a small admittance fee, they would pay their own expense of house-rent and care.

In her previous planning she had hoped to have a home sufficiently ample to accommodate all she might collect, but her success in that direction had so far exceeded her expectations and the improvement of their finances, that it was evident, unless her work could be made self-sustaining, much of it must be disposed of, and further labor in that direction resolutely abandoned. Hitherto her work as a naturalist had been regarded as little more than a pastime between hours full of other duties and labors—a recreation, however, obtained under such protest from circumstances and often from friends, that nothing but an irresistible passion, united with tireless energy, and an unconquerable will, made her resume it when, through discouragement, it had often been put aside. The sight of a new specimen always affected her, as the smell of alcohol is said to affect an inebriate, and she would sacrifice any amount of personal comfort, and put forth any degree of extra effort to obtain and preserve it. After numerous family consultations it was decided that, instead of giving up what she had done, she should attempt an enterprise having a much more extensive aim than simply the preservation of the fauna of her chosen State.

Her observations of the differences made in animal life, by climate and surroundings, had long made her wish for some museum, which, from its arrangement and classification, should enable them to be studied with greater ease and accuracy than was then possible.

She now resolved to attempt the founding of an institution that should meet this demand.

Its specimens, if artistically mounted and arranged, would interest the young, and awaken in them a love for a culture within the reach of all, in its nature wholesome and refining. She also hoped that it might be of service to those scientists who are interested in the solution of problems that await, in suspended judgment, the verdict of greater knowledge than the world now has. She trusted that, when she should so far succeed as to make the utility and practicability of her design apparent, she would receive the liberal assistance of the public, especially all those interested in higher education.

To diminish the liability of pecuniary failure, however, it was determined to add a collection of foreign curiosities. It seemed desirable to procure these upon the Pacific coast, as most of the population of Colorado is from the East and South, and would feel more interest in curiosities that naturally find a market in San Francisco. Through the kindness of a friend a ticket was assured her to that city. She also came into possession of some property she had inherited; and as the spring opened, the work of collecting for the projected museum became an acknowledged business. Exchanges of duplicate shells, skins, etc., were made with naturalists in many places both East and West. Dr. McL—, a man of some experience as a naturalist, was engaged;[100] and accompanied by him and Mr. H—,[101] a gentleman of ornithological tastes, both Mr. and Mrs. Maxwell set out to collect specimens of

---

100. Dr. W. D. McLeod. Maxine Benson notes that no biographical information can be found on McLeod beyond simple mentions of his name in newspaper notices.

101. It is unclear if the Mr. H— mentioned here is J. Clarence Hersey, mentioned later (see note 126).

everything needful to a complete representation of the natural productions of Colorado. Of their many varied adventures I shall give but a few of those most distinctly remembered.

19

SOUTHEAST EXPEDITION. STRONG EXPRESSIONS. A SNAKE
SCARE. BULL-SNAKE. PHILOSOPHY IN THE SADDLE.
"THUNDER-PUMPERS." BLUE HERON NESTS. COMMUNISTIC
BIRD. WOMAN'S TRUST. "MRS. NIMROD'S" DISCOVERY.
INVISIBLE REALITY. MANNISH FLING. SKUNK KITTENS.

Their first trip was out on the plains to the southeast of Boulder, in the neighborhood and along the banks of the Platte. After securing a number of varieties of petrified wood, shells, Indian curiosities, etc., etc., they reached a point where some cotton-wood trees shaded the river's bank. Upon the trunk of one a pair of agitated flickers was discovered. Flickers, permit me to explain, are birds of the woodpecker family.[102] Their coats are of a yellowish brown, profusely adorned with round black spots. They wear crescent bibs of velvety black, and in the Eastern and Middle States ornament the under side of their wings and tails with bright yellow, and wear black-check patches. In the far Western States they change these colors for red. They are of especial interest to ornithologists, because there is a large region of [the] country in which a variety occurs having some of the characteristics of both the eastern and western forms; and the question whether in it may not be discovered one of the "missing links" about which there is so much

---

102. Flickers belong to the genus of woodpeckers known as *Colaptes*.

agitation, the change being due to climatic influences which terminate in yellow-shafted flickers at the East and red-shafted ones at the West, is one which a whole school of modern philosophers would give no little to have decided in the affirmative. If it cannot be, is the change due to hybridization? If so, what then?

There is altogether too much involved in the discussion of that question to introduce it here, especially as we are to imagine Mr. H— attempting the ascent of the tree upon which the flickers were seen, it having been determined that a small hole in the under side of a large limb, about ten feet from the ground, must contain their nest.

Mr. H— was one of those individuals who seem to possess an extra amount of energy which is only prevented from injuring them by exploding in adjectives and strong expressions. The party were not at all surprised to hear him exclaim, when reaching the cavity, which feat was performed by clinging, his body stretched at full-length on the limb—

"Weeping Jeremiah! why couldn't those birds have made this hole big enough for a body's hand? I say, Mr. Maxwell, I've got to have that hatchet. Jerusalem! if a body had much of this business to do, he'd regret his ancestors didn't stop developing while they had prehensile tails to hang on to limbs by. How in the name of the great Crump-and-curmudgeon is a fellow to chop and stick on to a place like this? Stand from under, everybody! I don't want to be hung for breaking anybody's neck but my own!" and he hacked away vigorously for a few minutes.

Dropping the hatchet, he was about [to] thrusting [sic] his hand into the enlarged opening, when he drew back with a horrified scream, exclaiming:

"Red-hot demons! there's a *snake* in this hole!"

"A *snake?*" echoed the trio on the ground.

"Yes, by the jumping John Rogers! He poked his head up just as I was putting my hand in on to him!" and he began to descend.

"Hold on a minute, H—. If he is quiet now, give him a dose of chloroform and bring him down with you," suggested Dr. McL—.

"All right," he replied, "only be quick. This climbing trees for snakes is rather pokerish business."

A bottle of the fluid and some cotton were reached up to him, and the latter, after being well wet with the anæsthetic, was pressed firmly over the mouth of the hole.

CHLOROFORMING A SNAKE.

FIGURE 19.1.
Chloroforming
a snake

"There, I guess that will cap his quartz for him!" he remarked in a few minutes. "Get out your snake-box, and I'll fish him up."

"You mean you'll

> " 'Take him up tenderly,
> Lift him with care,
> Fashioned so slenderly,
> Scaly and bare—' "[103]

parodied the doctor.

"That's about it. Ugh! this is a dainty dish to set before a queen," he said, depositing the stupefied reptile, which he held by the head, wrapped in cotton, in the box at Mrs. Maxwell's feet. "There," making her a bow of mock

---

103. "The Bridge of Sighs" (1844) by the English poet Thomas Hood (1799–1845): "Take her up tenderly, / Lift her with care; / Fashioned so slenderly, / Young, and so fair!"

solemnity, "I wish you much joy, madam; wreaking upon that fellow the hereditary vengeance your sex owe his family; on account of the entanglement into which his primal progenitor beguiled your first fair representative, you know."

"Thank you," she bowed in return. "I can't say I feel sufficiently inspired with that revengeful spirit to begin operations just this moment." And she regarded the great spotted reptile with a slight shiver of disgust—very womanly, but quite unbecoming to a naturalist. "Shut him up, and we will take him into camp."

The snake-box was a prearranged affair with a sliding cover, and as Mr. H— stooped to close it he paused to give his sleeping trophy a closer inspection, remarking as he did so:

"He isn't so pokin'. I believe he's what plebeians call a bull-snake, and an unusually likely member of his family; don't you think so, Mrs. Maxwell?"

"He seems to be in very good condition," she replied; adding, "of course there were no eggs in the nest?"

"Not an egg. Don't you suppose this chap went up there to gather them?" he asked, shutting the reptile in his box.

"Certainly. You know the serpent's reputation for wisdom. 'Great minds run in the same direction.' We wanted the eggs; so did he," she replied, settling herself in her saddle, and gathering up her bridle-reins to continue their explorations.

If any one entertained any doubt as to the nature of the snake's errand up the tree, it was removed when they reached camp. Owing to the effect of the anæsthetic, or to sickness caused by riding, he was found to have disgorged five young flickers.

A few days after this, in passing down the Platte, the party saw some singular-looking large birds, but failed to get near enough to them to determine what they were. Calling at a house, Mrs. Maxwell found a transplanted "Down-Easter," and essayed to get some information with regard to natural history from him.

"We saw some large birds above here on the bank of the river," she began. "I wonder if you take enough notice of such things to tell us what they were?"

"Wal, I calculate I kin if I kin make out which kind you mean. There air several sorts round here. Wasn't crows, was they?"

"Oh, no," she replied, "they were much larger than crows. They had long wings and legs."

"Sorter dragged 'em after 'em as they flew?" he interrupted, and, reading an affirmative reply in her face, he announced:

"Them, ma'am? Them's *bull-geese*."[104]

"Oh—ah—did you never hear any other name for them?" she hesitatingly asked.

"Wal, yes, I did once. There was a feller along here a spell ago that pretended to know a sight about everything, and he called 'em *something*," and the old gentleman scratched his head thoughtfully; "but I can't just recollect what it was. He found another kind of long-geared bird down about that flat—thunder-pumpers.[105] They ain't so big as the bull-geese, but they're about as much set up, and I calculate they git their livin' pretty much the same way."

"I don't recognize them by that name," Mrs. Maxwell replied, "though I presume I may have seen them."

"Wal, maybe you've bin used to callin' 'em shied-pokes, or stake-drivers. Both them names is pretty common fur 'em out here. You must'er heard 'em—they go boom, boom, boom; make a sight of noise when they git at it."

"Oh, I think I know what you mean: a yellowish-brown bird, with long head, neck and legs," she said, as a vision of a newly-killed bittern flashed over her mind.

"Yes, yes, that's it. They ain't so stilted up as the bull-geese, but there ain't much but legs to any of 'em. You seem to be sorter curi's about birds, maybe you'd like to see some of 'em close by?"

"Indeed, I should."

"I hain't bin down there myself, but the boys say that in the big grove on Henderson's island, the bull-geese air nestin', and there's a *sight* of 'em among the trees."

The last clause of the instructive conversation was gratefully received. That the birds he referred to were a variety of wader, Mrs. Maxwell had no doubt, but could gather no idea from the name whether they were herons, cranes, storks, or ibis.

Upon reaching the designated spot the uncertainty was dispelled. A colony of great blue herons were nesting there.

---

104. Great blue heron (*Ardea herodias*).
105. American bittern (*Botaurus lentiginosus*).

The trees of the grove were very tall, their lower limbs being twenty-five or thirty feet from the ground, and the nests were in their tops; so how to reach and explore them was a difficult problem. They solved it by attaching a piece of twine to the end of a ramrod and firing that, instead of a bullet, over a limb of a tree. Once having the twin over a branch, a rope ladder was tied to it and drawn up. Mr. Maxwell, ascending it, found the herons had reduced co-operative housekeeping from theory to practice.

Each of the large trees held from one to half a dozen great nests, built of sticks and carelessly lined with grass, and each nest held from two to six young occupants. These were of varying ages: some hardly out of the shell; others certainly a week old, and others still more mature. As one pair of heron produce but two eggs in a season, it was clear that several couples must be uniting their parental labors in each of the more populous nests.

Could he have discovered their system of division of labor, who can say how much it might have done toward the solution of some of the vexed social problems of the day!

No dismal foreboding of inability to provide a nest for his bride shuts [a] young heron's bill as he poises himself upon one leg in sentimental mood beside the bird that ruffles his feather with admiration! He can lay his heart and freshest frog at her feet with impunity. Nor need visions of long, weary days and nights of close confinement to a nest, full of unrelieved care, deter her from accepting both with alacrity. Whatever "corners" may occur in twigs, he can surely provide enough for a third of a nest. No spectre of bills for hired help, or of his young wife becoming a nervous, rusty-feathered old bird before their first brood is fledged, need haunt his nuptial dreams, for other maternal wings will wait with eager tenderness to take her place over their angular, fuzzy little idols.

Ever-to-be-envied biped!

One day, while upon their journey home, Mrs. Maxwell brought the party to a halt by signaling game ahead.

You have always heard of woman's devotion; well, it is no illusion. The half of it can't be told. No one knows it but women, and they haven't egotism enough to repeat it.

If it is a man to whom one of them is devoted, he cannot treat her with such cruel indifference and neglect—he cannot do a thing under the sun so mean—but she will find some excuse for him, if there is a foundation enough for an excuse so that even a foot of her fancy can fasten upon it. If there is not, ten chances to one she will forgive him, *simply because she wants to*, with an indifference to reason that is fairly sublime.

There is only one way she can avoid doing so, and that is to persuade herself that she has been deceived in the person, and has been worshipping an ideal which the man only reminded her of. Then she is at liberty to hate him.

If she is devoted to dress, men don't need any information on that subject. If they don't fancy that direction for the sentiment, they should be noble and attractive enough to monopolize it themselves.

The devotion is the same, whatever it is given to. If it is to science, as we have seen, it will take a woman repeatedly through hardships enough to kill her if endured without its enthusiasm, and she will grow stronger every day; it will make her forget that the most repulsive work is disagreeable; it will enable her to skin turkey-buzzards and mount skunks! How great is the power of woman's devotion!—Mrs. Maxwell has *five* of these latter animals in her collection.

I am perfectly aware that this is a subject—not the devotion, but that pertaining to the quadrupeds—to be handled with perfumed gloves; but I am obliged to state that two members of the most unpopular branch of the family, *Mustelidæ*[106]—a devoted mother and her young—were the objects for which Mrs. Maxwell ordered that interruption of their homeward progress[.] (I trust this is stated with sufficient delicacy!)

"What do you see Mrs. Nimrod?"[107] asked Mr. Maxwell, stopping his horses.

"The prettiest old skunk and her kitten," Mrs. Maxwell replied, dismounting from her pony, a restless little beast; and taking her gun from its supports on the side of her saddle.

"Skunks!" exclaimed Mr. H—, jumping down from his seat of the baggage. "Shades of Arabia the blest! you don't mean to go after them!"

"Precisely my intention."

Striking an attitude of despair, he exclaimed:

---

106. The family Mustelidæ includes weasels, badgers, otters, ferrets, mink, and others. In Maxwell's time, skunks were considered part of the Mustelidæ family; they are now grouped in the family Mephitidæ.

107. Nimrod was the great-grandson of Noah and was noted as a great hunter.

" 'What though the spicy breezes
Blow soft o'er Ceylon's isle'[108]

"They're too eternally far off to be any relief to us now. Doc., are you prepared to die from asphyxiation? That woman means business, and we might
as well be preparing our last words."

But his remarks were lost on her ears, as she started over the level open
plain to get within range of a critical specimen. As there was nothing to do
but wait, Mr. H—, with the remark that "Mrs. Maxwell's game wasn't of a
kind a feller would particularly hanker after a hand in killing, still, if skunks
were the order of the day, it wasn't quite the thing to leave her to face them
alone," took up his gun, and, overtaking her, remarked,

"I suppose you've no objection to my being in at the death? Should you be
overpowered by an invisible reality (!), you might need some assistance."

"Oh, don't you be alarmed! Even skunks don't resort to extreme measures,
unless badly frightened, or in very close quarters," she replied.

The little animals were in plain sight, and were not long in discovering
their approaching enemies. The young one could run but slowly, and the
mother would not leave it; but, in her solicitude, ran back and forth, always
keeping her body between it and their foes.

"Pretty, ain't they?" said Mr. H—. "Prejudice aside, I think anybody would
say the old lady is gotten up in a 'nifty' manner. Dress—sable, striped with
ermine—and that plume! My! it must make every female in her neighborhood sick with envy, every time they see it!"

"How perfectly mannish you are, to end with a fling at feminine vanity a
remark which shows you yourself think of nothing but external appearances!
See the poor creature's anxiety for her kitten. It is certainly more charming
than her dress. I declare it is a shame to kill anything capable of manifesting
so much affection. But she must die some time, and if that time is now, she
may be saved the pangs that are so often caused by ungrateful children."

"So, you don't imagine the youngster any more appreciative than I of spiritual graces! Well, if we are a 'bad lot,' we don't want to get too near together;
can't we hit them from here?"

"I guess so. What kind of charges have you in your gun?"

---

108. "The Missionary Hymn" (1820) by the English bishop and poet Reginald Heber
    (1783–1826).

"One barrel B.B., and the other No. 10. What have you?"

"Buckshot, and No. 7."

"No. 7 will bring them, and won't tear them either."

As the report died away, he stepped forward and picked up a couple of specimens no more offensive than two rabbits, remarking, as he proceeded to remove all possibilities of the animals' making themselves obnoxious in future,

"I think that job was done up pretty neatly, Mrs. Maxwell. Hunting skunks isn't such bad sport, after all, if you manage it right and are a sure shot."

Her other three specimens had a more disagreeable history; but we drop the curtain of silence over their capture. One was a beautiful male, and the other two pretty little spotted creatures were a pair of a different variety.

20

SIREDONS. EMBRYOLOGY. INTERESTING CHANGES.
MYSTERIES. POPULAR EDUCATION.

After this trip of three or four weeks upon the plains, in which were secured a great number of birds and mammals besides those already mentioned, they made several excursions into the mountains, for minerals and specimens of animals which frequent high altitudes. *"Siredon"*[109] was the word that allured them to the banks of a lovely little sheet of water, called Gold Lake, far up among the heights. Its depths were crystal clear, very cold, and peopled with speckled trout and siredons. The latter they caught with a hand-net or a trout-hook.

"You understand what siredons are, I presume?" remarked Mrs. Maxwell, when I asked her for the details of the excursion.

"Oh, yes, I suppose so," I said. "They are some of those alcohol specimens, ain't they? A variety of fish, I believe. I never thought to ask you which jar they were in, and may not be able to describe them. I don't remember, either, what you said their common name is, or whether they are good to eat."

---

109. The larval form of a salamander.

"Good to eat! Snakes and lizards! What *are* you thinking of?"

Her face was a picture of disgust and astonishment. That the animal king-dom might contain something I had not heard of before, began to dawn dimly upon my mind.

"Why," I stammered, "isn't *siredon* one of the scientific names for shiners, pumpkin-seed, or something of the sort?"

There was a pause, suggesting that the depth of this freshly-revealed igno-rance was hopelessly profound.

"Shiners, indeed!" at last she said. "Understand, siredons have legs!"

"Legs?"

"Yes, legs! In many respects they resemble fish—they are long and thin like them—but they have *four* well-defined legs. They have gills, too; and, what is very strange, these gills are long, feather-like processes, on the outside of their necks."

"Indeed! Why don't they protect them, as fishes do, or else dispose of them, like respectable batrachians?"[110] I questioned, thinking to remind her that I was not the only person who did not know everything.

"They have been found to do the latter, under very favorable circumstances; but, as a rule, they remain in a permanently larval state," she replied.

"Legs! Permanent larvæ! Gills on the outside of them! Do tell me: are they like anything else on earth? I confess, I'm completely confused!" I exclaimed.

"They are quite an exceptional race of beings. You could understand their peculiarities better, if you knew more of embryology; but, as it is, you do know that no animal passes its entire existence in a mature state."

"Your remark," I said, "corresponds with my observation of at least the mental condition of the human species."

She did not notice my interruption, but continued,

"With the majority, the external form they possess when they leave the embryo state is essentially the same as they have at maturity, though there is a large class of insects, and a few vertebræ, that pass quite a period in a larval state—that is, having an immature shape that will be more or less changed before they reach the highest form they are capable of assuming. The cater-pillar and tadpole are examples of this."

---

110. Group of amphibians including frogs and salamanders.

"Oh, yes, I know the tadpole seems to be hatched a fish. It has only a round hole for a mouth, lives wholly in the water, and breathes like them by means of gills."

"Yes, but gradually all this changes. The mouth widens and becomes adapted to the seizure of prey; the gills disappear, and lungs are developed; and, instead of breathing water, he instinctively seeks another element of respiration; legs grow; the tail, grown useless, disappears; and the metamorphosis is complete.

"Now, suppose, at an unfinished period, this change should be suspended, and the little being should feed and swim on, produce young, and, in fact, complete the usual circle of an entire life without further development; and you have an idea of what is commonly the history of the little batrachian, called the siredon. It is usually a permanent larva. Formerly it was supposed, because it reproduced in this state, that it could not be possible that it ever reached a higher one. But Professor Baird, Professor Marsh[111] and others have proved that, under favorable circumstances, the change is completed, its gills disappear, and it is able to live on land as well as water. Why! what is it? You look as though you were under a spell, and your thoughts at least had left this world!"

"I did not know that any being had quite such a history. It thrills me! I was thinking of the wonderful analogy between these modes of animal development and our intellectual growth—of how we change, and the wistful longing with which we all think of the probabilities of another change, that shall usher us, with new forms, into a new element. I was wondering if larval batrachians might not know something of our unrest. When some mature one touches them in springing up to heights they cannot reach, may not their still immature forms thrill with prophetic longings for a greater power, and a wider sphere, as do our souls under the touch of some master mind—as do the greatest intellects under the awe of some fresh revelation of more than mortal wisdom?—If, in fact, we are not all 'permanent larva'—man's whole body, like the tadpole's tail and the siredon's gills, merely an appendage to fit him to his present surroundings?"

---

111. A regular correspondent with Maxwell, Spencer Baird (1823–1887) was a naturalist and the first curator named at the Smithsonian Institution; he served as assistant secretary of the Smithsonian from 1850 to 1878. Othniel C. Marsh (1831–1899) was a Yale University professor of paleontology.

"You are probably," she replied, "repeating the emotions passed through by some ancient poet, when he first learned of the changes in a butterfly's life, and made it from thenceforth a symbol for immortality. You cannot have forgotten all the beautiful illustrations drawn from the dragon-fly and the chrysalis?"

"Oh, no! but I am so miserably practical, none of those ever touched me, as what you tell me of the siredon does. None of those were like us—completing the whole circle of a life; birth, growth, reproduction—all the functions that are necessary to a continued series of existence, before they reached their highest state; I did not know that any creature did, or could. So your little siredon, who fills all the terms of animal life that our genus does, with still before him a higher form of existence, only awaiting right conditions for its realization, fascinates me. He indeed proves that nature is not always content with the simple completion of the circle of being, but in some cases may add to it, that for which we so deeply yearn—a physically unnecessary, but still higher, a more perfect stage of development." A vision of vanished faces and absent forms my arms may never clasp on earth again was with me, and a wave of that passionate longing—which only those who have felt it can understand—for life in yet another element—to which I might believe the silent ones had gone, and to which the absent ones and I might go—dashed its spray in my eyes, and filled my throat with an unvoiced sob. "Oh," I cried, "that science as well as revelation, would assure us of the possibility of life in a higher state of being!"

"It may, some time," she replied; "I do believe that there is one infinitely wise mind, and that science is Its latest prophet, and that we should listen reverently to her voice, though so young, it can only lisp the beginning of a wondrous message." At length I said:

"I am in sympathy at last, with your long rows of glass jars, confirmation of what hopes, dear to all human hearts, may not be corked in with some repulsive-looking reptile, or batrachian!"

"It seems to me," she replied, "that the eyes of those who spend their lives hunting for truth among Greek roots in the subterraneous darkness in which they grow, are dazzled by the radiance of Nature so that they cannot see that in her hand, too, is found that for which they seek. *Science* must have workers, and to secure them, common schools and colleges must have natural history collections and other facilities for awakening in the minds of the young a love of personal, patient observation of nature in all her features."

While the meagre advantages in this respect offered by the schools of her girlhood, and the fact that the energy of so much of her life had been distributed in such a diversity of ways, were matters of much regret, she still determined to do her share toward awakening this passion by making at least one department attractive; and *Taxidermy, as a fine art, subservient to science,* became the work of her life.

21

SNOWY RANGE EXPEDITION. SNOWY RANGE
FLORA. RASPBERRIES JULY TO OCTOBER. LIMITLESS
PROSPECT. THRILLING STORM SCENE. PTARMIGANS.
PTARMIGANS AND HARES. GRASSHOPPERS.
BIRD AND BEAR FOOD. LAKE OF FIRE.

Mrs. Maxwell's next work, after securing the siredons, and a variety of other objects of interest, at Gold Lake, was in a region very different from any we have yet described, namely: that portion of the Snowy Range which lies above timber-line.

Although the plains are almost perfectly tree-less, the Rocky Mountains are well wooded; their sides and gorges, in most places, being covered with pine, spruce, cedar, and fir trees. These are of such persistent growth, they appear almost up to the limit of perpetual snow, growing even where the drifts lie deep about their roots nine or ten months in the year. Still, as this altitude is approached, their size gradually grows less, their trunks are twisted and gnarled; and, as the fierce northwest winds prevent branches appearing upon that side, the other side is densely covered by preposterously long ones. Finally, dwindled to mere shrubs, their branches parallel with the ground and nearly upon it, they disappear. This extreme limit of tree-growth is called timber-line.

Almost the only vegetation found above it is clumps of grass, its blades rarely an inch in length, and patches of a kind of mossy plant, bearing tiny, fragrant blue or white blossoms, which open as soon as they are comfortably out of the ground.

For reasons belonging to the province of Physical Geography, we have no glaciers, and the perpetual snows of our lofty mountains are gathered into vast fields or banks, in places where the rocks or the contour of the ground protects them from the warm west winds. From their sun-eaten edges rills of the purest water leap down to lakes or ponds, which are their children, and which the besieging summer has only parted from their icy embrace for a few brief weeks. Where they extend down some valley below timber-line, as they often do, one can date each rod of ground the heat has won from them, by the age of the vegetation that has sprung up on it. Grasses of the deepest, tenderest green, and flowers of the most exquisite hues grow almost up to their very edges.

In the immediate vicinity of one of these vast snow banks, I one August day gathered twenty-four varieties of plants and flowers. Among them were fragrant shooting-stars, graceful blue harebells, large columbines in the daintiest shades of purple and white, and many flowers peculiar to the Rocky Mountains, but which ceased to blossom in their lower valleys and cañons in May and June. These months had but just reached that altitude. It was delightful sliding down those long snow-banks with the August sun overhead, and June's wealth of verdure and flowers before one's eyes!

This tardy arrival of the months to the high altitudes is very convenient for those who enjoy a long berry season. To illustrate: The inhabitants of Colorado the blest may begin picking red raspberries in July, and, by changing their elevation, continue the pastime until October. The very late ones grow on bushes hardly six inches high, just below the timber-line, and may have to be gathered in a snow-storm if picked at all.

Stern and forbidding as the region above them may appear, it is not without life and attractions. Ptarmigans, little chief hares, and marmots, frequent the rocks, and its immediate scenery, and the landscapes visible from its peaks, cannot be rivaled.

Locating their camp among the dwarfed evergreens, a mile or more from the top of the range, Mrs. Maxwell and her collecting party proceeded, one morning, to climb to its summit—the crest of a lofty peak overlooking the Middle Park.

As they made the ascent, now crossing snow-fields, dusty and crystalline with age and exposure, now picking their way over masses of huge, irregular rocks, every few steps pausing, because of the rarefied air, to regain their breath, each foot in advance increased the extent of a prospect that seemed limitless. With not a film of haze, or a cloud shadow, over all the vast expanse, beyond the crests of myriads of mountains, as far as the eye could reach to the east, stretched the ocean-like plains. On either hand rose sister-peaks, their snow-fields flashing back the morning sun, which revealed their huge rocks and chasms, in all their stern and naked grandeur. The mountain-tops had never known a morning more faultlessly calm and radiant, yet, as they proceeded, their ears were surprised by the sound of thunder and of rushing wind, at first indistinct, but increasing in power and clearness, as they advanced. Reaching the edge of a precipice overlooking the Park, they found themselves standing far above the clouds. These were gathered in the fierce commotion of a storm, hundreds of feet below them, eddying, rolling, tossing to and fro, the crests of their broken billows white and glistening, their caverns dark and murky, the sharp lightning cutting all, through and through, with sabres of vivid fire, each stroke accompanied by peals of deafening thunder, intermingled with the hoarse voice of rushing winds, the whole a spectacle, grand and beautiful, beyond the power of words to describe!

Awed in its presence the little party were, for some time, silent, but, as the voices of the storm grew less deafening and continuous, their emotions took form in words.

"Is it not grand?" said Mrs. Maxwell, as she leaned over the brink of the precipice, and gazed with rapt face upon the tempest below her.

"It is, indeed!" replied Mr. Maxwell. "Had this scene been the object of our coming here, we should be amply repaid for our long, hard climb. Now we can see what is meant by rising above life's clouds and storms."

"Yes," she said, "who, looking *up* to these clouds from the valley below, could imagine this dazzling, sunlit picture? I wish I could *know* that the storms and clouds of life had such a radiant, glorified side, and that from the calm heights of this positive knowledge, I could look down upon its roar of conflict and rain of tears, and see that *all* is needful and therefore well."

"Ah, Mrs. Maxwell, you echo a very deep wish in many a heart," said the doctor; "but most of us weak mortals feel as little hope of its realization as you would expect, had you wished, as some vagrant poet did, to be lying,

"With idle hands, unvexed by care,
On yonder cloud's white fleecy breast,

'Mid depths of blue, sunflooded air,
Entranced in blissful, dream-filled rest."[112]

"What a wish for Mrs. Maxwell!" exclaimed Mr. H—. "Jerusha crickets! she wouldn't more than get down there before she would be seizing some of that lightning, and jabbing it down among the clouds, to see if she couldn't kill the monster that roars so, and secure a specimen of thunder to stuff!"

The spell was broken. Mr. H—'s idea was so absurd that, with a laugh, they turned from contemplating the storm to the execution of their business there—the securing of ptarmigans and little chief hares. The latter are commonly called conies, and are found only on the barren wastes above timber-line. Having no foliage under which to hide, nature kindly protects the creatures who know no other home than those heights, by dressing them in colors that harmonize so perfectly with their surroundings, that it is almost impossible to see them when silent or at rest. The little hares, creatures about as big as two-thirds of a rat, minus the tail, make a shrill, chirping noise, which at first would be mistaken for the note of some bird or insect. They burrow under the rocks, and the openings of their holes are usually surrounded by quantities of grass, which they have either removed from their nests, or are curing for use in winter.

Much of their time in summer is spent in laying in supplies, and in sunning themselves on the rocks. Mrs. Maxwell would hear their voices upon all sides of her, yet neither by sight nor ear be able to detect the exact spot from which any one proceeded. At length, her ear becoming more practised, she would decide by it upon a location, cover it with her gun until some movement would disclose the little creature—a variation of aim, a touch of the trigger, and a specimen of unusual interest to naturalists was hers.

The ptarmigan, being usually silent, is still more difficult to capture. This crooked name belongs to a pretty, graceful bird of the grouse family, which is remarkable for appearing in four different suits during the year. This unusual devotion to dress is not, however, due to vanity, but to the necessity for protection from observation. Its summer dress is mottled rock-brown; as the season advances and the snows of autumn fleck the rocks with white, pure snowy feathers appear in the sombre plumage; and when the reign of winter is fully established, their presence is not to be detected by any spot on

---

112. These lines of verse appear to be of Dartt's creation.

its ermine mantle, for they are not less white than it. Their spring costume is the same as that worn in autumn. Their summer food is said to be largely composed of grasshoppers.

At times, during the warm months, the great snow-fields and barren, rocky wastes of their upper world, will be brown with these insects.[113] It is then that birds and bears find the cold drifts luxuriant tables, from which they may feast. It is a well-known fact that bears share John the Baptist's *penchant* for locusts and wild honey.[114] As the latter is not a production of Colorado, a double portion—yes, doubled several times—of the former luxury is often provided them. For, be it known, those grasshoppers are not of the same family as the innocent little fellows in green jackets, that skip and chirp away their lives in eastern meadows. Quite otherwise. They are the brown-coated, insatiable eaters of ancient pedigree, known as long ago as—the time of Adam, for aught I can tell—as [*sic*] the irrepressible, devouring locust.

Where they are manufactured, to be coming over the range in July and August no living being knows. But they are, many seasons in such numbers as to perfectly illustrate those lines of an old hymn, which, speaking of evil spirits, says,

"They swarm the air, they darken heaven,

And rule this lower world!"

Standing upon some height, from which the whole earth seems spread out before one, and only its inconvenient shape and lack of focal distance in the eye prevents one from seeing the Atlantic waves break off the coast of Cape Cod, one can look up and see the air above and around them, as far as the eye can reach in every direction, filled as with snowflakes, with the myriad wings of these terrible pests. The frosty morning and evening air of that altitude does not agree with them, and they are compelled to camp, by thousands, on snow-fields or wherever the cold happens to overpower them. Then the birds fill their crops, and the bears, with greedy joy, lick them from the great drifts.

---

113. The Rocky Mountain locust (*Melanoplus spretus*) is a now extinct species of locust that swarmed in large number in the western United States, including Colorado. The 1870s experienced the last recorded major swarms of the insects, which are believed to have become extinct in 1902.

114. In the Gospel of Mark, John the Baptist is described as living on locusts and wild honey.

Has the cold killed them? Ah! by no means! Don't every Coloradoan wish it had? It has only stupefied them. The next day's warm sun restores their *vivacity*, and they continue their flight toward the green plains, which lie in inviting defencelessness before them. Once there, they will rattle like hail against windowpanes, settle like brown, volcanic ashes on lovely gardens and growing fields; before each approaching footstep they will rise and part, a living cloud.

Safe in their individual insignificance, they are overpowering by their infinite number. Their coming used to bring consternation, and their going leave despair, for they left embedded in the earth they had devastated of every growing thing, the assurance, that, with the opening of another spring, their number would be duplicated a thousand times.

But this planet holds few difficulties, that man, with time in which to exercise his ingenuity cannot master. The young grasshopper, born in Colorado now, awakes to a struggle for existence his progenitors of five years ago never dreamed of! Deadly kerosene floats on the ditch he must swim for his breakfast; his infant form is remorselessly stuck to tarred blankets in the wheatfield, whereon he would lunch; and winged machines fan him into a lake of fire as he essays to dine. For his annoyance and extermination neither money, labor, nor research is spared; farmers hatch numberless broods of fowl to devour him; Congress sends commissioners to investigate him; States meet and sit in council upon him; China and the ends of the earth are importuned for receipts for vile smells to harass him; the wisdom and experience of all ages and climes are invoked to haunt and torment him. I submit, the future of the locust in America looks dark!

22

---■-■---

After a number of days spent, either above timber-line or in the immediate vicinity below it, the party turned their faces homeward. Their excursion had been a successful one in many respects, especially in securing semi-Arctic birds in summer plumage. Their good fortune did not forsake them as they descended to the lower regions of trees and shrubs.

They were climbing a hill too steep to be ridden up, preparatory to descending one too steep to be ridden down, when Mrs. Maxwell, who was walking some distance from the others, came suddenly upon a female grouse with a brood of little ones. Instantly there was a note of alarm given by the old bird, and the chicks disappeared as if by magic, while the mother, feigning lameness, fluttered away. She was soon secured; then came the task of finding the little ones. Seating herself where they disappeared, Mrs. Maxwell was perfectly still, for what seemed to her a very long time, although it was probably not more than ten minutes before any unusual sound met her ear. Then she was delighted by tiny shrill peeps, evidently coming from eight or ten places around her. With ears practised by recent cony-hunting, she noted one spot and made a minute search among plants, sticks, fallen leaves, and underbrush, and was rewarded by the capture of a little downy grouse. This waiting and searching was repeated until nine were captured. Then a longer pause than any before made convinced her there were no more.

They, with the mother-bird, form the group referred to by H.H. in the first part of this volume, and are indeed very interesting. Saturday night the party reached Boulder, and their combined exploration terminated.

23

OFF TO CALIFORNIA. HARDSHIP INSIGNIFICANT. COMFORT
DISREGARDED. SEA-CAPTAIN'S WIFE. ANTIQUE ARMOR.
EMIGRANT TRAIN. SALT LAKE. CIVIL TREATMENT.

The next Wednesday a quiet little lady, in soft brown travelling suit, was seen seated in a train bound for California.[115] No one of her travelling companions could have suspected that six days before she sat, gun in hand, on a rock hunting conies amid the snow-fields they could see glimmering in the distance. Yet such was the fact.

When seen away from home and conversed with upon topics of general interest, one might have thought Mrs. Maxwell's specialty, if she had one, was the growing of forests, the general development of the Territory which she had chosen as her home, or, perchance, the highest culture of humanity. Certainly only those who, like her, were interested in zoology or some of its kindred sciences, would have suspected her devotion to that study.

---

115. In an effort to flesh out her collection of "foreign curiosities" for her Rocky Mountain
    Museum, Maxwell traveled to California in August 1873. She chose to go to the Pacific
    Coast because she assumed that since most of the visitors to her museum would be
    from the Atlantic Coast, she would find in California artifacts more interesting to her
    potential visitors.

The thread of life has many strands. No one is ever naturalist, artist, *any-thing*, alone. There are other sides, or even the character most absorbed by one idea, so striking, that being seen in other relations than those of its specialty, one almost forgets that it exists. Probably few persons ever gave themselves with more passionate devotion to a pursuit, than did Mrs. Maxwell to the execution of her favorite project, yet so quietly and unostentatiously did she work, that until the opening of her museum, many of her friends and neighbors hardly knew she cherished plans that differed from their own. So shy was she of any display of skill unusual to feminine fingers, that few people ever saw her fire a gun, and many, who thought they knew her well, would hardly credit their ears when, in answer to the inquiry where she procured certain specimens, they were informed she shot them herself.

"What! can you shoot?" would be their astonished exclamation.

Her quiet "Sometimes, when necessary," accompanied by some remark tending to lead the attention to other subjects, was never questioned; nor [*sic*], after further conversation with her on her favorite topic, did it seem a matter of great importance; only a step in securing an end, which, in the light of her enthusiasm, seemed so great that any act, adventure, or hardship necessary to its advancement, was a matter of comparative insignificance.

We cannot give in detail the many annoyances, pleasures and adventures through which she passed during the six months of her stay in the Golden State; neither make grateful mention of all the many persons to whom her success was largely due.

They will always be remembered with gratitude, for they gave her assistance in securing an end far dearer to her than personal comfort. Indeed, comfort was something quite disregarded. So intent was she upon securing as many objects of interest as possible for the proposed museum, that she often spent for them the means which should have been used for her physical needs, renting a cheap room and subsisting upon such food as cost least. Indeed, so occupied were her thoughts in other directions that, after breakfasting, the necessity of eating would often be forgotten for the rest of the day.

Under such circumstances, of course unsuspected by them, the interest and elegant hospitality of gentlemen and ladies whose culture and urbanity it is a pleasure to recall, was something indeed to be appreciated; and it should be a comfort to all who are giving themselves unsparingly to any great cause, that the world holds not a few who find their highest pleasure in doing honor to those who personate ideas, irrespective of their circumstances or surroundings.

Among this class of the world's real nobility Mrs. Maxwell found friends, who were ready to accompany her in her search for curiosities into all manner of out-of-the-way places. In collecting these among the Celestials,[116] Mr. Locke, the Chinese interpreter, gave her the advantage of his influence and knowledge.

The wife of an old sea-captain, Mrs. B—, discovered, upon meeting her, that her projected enterprise was the very object for which, unconsciously, she had been for years preserving foreign curiosities, and so generously put them into her possession. Mr. G—, a German naturalist connected with Woodward's Gardens, gave her the liberty of that institution, and also introduced her to Mr. B—, a wealthy merchant of ornithological tastes, who helped her out of a dilemma.[117] She had visited the Big Trees, the Geysers, and very many other places, and wherever she had been, Indian curiosities and all manner of objects had adhered to her fingers, until her acquisitions, when boxed for home, weighed over one thousand pounds.[118] What was her dismay to find, when she had reached the extreme limits of her purse, that these treasures could not budge an inch from San Francisco without the freight upon them was prepaid, or some one, who had the "open sesame" to railroads, would be responsible for its payment. Mr. B— very kindly appeared as that individual.

A short time before her own departure, in visiting with her friends Mr. and Mrs. W—, a place where Japanese curiosities were sold, she saw a quaint old armor, once the glory of some hero of that far-off land. Its workmanship was very strange, but its price, taken in connection with the fact that her fare home would be one hundred dollars, put it hopelessly beyond her reach.

---

116. A nineteenth-century slang term for Chinese persons.

117. Developed in the late 1860s by hotel operator Robert Woodward, Woodward's Gardens had become a premier attraction in the San Francisco area by the time Maxwell visited. Its curator of gardens was Ferdinand Gruber, a German-born taxidermist. Robert Woodward (1824–1879) became rich during the 1849 California Gold Rush. Woodward's Gardens was immensely popular and operated from 1866 to 1891. In addition to a museum, the attraction also featured an art gallery, zoo, and aquarium.

118. Calaveras Big Trees State Park, located west of San Francisco, and the Geysers, located north of San Francisco.

Soon after having purchased her ticket, her eye happened to fall upon an advertisement for the same on the emigrant train for fifty dollars. Instantly that old armor, from being a coveted article, beyond hope of possession, became a necessity, without which life would lose half its charms! The next morning found her negotiating an exchange of tickets.[119]

Not without great difficulty, and the repeated assurance that she would regret it, she succeeded in obtaining the favor of trying a new mode of conveyance, and at the same time regaining the means to buy the interesting old relic.

She then hastened to Mr. W— to get him to assist her in making the purchase. Here she felt herself in rather an embarrassing position. She had promised to accept Mrs. W—'s proffered lunch for the journey, and knew that she and her husband expected to see her on board the cars. Would they care to accompany her to an *emigrant* train, and would they think her procedure quite sane?

Their remonstrances were both deep and earnest. "Why didn't she let them know how much she wanted the armor when she first saw it?" they questioned. "They would have been happy to provide the means to secure it."

As it was, they urged her to let them get a first-class ticket in exchange for the one she had, insisting that she should not impose upon herself the discomforts of such a journey. But her mind was made up. With the insatiable demands of her new enterprise upon her, she would incur no debt, even to the best of friends. So the Japanese merchant took the price of the comforts of her coming journey, and in its place the old armor, with all its battle-marks, and the title to its unknown romance and adventure, came into her possession.

Gorget and breastplate, helmet and greaves—with such defence, what discomforts could compel a surrender? But, that these might be as few as possible, Mrs. W—; with her unvarying kindness, procured a huge lunch basket and filled it to the brim, and both she and her husband did all that could be done to make her as comfortable as might be during the weeks she would be on the road.

And queer weeks they were! The strong points possessed by most of her travelling companions were, their power to endure heat and bad air, and

---

119. Maxwell paid thirty dollars for the suit of armor, exchanging her original ticket for a lower-priced ticket.

their fondness for whiskey and tobacco. The majority of the masculine portion passed the time in smoking, consulting familiar spirits—evoked from pocket-flasks—and seeing how much wood could be crowded through two immense stoves; the attention of the feminine portion was given to the wants and vocal exercises of a number of small children; while Mrs. Maxwell passed her time (it was January) in a struggle between suffocation and the cold from an open window. As, through the entire journey, the car was frequently switched off on to side tracks, to wait for its passengers knew not what, existence, even in the conscious possession of an entire suit of ancient armor, grew to seem not wholly an unmixed blessing.

A most agreeable respite was taken, however, in a stay of a few days at Salt Lake, where through the kindness of friends, she procured some valuable minerals and other curiosities, and had the pleasure of making the acquaintance of five forlorn widows and their numerous children, all left in a bereaved condition by the death of one frail man!

During the remainder of the journey the objectionable features of her mode of travelling were intensified rather than diminished, and, though the conductors did all they could for her comfort, some days before she reached Cheyenne she was suffering intensely from a cold. The wife of the last conductor before reaching that place chanced to be on the train, and insisted upon taking her home with her for a night, and then passing her to Cheyenne in a car better adapted to human comfort, and thus her experience as an emigrant terminated.

During the entire journey Mrs. Maxwell testifies to having been treated with the utmost deference and politeness from every one, and she would gladly add her experience to substantiate the testimony of so many others, that a woman who is womanly and thoroughly respects herself, can go anywhere, and travel in any way she finds necessary—in America, at least—without fear of incivility or disrespect.

24

OPENING OF MUSEUM. LIVING RATTLESNAKES.
FRATERNAL BEARS. SNAKES KILLING MICE.

Soon after reaching home, the citizens of Boulder proffered her the use of a hall for her museum. Into it were removed the many specimens she had mounted; the curiosities she had procured; a multitude of ores and minerals, contributed by those interested in the mines of the territory; those collected by Mr. Maxwell, Prof. G—, and Dr. McL—[120] during her absence; cabinets of foreign minerals and shells, and specimens of all kinds of productions, presented by other individuals who were kindly interested in the success of her enterprise. In classifying and arranging the departments of conchology and mineralogy she was assisted by Prof. G—and the Colorado State geologist, J. A. S—.[121]

The following account of the formal opening of the museum we copy from the *Boulder News* of that date:[122]

---

120. Along with McLeod, John W. Glass was hired by Maxwell to assist with collecting animal and mineral specimens for the Rocky Mountain Museum. As with McLeod, there is a lack of biographical information on Glass.
121. J. Alden Smith, a Colorado territorial geologist.
122. *Boulder County News*, June 5, 1874.

"The event of the week was the opening of the Rocky Mountain Museum,—an event celebrated with flags and music, as befitted an occasion so significant of benefit to this country. The Boulder brass band and the string band were out. The exhibition itself created quite a sensation; the collection of curiosities and specimens being unexpectedly full and fine. Mrs. Maxwell is indefatigable in her profession as taxidermist and collector in natural history. As one of the visitors last evening enthusiastically remarked,—'Why, she has everything in air, sea, earth or under the earth imaginable.'

"It is well called the 'Rocky Mountain Museum,' as she and her assistant, Professor Glass, have laid the whole Rocky Mountain region under tribute for representatives of its fauna, fossils and minerals. Her visit to the Pacific coast last season was for the express purpose of collecting, for this museum, relics, curious specimens and objects of interest in natural history; and it is wonderful how much her tact and energy have accomplished. Every beast of the forest and plains, from the big buffalo and huge cinnamon,[123] to the field mouse and the mole; every bird of the air; rare fishes and shells from the seas; barbarian armor, and relics, and nameless things, arranged with infinite patience and cunning art."

Of its appearance, and the impression it made upon one quite unacquainted with Mrs. Maxwell, or any of the circumstances we have narrated, H.H. has already spoken.[124]

Before many months passed, among the attractions (?) added to the museum, were a number of living rattlesnakes, and a couple of bear cubs. The mother of the latter was killed at the time of their capture. Ten days or more after her death, her skin being mounted, was placed in the museum. Mrs. Maxwell, to test her work and to see whether the cubs still remembered their mother, let them out into the room where she was. Selecting her from the other animals, they ran, whining, and jumped about her, licking her face, and seeming overjoyed at finding her again. But when conscious that she would not return their caresses, their grief was touching in the extreme. Standing up and stroking her face with their little paws in the most pleading

---

123. Cinnamon is a subspecies of American black bear found in the western United States and Canada.
124. Helen Hunt, "Mrs. Maxwell's Museum," *New York Independent*, September 23, 1875, n.p.

manner, they licked her nose and cheeks, and moaned like two heartbroken children. It was more than Mrs. Maxwell could endure, and with tears of sympathy for their disappointment, she took them away.

They were about the size of large cats, when taken, and at the time of their death were nearly half-grown. This event occurred in a melancholy manner. With mistaken kindness they were permitted to exercise their natural instincts for burrowing, and proved themselves much more expert in the art than one, from their youth, could have anticipated. They passed under the coal-cellar wall and came so near the surface of the street upon the outer side, that a horse broke through and was precipitated upon them.

Although Mrs. Maxwell believes bears to have such an element of uncertainty in their characters, that one could never be quite safe in their power, still her acquaintance with them proves they have many winning ways, and she became very much attached to her little pets. They were as playful as two kittens, and, in their amiable moods, exceedingly loving. Notwithstanding they could not eat in peace, if there was no food about and they were good-natured, they would fold each other in their tenderest embraces. Nothing could be prettier than to see the two little shaggy cinnamon-colored creatures, stretched out side by side with their little arms about each other's necks, and a very laugh in their small, black eyes, hug and caress each other. Then they would be so gracious to their human friends when they felt in a condescending mood.

Her other pets, the rattlesnakes, were gifted with entirely different dispositions. Whereas the bears were very demonstrative, these seldom expressed any emotion, and never quarrelled about the mice which were given them for food. They would never eat these unless they themselves killed them. This they did by striking them with their poisoned fangs; and here a curious fact may be noted.

Their venom, so deadly to other creatures, is harmless to themselves; as is proven, not only by their eating mice so killed, but by the fact that one of them bit itself and was not injured. A man was so foolhardy as to hold it in his fingers by the back of its neck. In its desperate efforts to bite him, it struck its fangs into its own body, drawing blood, yet showing no sign of being poisoned.

They never molested snakes or other reptiles which were put into the case with them, no matter what their size or family. Like most other venomous serpents, they are ovoviviparous;[125] and soon after the capture of the first rattlesnake, she made Mrs. Maxwell the happy possessor of eleven young ones; however, only six of them survived any length of time. These were subjects of especial interest and attraction, and Mrs. Maxwell had great hope through them of determining some vexed questions concerning their species; but unfortunately three of them were devoured by mice given to the old ones for food. The other three died, one after the other, the last at the age of eleven months. The remarkable thing about their history is, they were never known to have taken any food, although every effort was made to find something the little things would eat. With the old ones she had nearly three years' acquaintance; and many pages might be written about them, were snakes only universal favorites.

---

125. Ovoviviparous refers to animal species whose eggs develop and remain inside the mother's body until they are ready to hatch; the young are born alive.

25

VALUABLE AID. MOUNTAIN RATS.
STEALING AND HIDING. LOST STOCKINGS.

In the spring of 1875, Mr. Hersey, a young naturalist, came to Mrs. Maxwell's assistance, and they arranged to alternately take charge of the museum and to collect for it.[126] He was, like her, inspired with an enthusiastic love of discovery, and was untiring in his researches, traversing, alone, mountains and plains, camping wherever night overtook him, in his tent, with miners or in their deserted cabins. Once, while occupying one of the latter, the mountain rats—little animals, so common in that region, that an account of their "tricks and manners" must not be omitted—treated him very uncivilly.

Not in the least appreciating his efforts for a better understanding between men and animals, they ungraciously picked his pockets as he slept! Taking out his pocket-book, they nibbled its cover, carried off its loose notes, and so thoroughly appropriated a five-dollar bill that no trace of it has been discovered from that day to this!

---

126. J. Clarence Hersey was hired by Maxwell in 1875 as an assistant to help her collect specimens. Originally from Vermont, Hersey moved to Colorado in 1872.

This family of rats would disdain acknowledging even distant relationship to the wharf variety. Haven't they hair on their tails? Yes, indeed—quite a fringe of it; and, then, their complexion is as much as a shade lighter. So they are by no means to be confounded with ordinary rats. They would be quite as pleasant neighbors as squirrels, only they have kleptomania in a malignant form!

They will steal everything they can manage, no matter how useless to them.

Not long before the museum opened, Mrs. Maxwell wished to use some dried apples. She knew she had placed a large panful, about eight quarts, in her pantry but a few days before, and was somewhat surprised to find it empty, and the apples nowhere to be found. Thinking some one of her family had put them away, and having no time to investigate the matter, it was forgotten. Soon after, while rearranging the rockwork that formed the foundation for the bird-tree in her parlor, she discovered that, between the boards that supported the rocks and those that covered the carpet, underneath, the rats had stored a large quantity of leaves, missing garments, etc.; and there, in a nice pile quite by themselves, were all those dried apples!

The house was yet unfinished, and their passage from room to room was not so very difficult; yet, as the pantry was in the story below, and in an opposite corner of the house, their removal showed some industry, to say the least.

The apples were taken down-stairs and put in a more secure place until Mrs. Maxwell could show them to some of her friends, as an illustration of rat-work. When looked for, for that purpose, behold! they had disappeared a second time! Imagine her disgust, upon looking under the rocks, to find those *very* apples again, in the very place from which she had removed them—this time mixed with dried cherries, grapes, blackberries, pine cones, spoons, forks, broken crockery, pieces of tin cans, and a little of almost everything they could find, either in-doors or out!

If her acquaintance with that particular family ceased here, her knowledge of the tribe did not. Later in that year, as she and her husband and party were returning from the Middle Park, they camped one night in an empty house in the deserted mining camp, Excelsior. This place is so near the Snowy Range, and it is so beautiful, that its houses usually have summer occupants, as sea-side and mountain cottages have in the Atlantic States. But such visitors had been gone for some weeks, when their party made one of these houses do duty as hotel. Mr. Maxwell was the first to make his toilet in the morning, and after spending an unusually long time about it, inquired:

"Mattie, have you done anything with one of my socks?"

"It's altogether probable I have," she answered, rubbing her half-open eyes. "There are so many fascinating things I could do with that 'inviting piece of your wardrobe!'" and she noticed his helpless, perplexed-looking face with amusement.

"Oh, pshaw! Now be in earnest. I've looked everywhere, and I can't find it."

"I am ready to believe you. The room looks as though either a man had been looking for something, or a whirlwind had been having a frolic here! You have probably buried it under something."

"No, I haven't. I pulled them both off right here, and one was all right, but the other was gone."

"Well, hand me the valise, and I'll get you another pair. And, as not a soul has been in the room during the night but ourselves, we will call this a decided case of spirits or rats."

When Mrs. Maxwell came to prepare for breakfast, she found herself repeating Mr. Maxwell's experience. She shook and folded every article in the room, but not a sign of stockings appeared.

"Ready for breakfast?"

"No," was her reply.

"Why, what's the matter? I thought you could dress in five minutes any time," said Mr. Maxwell, re-entering the room.

"The rats have carried off my stockings!" and her face wore a comically deprecating look, as she stood on a folded blanket, exploring the depths of a valise on a stool before her.

Mr. Maxwell's reply was a laugh, and the question, "Shall I comfort you as you did me a few minutes ago?"

"No, I thank you," she replied. "I had rather you would spend your energy in helping me hunt them up."

"Oh, fie! let them go."

But Mrs. Maxwell wouldn't. She proposed to discover what

"Ways that are dark
And tricks that are vain"[127]

---

127. "The Heathen Chinee" (1870) by the American writer Bret Harte (1836–1902).

had been practised by those rats. The search began by removing a board from the chamber floor wherever a hole suggested the possibility that rats had passed that way. And what things they discovered! Leaves, sticks, stones, fragments of all kinds of small wearing apparel; not only Mr. Maxwell's sock, but pieces of many others, purloined from former victims; everything but Mrs. Maxwell's own property.

"Well," said Mr. Maxwell, as they lifted the last board, "I think you will have to give up now."

"By no means," she replied. "There is the loft over the lean-to. I'll have a candle, and explore that."

She did, and found all that Dr. Coues mentions in the appendix, and also her own property and a handkerchief belonging to Miss E—, the other lady in the party.[128]

---

128. See appendix, "Notice of Mrs. Maxwell's Exhibit of Colorado Mammals. Prepared by Dr. Elliott Coues, U.S.A."

26

———————

The trip into the Park, just referred to, was one of particular interest from the territory explored and the number of valuable additions made by it to the museum.

The party at first consisted of Mr. and Mrs. Maxwell, an editor and his son, and a Miss E—. Mr. Maxwell took the baggage, and went over the toll-roads, while the rest of the party, on horseback, tried the merits of a new pass, proposing to meet him at Willow creek in the Park.

Leaving Mr. Maxwell at Nederland,[129] a little village so christened by a Holland mining company, Mrs. Maxwell joined the other excursionists at Caribou—the place where said Hollanders took ore from a silver mine, which they purchased for the trifling sum of three million dollars ($3,000,000)![130] The location of the town, like the valuation of its mining property, is rather

---

129. Located west of Boulder, Nederland, Colorado, started as a trading post between the Utes and European settlers in the 1850s.

130. Caribou was a silver mining town located a few miles north of Nederland.

high! It is so near timber-line in fact, that a ride of three or four miles to snow-fields is a common Fourth-of-July recreation.

Starting from there early the next morning, our travellers soon found themselves shivering under the August sun amid the bleak, rocky wastes of Dartt Pass. This pass is one of the few points where it is possible for men and beasts to cross the vertebræ of our continent. Its elevation is 11,300 feet above the sea. As its trail had but just been located by Mrs. Maxwell's father—for whom it was named—and sufficiently worked and marked that it could be called passable, she and Miss E— were the first women who ever panted in its rarefied atmosphere while drinking in the grandeur of its wild desolation. Considering the discomfort through which this distinction was purchased, few of their sex will envy them its enjoyment. Climbing heights, whether material or spiritual, has been repeatedly proven to be difficult work. In this case it was emphasized by a light snow, which had fallen to the depth of several inches the previous night. Their first ascent lay over a spur of the range so steep, that sympathy for their horses, together with the difficulty of remaining on their backs, prompted them to walk. The snow made this by no means an easy task still harder, for as the day advanced it grew soft and slushy, penetrating their boots and making the half-concealed rocks so slippery that their feet were not the only portions of their bodies brought in frequent contact with them. Climbing a few rods, then pausing to let their panting horses get breath and to fill their own lungs with the light, cold air, they slowly advanced until noon, when they reached a gulch, at the bottom of which were a few trees and a little stream of water. They were obliged to stop here to recover a missing gun, and remained until the next morning, when, at dawn, they resumed their journey.

They found the ascent of the main range still more difficult than had been that of the spur. I shall not assert that their trail—it didn't pretend to be a road, and was not marked by a track, but merely by piles of stones put up at intervals—I shall not assert it was *absolutely* steep and bad, for I find that adjectives, when applied to high-ways, are quite as relative as when used elsewhere.

I have known farmers in Massachusetts [to] stay at home a week, rather than venture over the mud of roads that, to my eyes, accustomed to the depth to which mother earth softens at the touch of spring in Wisconsin and Illinois, seemed remarkably good. In these latter States I have known roads that bore the reputation of being next to impassably steep and sideling; yet which, after travelling along mountain-sides in Colorado, where the large wheels of a wagon had to be placed on its lower side, and the smaller ones on its upper side, and the vehicle then steadied by ropes wound around trees to keep it from overturning, seemed only sufficiently uneven to give pleasant diversity—I wondered, in contrasting the two, that any one should think of complaining of such trifling inequalities. So about this trail over Dartt Pass I shall make no absolute assertion. A traveller among the Himalayas, or even the higher Andes, might have called it very good, and have regarded any other statement as simply evincing a lack of experience in the possibilities of travel. It is true, when their horses were a halter's length behind them, they had to look below the level of their own feet to see those patient beasts' advancing ears; but I dare say they were fortunate in being able to see them even then!

In many places, too, the poor creatures found it almost impossible to pick their way over great beds of rocks, or to squeeze between their sharp edges: but then the rocks were firm, or it might have been worse.

Even Mrs. Maxwell's experience verified this, for once, when she and some friends crossed the range, they came to a place where the stones had a trick of sliding, and a poor packed donkey was given a gratuitous ride twenty-five or thirty feet down the mountain-side, and only prevented from being dashed to pieces over a precipice by the moving stones clogging for a few moments. A single movement would have started them on, but poor Jack was so terrified that he lay perfectly still until a man, risking his own life, crawled to a point where he could throw ropes about the poor brute, with which to draw him up. And once, on another trip, the whole party slid down a mountain-side into a lake, which they were obliged to ford as best they could, and from whose imprisoning valley they were twenty-four hours in finding a possible way of escape.

Without diversifying their ascent by any such exciting episodes, they toiled on until at length they stood upon the summit, where falling snowflakes part company, to meet again only when the waves of commingling oceans touch. For a time all was forgotten save the magnificent prospect spread out before them. On one side the valleys of the Park, with their distant walls of snowy peaks; on all other sides innumerable mountain tops—the near ones white and cold, the far-away ones purple and dark, melting at the east into the distant, cloud-like plains. But the necessity of reaching, before nightfall, the evergreen depths and bits of emerald meadows that lay far, far below, compelled them to hasten on.

As they approached timber-line they saw clouds gathering, and quickening their pace, selected for a camp the first spot where wood, water, and grass in suitable proximity could be found.

Expecting to meet Mr. Maxwell and the wagon so soon, they had undertaken the trial of this pass with no other baggage than could be packed at the back of their saddles. A fly—a strip of canvas, twelve by eight feet, which could be rolled with their bedding—was their only substitute for a tent. With nothing but it for protection, what was to be done? To spend the night drenched by an icy rain, at an altitude where one's clothes would freeze as soon as wet, was a prospect calculated to dismay any one but a soldier or a pioneer.

Much has been written and said of the hardships of frontier life, and many people are disposed to regard the pilgrims who landed on Plymouth Rock, the settlers who first faced the perils of our western frontier, and the heroes and heroines of "Fox's Book of Martyrs,"[131] as all belonging in the same catalogue—people who are to be admired and revered, but not at all to be envied. I have no objection to this classification, but I would remind those who make it that nature never forgets to put in her compensations. Who would not be almost willing to be burned at the stake to know that sublime love and faith that can make pain a joy, because borne for the Being one adores? Who would not be glad to be brought, for a time at least, face to face with the unconquered wilderness, to know they possess the power to subjugate it?

Frontier life *has* its hardships, and they are neither fewer nor more easy to be borne than has been pictured, but their shadows are interwoven with many lights; and one of the brightest is the knowledge gained of one's own resources. Nothing is more gratifying to a person than to know he has met difficulties and conquered them, until, like Alexander of old, conquest has become a habit; and he would court, rather than shun, obstacles, and weep, were there no more to conquer.

This knowledge is a reward for frontier life by no means to be lightly valued, for, to feel equal to an emergency, is to convert it from a terror to a delight.

---

131. Foxe's *Book of Martyrs* (1563) by the English historian John Foxe (1516–1587).

That the storm which threatened them would be severe, and that their resources for meeting it were very meagre, Mrs. Maxwell was perfectly aware, but the fact did not disconcert her.

How the problem of shelter was to be solved, she had at first no idea beyond the one that it was to be done. I speak of Mrs. Maxwell assuming the question; Miss E—'s previous experience in out-door life had been very limited, and in making an inventory of his many virtues, Mr. B— protested that ingenuity was not one of them, his supply being as small as that in the possession of any average mortal.

The first step taken was the selecting of two trees, growing near enough together so that a corner of each end of the fly could be securely fastened to them about five feet from the ground. The lower side was pinned firmly to the earth and with hatchet and sticks a little trench was dug along its edge to conduct the water away. This was for protection on the windward side. Mrs. Maxwell's blanket-shawl, opened to its full length and pinned to the upper edge of the fly, shut in the open side. Saddle-blankets and corn-sacks, which had held grain for their horses were called upon to enclose the ends. A paper of pins was used to fasten the various parts together; hair-pins, taken from heads feminine, doing duty where the other kind was too small.

The house being completed, it was quickly furnished; a carpet of boughs was laid on the floor, the blankets for two beds spread, and into the space between them the saddles, bridles, guns, ammunition, provisions, and their only cooking utensils—a coffee-pot and frying-pan—were placed. Though they had not an inch of space to spare, they passed the night as comfortably as though a wild storm of wind and rain had not swept around them.

The exciting question for the next few days was, "Where is Willow creek?" They found, upon comparing notes, that no two of them had been directed to follow the same route, and it was doubtful if they had been told of the same place. There were no houses at which to inquire, and the two or three hunters they met gave such conflicting directions, that it was probable each of them meant a different stream. All the creeks in that vicinity emptied into Grand river, and all were edged with willows, so that the name could properly be applied to any one of them.

After spending two days in search and fording the Grand—at this point a dangerous feat, as its bottom is formed of large, round, slippery stones, and its waters are very swift and deep—chancing to meet a traveller, they learned from him that a man with a team, answering the description of Mr. Maxwell and his outfit, was on the way to Grand lake. As they were out of provisions they took as direct a line as possible for that spot, where they found the individual.

The special object of the trip with Mr. and Mrs. Maxwell was to get elk, and as they were not at all familiar with the different localities in the Park, and the season was already so far advanced that within a couple of weeks a storm might render the Snowy Range next to impassable, they hired a professional hunter to assist them. He assured them he knew the exact locality in which to find elk, and would kill some in a day or two at most.

He spent three days without seeing even a track of one; then he reported having killed one, but said, "It had the scurvy so bad its skin wan't good fur nothin', its meat a dog couldn't eat, and its horns was broke!" a state of demoralization which, he assured them, quite disgusted him with the pursuit of that graceful animal, and compelled him to ask for his five dollars per day and to retire from business.

In the meantime Mr. and Mrs. Maxwell had not been idle, but had collected minerals, animals, and birds. About the time of the departure of the disgusted Nimrod, Mr. B— and his son left them, much to their regret; and they removed to another point where two hunters were employed. The new apostles of Diana[132] saw tracks and sights, and heard sounds, and even went so far as to fire at a supposed elk; but, after several days hunting, reported nothing more tangible than their bill. Mr. and Mrs. Maxwell and Miss E— then removed to the Hot Sulphur Springs.

These, for years, have been the central point of attraction to tourists visiting the Middle Park. Whether they are more or less curious than others of their kind, I am not prepared to say. I can only state, positively, that their odor is abominable, their waters very clear, and quite too hot at first touch for comfort; but one gets used to it after a few moments, and finds the sensation of being gently parboiled very delightful.

This was not their first visit to the locality. Years before during their first residence in Colorado, Mrs. Maxwell had accompanied her husband and a party from Central City, and she is said to have been the first white woman ever there. The authority for such a belief is testimony of a couple of trappers,

---

132. In Roman mythology, Diana is the goddess of the hunt.

who had practised their vocation in that region for years, making the springs their head-quarters. Visiting Central with furs, immediately after her return home, they inquired what white woman had been there, averring that one had certainly tried a bath in the springs. The person of whom they inquired, thinking their assertion very improbable, demanded how they knew.

"We saw her tracks in the sand where she came out of the spring," they replied.

"Pooh! If that's all the evidence you have, you needn't bet very high on the woman! The tracks were doubtless a boy's."

In answer to this remark one of the buckskin-clad reporters drew himself up to his full height, which was not diminutive, and, with the playfulness of a grizzly bear, demanded—

"See here, mister, do you see them air?" opening his mouth and pointing to two tobacco-stained fangs, "them's eye-teeth, and you'll take observation they're cut clean through."

"Well, yes. 'Pears like you *are* through teething," the man replied.

"I allow I be! and when I sez a thing you may stake the drinks that I knows what I'm talkin' 'bout. I hain't watched tracks these thirty years without known' what kind of critters they belong to! Them tracks was too narrer for their length fur any boy!"

"Oh," the Central man replied, "I wouldn't want to misdoubt your word, but you know there ain't mor'n a dozen or so women in these parts, and a trip over there wouldn't be a likely one for any of 'em to take. If they were only tracks of naked feet, I don't quite just see how you could tell they weren't a squaw's?"

"Why, bless you, mister, that's easy 'nough. I'm s'prised anybody should have any trouble over that. Squaws turn their toes in and white folks don't. The jaunt ain't a very likely one for 'em to take, I allow, and none of 'em ever took it afore, I know; but if you jest inquire 'round enough, you'll find out some white woman made it. You may bet your bottom ounce of dust on that!"[133]

---

133. This passage mirrors the earlier scene in which Maxwell is initially mistaken for a Native American (chapter 8). It simultaneously speaks to the fact that Maxwell's activities were outside the norm for white women settlers and to a preoccupation with ensuring that, despite those activities, Maxwell was definitely a white woman. As noted in the opening of the book, questions of "Is she a half-breed?" and "Is she an Indian?" were frequently raised by the public.

They inquired, and found Mr. and Mrs. Maxwell had just returned from there.

At that time the springs were just as nature made them, and their hands were the first to begin a series of innovations, which have ended in completely changing the original aspect of the spot. They only made the water of the upper spring fall into the deep, rock-formed basin of the lower one, so that when it was converted into a bath-house, by putting a pole across it and covering it with canvas, shower-baths could be *endured* as well as other varieties. But recently others have erected a bath-house, supplied with all modern conveniences.

Alas for the poor Utes! They can no longer submerge their sick horses, pappooses, and puppies in its purifying waters! They were said to hold them in great reverence as possessing powers little less than miraculous. To judge from their appearance, they hold water, wherever found, as too sacred to be used except in a last extremity. It is useless to longer imagine that the picture memory holds of their utter ugliness and filth can ever be changed. Hot chemicals are no longer possible to them, and cold water would be powerless on a Ute![134]

Mrs. Maxwell's party made this location their head-quarters for a while as they continued their search for elk. A new set of hunters were employed. They, like the others, "knew *just* where elk were to be found." "Nobody *ever* went to that place that didn't see elk!" The party went with them, and their combined efforts resulted in finding some old tracks.

A dash of intense excitement, however, was given their fruitless search, for they came upon a cinnamon bear, and all gave it chase, firing at it several times. It was the only game, larger than a rabbit, they saw during the whole four days of their absence.

They then started for Whiteley's Peak, about forty miles distant. Most of the way there was no wagon-track whatever, and that necessary vehicle was as nearly bottom-side up a good share of the way, as the laws of gravitation would permit and allow anything to remain in it. The new hunters declared nothing saved it from being "smashed up" but the fact that Mr. Maxwell would sing instead of swear, in all the worst places!

---

134. The negative stereotypes about Native Americans in Dartt's writing were common among white settlers at the time. By depicting Native Americans as hostile, primitive Others, these stereotypes led white settlers to view the eradication and removal of Native Americans as both inevitable and beneficial.

The last possible point that the wagon could be supposed to reach, in a certain direction, was agreed upon for a camp; and when a day's journey distant, the hunters left them to pursue different routes to the spot, hunting as they went. Before many hours the wagon came to a rock upon which two antelope had been placed by a hunter, who knew it must pass that way, and at night a deer was reported killed. The fates seemed suddenly to have relented, for with the next night came the welcome news that two elk, a male and a female, awaited Mrs. Maxwell's attention at different points in the woods.

Here, when large game was killed, it was left where it had fallen, and she and Mr. Maxwell went to it on horseback, taking with them a pack-animal. It was her task to superintend and assist in removing the skin, to take the measurements and record them with observations in her note-book, and see that the skull and other necessary bones were prepared for preservation.

To accomplish this, the next morning, accompanied by Miss E—, they went to find the buck-elk. It was five or six miles to where it lay. Late in the day the parts necessary in taxidermy were put upon the pack-horse and secured there by ropes. Two of the other horses were packed, one with the body of a young deer, the other with part of a full-grown one, both killed in that vicinity, and they started for camp. In going down a steep hill-side the elk-skin pack began to turn, and before it could be adjusted a sight of the horns and the smell of the blood frightened the horse, and he began to kick, rear, and run. Stumbling, and being tangled in the pack he fell and rolled over down the mountain side, and as they watched him they thought he must surely be killed by the large horns being forced into his body, and certainly they must be broken among the rocks.

Mrs. Maxwell reached him just as he was struggling to rise, and, springing upon his head, held him down until Mr. Maxwell could unfasten the ropes and remove the offending pack. To their great relief no very serious damage had been sustained by either the horse or his load. The other horses also took fright, but Miss E—, with great presence of mind, succeeded in securing their halters and leading them away before they became unmanageable. After much petting and soothing they all became quiet, the load was replaced, and they proceeded to camp.

Here a hunter reported the discovery of a herd of mountain buffalo—creatures so rare that they had not thought of looking for them—and that he had shot one of the cows.[135] The next morning the men proposed that they hasten to the spot where it lay, without guns or other temptation, to spend an extra hour, secure the skin, and leave the female elk to the wolves, for all were growing nervous about recrossing the range.

It was not without many remonstrances that Mrs. Maxwell was persuaded to leave her gun; but she finally yielded, and set out unarmed. They were busy removing the skin from the cow, when, looking up, she saw only a little distance from her, a beautiful buffalo calf. It evidently belonged to the cow that had been killed, and it had stayed behind the herd to wait for her.

Probably there was never a time when strong language would better have fitted Mrs. Maxwell's thoughts, than while that little creature stood there within easy shot, and not a rifle or even a shot-gun within half a dozen miles! That variety of buffalo was so rare, the group would be so pretty with both mother and young, and above all it was too bad to leave the little creature to perish.

To leave the female elk, Mrs. Maxwell insisted, was not to be thought of by her; and, although it would take another day, so intense was her desire to save it, that the party remained. They were out of flour, and although supplied with the choicest meats and plenty of rice, the satisfied sensation of really having dined could not be quite realized by any combination of those two articles. Still there was no danger of suffering while they held out; and the next morning early found Mr. and Mrs. Maxwell and Miss E— picking their way over rocks and fallen trees, underneath gloomy evergreens, and through open grassy glades, searching for the wood where the elk lay.

At last it was found, and Mr. Maxwell having brought his gun with him, left them, to see if by looking about in the neighborhood of their trip the day previous, he could find the buffalo calf. In the meantime an icy rain, alternating with snow, had set in, and Mrs. Maxwell and Miss E—, who for a time assisted her, found their task of skinning the elk an intensely uncomfortable one. The chilling drops beat down on hands that were soon so numb that they could hardly hold the knife or be made to obey any command of the will that would not let them desist from work. Breathing upon her fingers to enable them to make any kind of figures upon a page so splashed by rain as

---

135. Wood bison, or mountain buffalo (*Bison bison athabascae*), are a subspecies of American bison that are larger and heavier than plains bison.

to be pretty much a blot, the measurements were recorded. Late in the afternoon the disagreeable work ended, and she joined Miss E— in her retreat under the thick foliage of a fir-tree, to wait for Mr. Maxwell's return. It must be admitted that a more forlorn-looking couple of human beings are seldom seen, than he found, dripping, shivering and listening to the melancholy soughing of the wind among the dark evergreens of that lonely mountainside! He had seen nothing of buffalo, either large or small, and the next day found them *en route* for home.

Into the shades of forgetfulness are remanded all the hardships, annoyance and suffering of that journey home. They were all that the most vivid fancy could picture, as connected with such a trip over such a country, at the beginning of winter. It will be remembered that the season, never wholly absent from the range, is fully reinstated there by the first of October, the time at which our excursionists returned. If any one thinks that specimens of Natural History cost nothing beyond the courage to shoot them, we can only recommend them to try procuring deer and mountain buffalo, bear and elk, preparing their skins, and transporting them over the mountains, as the best method of correcting such an erroneous opinion.

27

LEGISLATIVE INVITATION. RELUCTANT CONSENT. SKILLED
ASSISTANT. UNSPEAKABLE IMPUDENCE. NECESSARILY
DEAF. ATTEMPT TO STEAL. AMERICAN CHARACTER. RIFLE
PRESENTATION. BLANK FACES. MISREPRESENTATIONS.

In the autumn of 1875, soon after her return from the Park, her attention was called from collecting for the museum to its demands in another direction. Boulder was then a village of less than three thousand inhabitants; its many tourists, not expecting anything of the kind worth seeing in so small a place, failed to visit it in any numbers; and so, contrary to her hopes, she had been unable to make it meet the expenses of rent, etc. The greater number of inhabitants in Denver, and the generous proffer of assistance from a friend, Mr. P—,[136] induced her to remove it to that place. There, during the winter, was performed the laborious task of mounting, not only the elk and other large animals procured in the Park, but many skins obtained previously.

While still completely occupied in this work, and full of plans for the realization of her great desire to make the museum a permanent institution if possible, the Legislature of Colorado decided that the Territory should take part in the Centennial Exhibition, and began to make arrangements

---

136. John Pickel, a Denver businessman.

to represent its resources. Among these preparations was an official request that Mrs. Maxwell should place the Colorado department of her museum with their exhibit.

This action of the Legislature was not taken until it was almost time for the shipment of articles to be exhibited. Yet it was still some time before Mrs. Maxwell could make up her mind to comply with the request. It conflicted too decidedly with her cherished plans. In fact it really involved their abandonment; for, under the circumstances, it would be impossible to close the museum and give her time and the use of that department during the summer, and hope to return and regain the opportunity she then had.

Her friends urged that the success of her museum enterprise was still very precarious, as Colorado was not yet either sufficiently populous or wealthy to sustain an institution of its kind, even though she continued to give it all her time, energy and means. Should she exhibit her collection, and then sell it, some one else might continue her effort for comparative science in some other place.

At least she would be free to devote herself to some branch of her favorite study which should involve less exhaustive labor and expense. At length she reluctantly consented. However, in giving up her museum, she did not surrender the hope that she might be able, at some future time, to repay, by contributions to their knowledge of the natural history of their State, the great kindness of the many in Colorado, who had assisted her, either by word or deed, in forming her collection. Whether realizing this hope or not, her deepest gratitude will always be theirs.

We forbear to mention all the hurry and worry and work of the weeks that preceded her departure from Denver. It is enough that one morning she found herself and her docile menagerie set down in an unfinished building on the Centennial grounds belonging to the commonwealths of Kansas and Colorado combined, and was told that one side of one wing could be occupied by her, as soon as the wind and rain could be excluded. The main Exhibition had already begun, and all haste was desired in preparing the minor details. So, as soon as possible, Mrs. Maxwell began her work, and discovered that exceptional circumstances for a woman to work under were not yet at an end for her!

In the construction of her landscape, she was provided with the skilled (?) assistance of a negro who, under ordinary circumstances, was doubtless competent to drive nails! He certainly had the strength to do so, as Mrs. Maxwell was able to testify after he crushed her finger in a bungling attempt to drive one in a spot she indicated.

It of course seemed very strange to the visitors who were admitted long before her miniature mountain-side was completed, to see a woman in a working-dress using paste, pulverized ore, water, lime, gravel and ever-greens; yet, only by laying aside all fastidious notions of propriety, and all regard for her own comfort, and working for about two weeks, as nearly night and day as possible, was her exhibit made the attractive picture presented during the summer. The innumerable questions concerning her work, and the criticisms upon it, were not surprising, even though they were a hindrance and an annoyance. Of course, Mr. Smith and Mrs. Jones couldn't help wondering "What on earth that woman was doing on those rocks with all those animals!" and "what the whole thing was going to be, any way!" Nor could their neighbors from all over the Union help pouring out their inquisitive souls in torrents of questions. On the other hand, Mrs. Maxwell was absolutely obliged to be deaf to them, or her work would never have been completed.

This fact, however, was not apparently suspected by the visitors, who, anxious to know all that was to be learned at the great Exhibition, used every means in their power to attract her attention to their questions, poking her with canes and umbrellas when she was near enough to be reached, and assailing her ears after this fashion when too far from the rope stretched around her space to permit those appliances being used to advantage.

"Madam! Could you tell me what is the design of this work?"

No answer.

"*Madam!*" a little louder, supposing her to be somewhat deaf as well as pre-occupied.

"Madam!! I say!"

Still no answer.

"Madam!!!" with a spitefully suggestive accent of the last syllable, emphasized still more by a thrust with the end of his cane as near her as the rope will permit.

Still no sign that she was aware of the presence of any one in the building.

"Humph! She must be awful deaf, or else she hasn't any manners not to answer a civil question," he mutters, as he disappears in the crowd.

UNSPEAKABLE IMPUDENCE.

FIGURE 27.1. Unspeakable impudence

Those immediately behind him have been too much occupied to profit by his failure, and with curiosity all aroused by the strange creatures in frames or out of them, that she was at work with, at once begin:

"Mrs., will you tell me the name of the animal you have your hands on, and what you are making here?"

Another change in the beast's position, but no answer. The man behind him, inspired with the same zeal for knowledge, calls out:

"Hallo, there! Ain't this 'ere a buf'lo?"

And the woman by his side pipes up:

"If you please, miss, air these all Kansas critters?"

And a man behind them, provoked by her utter absorption in her work, exclaims:

"I say, ma'am! Can't you hear a civil question? I paid my money to come into this show, and I want to know about this here."

So the hours went by. Of course numberless questions were answered. When possible, without a waste of time, it was a pleasure to give all the information in her power, but she felt that her duty was first to the eyes of the public rather than their ears. From the moment this duty was discharged, until the Exhibition closed, her whole time was devoted to giving all the desired information in her power with regard to her adopted State, the animals, ores, etc., by which it was represented, and in superintending the sale of minerals and photographs of her collection, and, after a time, of herself. To the sale of these articles she had to look for the only pecuniary compensation for her time and labor—a compensation stipulated for before leaving Colorado. Yet to secure a monopoly of the views of her collection cost her a prolonged struggle. The arrangement of her exhibit was not fully completed before an attempt was made to steal and copyright pictures of it. It was only by great exertion that it was prevented, and attempts to repeat the outrage were made several times during the summer. Only the resolution gained by facing mountain storms and wild beasts enabled her to keep possession of this, the only source of income ever connected with her collection. That this promised to be a real source of profit during the summer may be guessed from the efforts made to deprive her of it. The fact that the Centennial Photographic Company had the exclusive right to manufacture views of exhibits, while a protection, was a great disadvantage, because they were utterly unable to keep her stands supplied. For this reason she was able to realize only a small part of what should have been hers. The idea of selling her own likeness was at first very repulsive, but the demand for it was so constant and the supply of views so limited, she felt compelled to yield a point, where her feelings simply were concerned.

The other division of her summer's work—that of replying to inquiries—though often very fatiguing, was far more agreeable.

While the character of the American people is relieved from any suspicion of monotony by a reasonable number of those who are very ignorant, or who possess the power of being disagreeable, for the most part its good humor and intelligence leave little more in that direction to be desired. There was never an hour, through all the summer, when there were not numbers of interesting and appreciative people eager to know all about her and her adventures, about the country where all her specimens were obtained, its climate, resources, agriculture, and mines; how the latter were worked; how the land was irrigated, etc., etc. Among those interested were many of the most cultivated people of our own country and from foreign lands, and the conversations were mutually pleasant and instructive. Often an hour or more would be passed with one party, examining not only the ores and curiosities of her own collection, but in showing them all of Colorado's exhibit. She was proud of its magnificent scenery, delightful climate, and wonderful resources, and was always happy to find those who were interested in learning about them. Many friends were thus formed and many tokens of esteem were received, both from persons in her own country and from visitors from abroad. Not the least among these, nor [sic] the most lightly prized, was a beautiful rifle, presented by those associated with her in the same building as an expression of their appreciation of what she had done "to make the Kansas and Colorado Exhibition a grand success."

But people who were capable of conversing intelligently about the remote corners of the earth were not the only persons who sought information, and we trust found some. More than one person asked, "How big a village Colorado was?" and there was quite an amount of curiosity as to whether it was "fur there," and whether "the Rocky Mountains were much higher than the one she had made;" whether the water of the little cascade was the genuine article; whether it, and the rocks over which it fell, were brought from Colorado; and one young woman put up a cup for some of the sparkling fluid, remarking as she did so that she "wanted to say she had had a drink of real mountain water," adding, as she complimented its coolness and flavor, that she never drank the "hydrant stuff when she could get anything else."

A very large number sought information with regard to the present danger of being scalped were they to venture to Colorado to hunt and explore its wilds.

Mrs. Maxwell grew to expect blank faces when people were informed that the animals they saw were collected for scientific purposes, and not for the sake of gratifying an abnormal desire to shoot things. But she, and her friends who had "lived West," *were* astonished at the number of apparently well-informed people who received the information that they were only a small part of a museum formerly established, and having the patronage of the people of Colorado, with looks of surprise and even polite incredulity.

"Why, these people seem to think the West is still occupied by Indians and ruffians!" was a usual exclamation of those from that locality, after standing for a time in her enclosure and conversing with the crowd. "Please do what you can to enlighten them."

In obeying this injunction, given for the benefit of people whom the growth of our country has quite outrun, Mrs. Maxwell took commendable pride in pointing to a large frame filled with photographs of the schoolhouses of Colorado. In those handsome structures she maintained there was an unanswerable argument against such utter lack of civilization as they supposed to exist so far from the Atlantic coast.

The source of the deepest annoyance to Mrs. Maxwell's family, which her presence at the Centennial occasioned, was an out-growth of this ignorance. To their intense disgust the newspapers persisted for some time in representing her as simply a female "Border Bill," and seemed willfully oblivious to the possibility that, coming from the Rocky Mountains, she could be other than what they termed her, "The Colorado Huntress"—a female of remarkable skill with a gun, and courage enough to shoot a bear!

But she had neither time nor inclination to correct assertions which she felt the reality of her life contradicted. Her present was too full of more urgent and agreeable claims. As every one of the many, many persons who visited the Centennial will readily believe, each moment of her summer was occupied. She was left no leisure even for her meals and the demand of her wardrobe. Some one was always waiting with an imperative demand to see her; and when at last the great Corliss engine[137] ceased its work, and the curious and beautiful things of the Exposition were removed, she found she had given memory few more of its wonders to retain than the recollection of the most interesting feature of it all—the many charming people who had visited or been associated with the Centennial.

---

137. The Corliss Centennial Engine was a steam engine that powered the exhibits at the Centennial International Exposition. The centennial ran from May 10 to November 10, 1876.

28

TASK COMPLETED. HER DAUGHTER'S EDUCATION.

The task I promised those kindly faces at the Centennial I would some time perform is now finished. If they take half the interest in my answer to their questions that their pleasant faces expressed in Mrs. Maxwell's work, I shall be satisfied and grateful.

The field in which she labored still calls for courageous observers and tireless workers. If this story of her adventures shall stimulate any one to a deeper love of her favorite study, whatever her future may be, she will deem her past a success.

To those in whom it may have awakened something of a personal interest in her, yet who may question what effect such an exceptional career may have had upon her as a woman, I present no theories. I can only say, through all these years, to her friends in trouble she has been simply a tender-hearted, sympathetic woman. Though she gave herself no rest, nor [sic] spared time for any pleasure, whether social or solitary, she gave months to the care of her mother when disabled by an accident, and in her busiest time had many days and nights for her sister's child when sickness came.[138] While hope lingered she knew no other thoughts than those that centred in the frail, sweet life they all so longed to keep. When all failed, and the baby form was laid in the shadow of the granite cliffs—Oh, grand, majestic mountains! guard well that little grave, and all the graves of sons that sleep beneath your care, too far away for mother's eyes to watch over them—it was to her the bereaved clung for comfort in their hour of bitter grief.

Before these and similar memories, and in the presence of ceaseless exertions and self-denials for her daughter's higher education,[139] let no one say that any worthy, noble pursuit need diminish the sweetness of true womanhood, or render the heart, once gentle and tender, harsh and cold. Devotion to frivolity, and the struggle for wealth, fame, or any unworthy end, may, *does* do this, but the quest for truth is a search for the divine, and can but ennoble the soul that makes it, though it leads that soul through depths and wilds no mortal ever trod before.

---

138. Mary Dartt Thompson's son, Clarence Thompson, who died as an infant.

139. Maxwell's daughter, Mabel, attended Oberlin College, in Ohio, in 1874 and later the University of Michigan in Ann Arbor and Wellesley College in Massachusetts. The Maxwell family had difficulty financing Mabel's education, and it was a driving force behind Maxwell's hopes that her collection could generate money.

Appendix.

NOTICE OF MRS. MAXWELL'S EXHIBIT
OF COLORADO MAMMALS.

PREPARED BY DR. ELLIOTT COUES, U.S.A.

I had the pleasure of inspecting Mrs. Maxwell's collection of the animals of Colorado, while the exhibit was in Washington during the winter of 1876–7.

My repeated visits afforded me both pleasure and instruction. I was glad to see a collection of our native animals mounted in a manner far superior to ordinary museum work, and to know that there was at least one lady who could do such a thing, and who took pleasure in doing it. While the collection embraced several specimens of high scientific interest, I regarded it as one of the most valuable single collections I had seen—for beyond the scientific value which any collection of the animals of a locality may possess, it represented a means of popularizing Natural History, and making the subject attractive to the public; this desirable object being attained by the artistic manner in which the specimens were mounted and grouped together. Faulty taxidermy has a great deal to do with creating misconceptions of nature in the public mind, and with rendering the study of Natural History unattractive. The best results may be hoped for when such skillful and faithful representation of nature, as these of Mrs. Maxwell's, come to be recognized as a means of public instruction.

With Mrs. Maxwell's kind permission I made for my own benefit some notes on the species of mammals contained in the collection, and I take pleasure in furnishing a list of the specimens, which she is at liberty to use in any way she may see fit. My identifications of the species are supplemented by some remarks partly based upon my own observations in Colorado in 1876, partly derived from my conversation with the intelligent and enthusiastic lady-naturalist herself.

FAMILY FELIDÆ

The Cougar, or American Panther.

FELIS CONCOLOR—LINN.

The collection contains two full-grown specimens of this great cat, sometimes called "the Californian lion," and much dreaded for its depredations upon live-stock. One was killed near Boulder by poisoning the carcass of a young horse which the panther had destroyed. The other was shot.

The cougar appears to be rather common in the mountainous portions of the State, where two or three are usually killed each year, but is only rarely seen on the prairie.

The Mountain Lynx.

LYNX CANADENSIS?

The most common Lynx of the Rocky Mountains in this latitude appears to be a modification of the Canada Lynx, *L. canadensis* of authors, and is perhaps entitled to varietal designation as a geographical race of that species. It may be named var. *montanus*. I have seen similar specimens from elevated portions of California. These Lynxes do not seem to be specifically separable from *L. canadensis*, but they are distinguishable at a glance from the *Lynx rufus*, which also occurs in the same locality. They are much more abundant than the *L. rufus*, and numbers are shot or trapped each year. Several well-prepared specimens are contained in the collection.

The Common or Bay Lynx.

LYNX RUFUS—RAF.

One specimen of the ordinary lynx of the United States—which, as just intimated, is not so common in Colorado as the preceding species—was shot on Câche-Le-Poudre creek at the eastern base of the mountains.

FAMILY CANIDÆ

The Great Gray Wolf.
> CANIS LUPUS OCCIDENTALIS—RICH.

One specimen, full grown, and in fine order. This animal is much less numerous than the following species.

The Prairies Wolf, or Coyote.
> CANIS LATRANS—SAY.

A very abundant animal in Colorado as in most other parts of the West, and occurring in the mountains as well as on the plains.

The Red Fox of the Plains.
> VULPES MACRURUS—BD.

Numerous specimens of this species, differing much in color, but all apparently referable to the animal described by Baird in 1852. It runs into many color varieties, as the cross and silver-gray, and in one case of which I learned the animal was pure black, with a white tip to the tail. One of the specimens in the collection is remarkably light-colored.

The Swift or Kit Fox.
> VULPES VELOX—SAY.

This is a common animal in Colorado, living in burrows on the prairie.

The Gray Fox.
> UROCYON CINEREO-ARGENTATUS—COUES.

Apparently rare in Colorado.

FAMILY MUSTELIDÆ

The Wolverene, or Carcajou.
> GULO LUSCUS—SAB.

It is only of late years that the presence of this remarkable animal so far south has been known. It ranges chiefly in the high north, where it is the most serious annoyance with which the trapper has to contend. The specimen in the collection was captured with a steel trap near Boulder. The animal resides in the mountains, and does not appear to be very rare.

The American Martin or Sable.

MUSETLA AMERICANA—TURTON.

Though not represented in the collection, I enumerate this species as one of the known animals of the State.

The Long-Tailed Weasel.

PUTORIUS LONGICAUDA—BD.

Several specimens of this interesting species, believed to be perfectly distinct from the common ermine, are contained in the collection. These illustrate very fairly the specific distinctions from *P. erminea*, being rather dark-colored, especially on the head, with the underparts decidedly tawny, instead of sulphury-yellow, abruptly defined against the white of the chin, and the black tip of the tail restricted to the terminal pencil. The species turn perfectly white in winter in this latitude, as well as farther north.

The Least Weasel.

PUTORIUS VULGARIS—GRIFF.

One specimen of this pretty little creature was procured near Boulder.

The Mink.

PUTORIUS VISON—GAPP.

This common animal is represented by several specimens.

The American Ferret.

PUTORIUS NIGRIPES—AUD. & BACH.

Mrs. Maxwell's collection contains several specimens of this extremely interesting animal, unknown to naturalists until within a few years. It was originally described by Audubon and Bachman; but subsequently lost sight of until recently, when a few specimens reached the Smithsonian from different localities in the West. It appears to be not at all rare in some portions of Colorado, especially about the plains at the foot of the mountains, where it lives among the prairie-dogs and feeds upon them. Two individuals were captured by being "drowned out" of prairie-dog holes, and another was trapped. It became quite tame, readily submitting to be handled, though it was furious when first caught. It was kept in a wire cage and fed on beef.

When irritated, it hissed and spat like an angry cat. It used to hide by covering itself over with the material of which its nest was composed, but at times, especially at night, it was very active and restless.

The Common Skunk.

MEPHITIS MEPHITICA—BD.

This animal is far too numerous in Colorado, especially about the settlements in the foot-hills and on the prairie.

The Little Striped Skunk.

MEPHITIS PUTORIUS—COUES.

Rather common in the mountains and foot-hills, but less so than the last.

The Badger.

TAXIDEA AMERICANA—BD.

In the specimens examined in Mrs. Maxwell's collection the white stripe runs down over the shoulders, showing an approach to the condition seen in the var. *berlandieri.* The species is abundant in the open portions of the State.

The Otter.

LUTRA CANADENSIS—CUV.

The otter appears to be a rare animal in Colorado. I did not find any sign of its presence during my tour in that State in 1876, and the single specimen in the collection was the only one of which Mrs. Maxwell had known.

FAMILY URSIDÆ

The Bears.

URSUS———?

These formidable animals are represented by a fine group of several specimens, in which three varieties may be recognized. One of the largest is a true grizzly bear, which was shot about forty miles from Denver. Others belong to the variety known as the "cinnamon" bear, and form an interesting group of two cubs crying over their dead mother. Another specimen is the black bear, perhaps of an entirely different species from the rest.

FAMILY BOVIDÆ.

The American Bison, or Buffalo

BISON AMERICANUS—H. SMITH.

The mounted buffaloes of this collection represent both the ordinary species of the plains, and what is known as the "mountain buffalo," by some erroneously supposed to be a different species. The latter are decidedly darker and more uniformly colored than the former, and were shot in September, 1873, near Whitely's Peak, Middle Park.

In 1876 a small band of buffalo still lingered in North Park.

The Mountain Sheep.

OVIS MONTANA—CUV.

A family group consisting of both male and female, and a lamb, shot on the main range near Boulder.

FAMILY ANTILOCAPRIDÆ.

The Antelope.

ANTILOCRAPRA AMERICANA—ORD.

I have nowhere else found antelope so abundant as they were in North Park during the summer of 1876. They were almost continually in view, and thousands must breed in that locality.

In one of the finely mounted specimens in Mrs. Maxwell's collection the points of the horns curve inward toward each other; the two together making a heart-shaped figure.

FAMILY CERVIDÆ.

The American Elk.

ELAPHUS CANADENSIS—DE KAY.

Represented by a fine pair shot near Whitely's Peak.

The Black-Tailed Deer.

CERVUS MACROTIS—SAY.

This is the most abundant of the Cervidæ in Colorado, and is represented by a fine group of two buck, a doe and two fawns.

The White-Tailed Deer.

CERVUS VIRGINIANUS—BODD.

One specimen, a doe from Câche-Le-Poudre creek. It is far less numerous in Colorado than the last-named species.

FAMILY SCIURIDÆ.

The family of the squirrels is very numerously represented in Colorado, both in species and individuals. No less than eight different species are contained in the collection.

The Tuft-Eared Squirrel.

SCIURUS ABERTI—WOODH.

This large and beautiful squirrel, equaling in size the cat and fox squirrels of the East, is common in the pine-covered mountains of Colorado. It is in this region peculiarly subject to melanism, this state being more frequently observed, than the normal coloration. Several specimens examined are uniform deep brownish black, while only one is of the ordinary grey color, with the black stripe on the side.

Fremont's Chickaree.

SCIURUS HUDSONIUS *var.* FREMONTI—ALLEN.

Very abundant in all the woods of the high mountains.

Four-Striped Chipmunk.

TAMIA QUADRIVITTATUS—WAGN.

An exceedingly abundant little animal everywhere in the mountains and parks.

Say's Chipmunk.

TAIMAS LATERALIS—ALLEN.

Common in the pine timber, especially in the rocky places of the higher ranges.

Large Ground Squirrel.

SPERMOPHILUS GRAMMURUS—BACHM.

This is a large and conspicuous species, with its long, bushy tail looking much like a regular tree-squirrel. It is common in rocky places on the foot-hills.

Thirteen-Striped Ground-Squirrel.

SPERMOPHILUS TRIDECEMLINEATUS—AUD. & BACK.

Very common in open places.

The Prairie-Dog.

CYNOMYS LUDOVICIANUS—BAIRD.

One of the commonest and best known animals of the country, the colonies of which dot the prairie on every hand.

The Yellow-Bellied Marmot.

ARCTOMYS FLAVIVENTRIS—AUD. & BACKM.

Apparently confined to the foot-hills and mountains, where it is common.

FAMILY MURIDÆ.

Rocky Mountain Rat.

NEOTOMA CINEREA—BD.

Found in abundance in the mountains of Colorado. They often come about the house and take up their residence, proving very mischievous and undesirable from their propensity to steal and hide everything they can get hold of and carry off. Among the articles which Mrs. Maxwell has found in their retreats, are bushels of weeds of various kinds, chips of wood, cow-manure, old stockings, tent-blocks and ropes, pieces of crockery, knives, forks and a broken doll.

The Bush Rat.

NEOTOMA FLORIDANA—SAY & ORD.

This species also occurs, and comes about the houses like the others, but the two do not seem to get along well together.

The White-Footed or Wood-Mouse.

HESPEROMYS LEUCOPUS *var.* SONORIENSIS—COUES.

A common species of general distribution in the West.

The Meadow Mouse.

ARVICOLA ?

A large species, and resembling *Arvicola riparius*, if not the same.

The Muskrat.

FIBER ZIBETHICUS—CUV.

Very abundant in suitable places in Colorado.

FAMILY ZAPODIDÆ.

The Jumping Mouse.

ZAPUS HUDSONIUS—COUES.

One specimen captured near Boulder.

FAMILY SACCOMYIDÆ.

The Kangaroo Mouse.

DIPODOMYS ORDI—WOODH.

One specimen taken near Denver.

FAMILY GEOMYIDÆ.

The Pocket Gopher.

GEOMYS BURSARIUS—RICH.

One specimen. The species is said to be abundant on the plains and adjoining foot-hills.

FAMILY CASTORIDÆ.

The Beaver.

CASTOR FIBER *var.* CANADENSIS—COUES & YARROW.

A group of several individuals, with specimen of large stump—about three feet in diameter and perfectly sound—cut by them. The beaver is still very abundant on many of the waters of the State.

FAMILY LEPORIDÆ.

The Mountain Rabbit.

LEPUS AMERICANUS *var.* BAIRDI—ALLEN.

Known also as "Snow-shoe" and "Maltese rabbit." This species is confined to the mountains and turns white in winter. In a specimen examined the roots of the hairs showed plumbeous, then a pale salmon or fawn color. The ears sometimes retain a blackish tipping or edging.

Common Jack Rabbit.

LEPUS CAMPESTRIS—BACH.

Very abundant on the prairies and parks of the State, but not found in the woods. This species is identical with that from the northerly parts of the West, but entirely distinct from the following.

Southern Jack Rabbit.

LEPUS CALLOTIS *var.* TEXANUS—ALLEN.

Said to occur in the southern part of the State as far north as the vicinity of Greeley. With the size and general appearance of *L.* Campestris, it may be distinguished by having the top of the tail black instead of white as in the foregoing species.

The Sage Rabbit.

LEPUS SYLVATICUS *var.* NUTTALLI—ALLEN.

Very abundant in the sage brush anywhere.

FAMILY LAGOMYIDÆ.

The Little Chief Hare.

LAGOMYS PRINCEPS—RICH.

Common on the mountains above timber-line.

Mrs. Maxwell's Colorado Museum.

Catalogue of the Birds.

The following is a systematic catalogue of the birds contained in the "Colorado Museum," prepared by Mrs. M. A. Maxwell, of Boulder, Colorado, and by her exhibited at the Centennial Exposition held in Philadelphia during the past summer. The collection consists of excellently mounted specimens, many of which were procured by the lady herself, while all were put up by her hands. It illustrates very fully the avian fauna of Colorado, while it bears testimony, not only to the great richness and variety which characterize the productions of the new State, but also to the success which has crowned the enthusiastic and intelligent efforts of a "woman Naturalist."

The collection embraces many species whose occurrence in Colorado was wholly unlooked for; such as *Nyctherodias violaceus*, *Garzetta candidissima*, and *Tantalus loculator* among southern species, and *Stercorarius parasiticus*, *Xena sabinei*, and *Œdemia Americana* from the high north; the latter, it will be observed, is a strictly littoral species, hence, its occurrence in Colorado, the very centre of the continent, is all the more remarkable.

Family TURDIDÆ: Thrushes.

1. Turdus migratorius, β. propinquus, (Ridgw.) Western Robin. a, ♂ ad.; b, ♀ ad.[140]
2. Turdis guttatus, y. auduboni, (Baird.) Rocky Mountain Hermit Thrush. a, ♂ ad.; b, ♀ ad.
3. Turdus ustulatus, β. swainsoni. Olive-backed, or Swainson's Thrush. a, ♂ ad.
4. Turdus fuscescens, (Stephens.) Tawny Thrush; Wilson's Thrush. a, ♂ ad.
5. Galeoscoptes carolinensis, (Linn.) Cat Bird. a, ♂ ad.; b, ♀ ad.
6. Oreoscoptes montanus, (Towns.) Sage-Thrasher: Mountain Mocking Bird. a, ♂ ad.; b, juv.
7. Mimus polyglottus, (Linn.) Mocking Bird. a, ♂ ad.; b, ♀ ad.
8. Harporhynchus rufus, (Linn.) Brown Thrasher. a, ♂ ad.; b, ♀ ad.

Family CINCLIDÆ: Water Ouzels.

9. Cinclus mexicanus, (Swains.) American Water Ouzel. a, ♂ ad.; b, ♀ ad.; c, d, e, f, young.

Family SYLVIIDÆ: Warblers.

10. Myiadestes townsendi, (Aud.) Townsend's Solitaire. a, ♂ ad.; b, ♀ ad.
11. Sialia sialis, (Linn.) Eastern Blue Bird. a, ♂ ad.; b, ♀ ad.
12. Siala mexicana, (Swains.) California Blue Bird. a, ♂ ad.; b, ♀ ad.
13. Sialia arctica, (Swains.) Rocky Mountain Blue Bird. a, ♂ ad.; b, ♀ ad.
14. Regulus calendula, (Linn.) Ruby-crowned Kinglet. ♂ ad.
15. Regulus satrapa, (Licht.) Golden-crowned Kinglet. a, ♂ ad.; a, ♀.
16. Polioptila cærulea, (Linn.) Blue-gray Gnatcatcher. a, ♂ juv.

Family CERTHIIDÆ: Tree Creepers.

17. Certhia familiaris, β. americana, (Bonap.) Brown Creeper.

Family PARIDÆ: Titmice or Chickadees.

18. Lophophanes inornatus, (Gamb.) Gray Titmouse. a, adult.
19. Parus montanus, (Gamb.) Mountain Chickadee. a, adult.
20. Parus atricapillus, β. septentrionalis, (Harris.) Long-tailed Chickadee. a, adult.
21. Psaltriparus plumbeus, (Baird.) Lead-colored Least Tit. a, ♂ ad.

---

140. All symbol notations in Ridgway's appendix are represented as close as possible to their appearance in the original printing.

Family SITTIDÆ: Nuthatches.

22. Sitta carolinensis, β. aculeata, (Cass.) Slender-billed Nuthatch. a, ♂ ad.; b, ♀ ad.

23. Sitta canandensis, (Linn.) Red-bellied Nuthatch.

24. Sitta Pygmæa, (Vig.) Pigmy Nuthatch. a, ♂ ad.; b, ♀ ad.

Family TROGLODYTIDÆ: Wrens.

25. Catherpes mexicanus, β. conspersus. (Ridgw.) Cañon Wren. a, ♂ ad.

26. Salpinctes obsoletus, (Say.) Rock Wren. a, ♂ ad.; b, ♀ ad.

27. Troglodytes ædon, β. parkmanni, (Aud.) Parkmann's Wren. a, ♂ ad.; b, ♀ ad.; c, d, e, f, g, h, young.

28. Telmatodytes palustris, β. paludicola, (Baird.) Tule Wren. a, ad.

Family MOTACILLIDÆ: Wagtails, and Titlarks, or Pipits.

29. Anthus ludovicianus, (Gm.) American Titlark. a, ♂ ad.; b, ♀ ad. [Breeding abundantly on mountains above timber-line, at an altitude of about 12,000 feet!]

30. Necorys spraguei, (Aud.) a, ad.

Family MNIOTILTIDÆ: American Warblers.

31. Dendrœca auduboni, (Towns.) Audubon's Warbler. a, ♂ ad.; b, ♀ ad.; c, juv.

32. Dendrœca coronata, (Linn.) Yellow-rump Warbler. a, ♂ ad.; b, ♀ ad.

33. Dendrœca nigrescens, (Towns.) Black-throated Gray Warbler. a, ♂ ad.

34. Dendrœca æstiva, (Gm.) Golden Warbler; Summer Yellow Bird. a, ♂ ad.; b, ♀ ad.

35. Parula americana, (Linn.) Blue Yellow-back Warbler. a, ♂ ad.

36. Helminthophaga celata, (Say.) Orange-crowned Warbler. a, ad.

37. Helminthophaga peregrine, (Wils.) Tennessee Warbler, a, ♂ ad.; b, ♀ ad.

38. Geothlypis trichas, (Linn.) Maryland Yellow-throat. a, ♂ ad.; b, ♀ ad.

39. Geothlypis macgillivrayi, (Aud.) McGillivray's Warbler. a, ♂ ad.; b, ♀ ad.

40. Icteria virens, β. longicauda, (Lawr.) Long-tailed Chat. a, ♂ ad.

41. Myiodioctes pusillus, (Wils.) Black-cap Green and Yellow Warbler.

42. Setophaga ruticilla, (Linn.) American Redstart, a, ♂ ad.; b, ♀ ad.

Family VIREONIDÆ: Greenlets or Vireos.

43. Vireosylvia gilva, β. swainsoni, (Baird.) Western Warbling Vireo. a, ♂ ad., b, ♀ ad.

44. Vireosylvia olivacea, (Linn.) Red-eyed Vireo. a, ♂ ad.; b, ♀ ad.

45. Lanivireo plumbeus, (Coues.) Lead-colored Vireo. a, ad.

46. Lanivireo solitarius, (Wils.) Solitary Vireo. a, ad.

Family LANIIDÆ: Shrikes.

47. Collurio borealis, (Vieill.) Great Northern Shrike. a, ♂ ad.; b, juv.

48. Collurio ludovicianus, β. excubitoroides, (Swains.) White-rumped Shrike. a, ♂ ad.; b, ♀ ad.

Family AMPELIDÆ: Wax-wings.

49. Ampelis garrulus, (Linn.) Northern Wax-wing. a, ♂ ad.; b, ♀ ad.

50. Ampelis cedrorum, (Vieill.) Cedar Wax-wing. a, ♂ ad.

Family HIRUNDINIDÆ: Swallows.

51. Progne subis, (Linn.) Purple Martin a, ♂ ad.

52. Petrochelidon lunifrons, (Say.) Cliff Swallow. a, ad.

53. Hirundo erythrogaster, β. horreorum, (Barton.) Barn Swallow. a, ad.; b, juv.

54. Tachycineta bicolor, (Vieill.) White-bellied Swallow. a, ♂ ad.; b, c, d, juv.

55. Tachycineta thalassina, (Swains.) Violet-green Swallow.

56. Stelgidopteryx serripennis, (Aud.) Rough-winged swallow. a, ad.

57. Coltyle riparia, (Linn.) Bank Swallow.

Family TANAGRIDÆ: Tanagers.

58. Pyranga ludoviciana, (Wils.) Western Tanager. a, ♂ ad.; b, ♀ ad.

59. Pyranga æstiva, (Wils.) Vermilion Tanager.

Family FRINGILLIDÆ: Finches, Sparrows and Buntings.

60. Pinicola enucleator, β. canadensis, (Linn.) Pine Grosbeak. a, ♂ ad.; b, ♀ ad. [Breeds on high mountains of Colorado.]

61. Loxia curvirostra, y. mexicana, (Strickl.) Mexican Crossbill. a, ♂ ad.; b, ♀ ad. [Breeds in Colorado.]

62. Hesperiphona vespertina, (Cooper.) Evening Grosbeak. a, ♂ ad.; b, ♀ ad.

63. Plectrophanes nivalis, (Linn.) Snow Bunting. a, ♂ ad., winter plumage.

64. Centrophanes lapponicus, (Linn.) Lappland Long-spur.

65. Centrophanes ornatus, (Towns.) Chestnut-collared Long-spur. a, ♂ ad.; b, ♀ ad.

66. Rhynchophanes maccowni, (Lawr.) McCown's Long-spur. a, ♂ ad.; b, ♀ ad.; c, juv.

67. Leucosticte tephrocotis, (Swains.) Gray-crowned Leucosticte. a, ♂ ad., summer pl.; b, ♀ ad., summer pl.; c, ad., spring pl.; d, ad, summer pl.

68. Leucosticte tephrocotis, β. littoralis, (Baird.) Hepburn's Leucosticte. a, adult, winter pl.

69. Leucosticte atrata, (Ridgw.) Aiken's Leucosticte. a, ♂ ad., winter pl.

70. Leucosticte australis, (Allen.) Allen's Leucosticte. a, ♂ ad., summer pl.; b, ♀ ad., summer pl.; c, ♀ ad., winter pl.

71. Chrysomitris tristis, (Linn.) American Gold-finch. a, b, ♂ ad., summer pl.; c, ♀ ad.

72. Chrysomitris psaltria, (Say.) Green-backed Gold-finch. a, ♂ ad.

73. Chrysomitris pinus, (Wils.) Pine Gold-finch. a, ♂ ad.; b, ♀ ad.

74. Carpodacus cassini, (Baird.) Cassin's Purple Finch. a, ♂ ad.; b, ♀ ad.

75. Carpodacus frontalis, (Say.) House Finch. a, ♂ ad.; b, ♀ ad.

76. Centronyx bairdi, (Aud.) Baird's Bunting. a, ♂ ad.

77. Chondestes grammaca, (Say.) Skylark Bunting. a, ♂ ad.; b, ♀ ad.

78. Pooecetes gramineus, β. confinis, (Baird.) Western Bay-winged Bunting. a, ad.

79. Passerculus sandvichensis, γ. alaudinus, (Bonap.) Western Savanna Sparrow. a, ♂ ad.; b, ♀ ad.

80. Junco Aikeni, (Ridgw.) White-winged Snowbird. a, ♂ ad.; b, ♀ ad.

81. Junco hyemalis, (Linn.) Eastern Snowbird. a, ♂ ad.; b, ♀ ad.

82. Junco oregonus, (Towns.) Oregon Snowbird. a, ♂ ad.; b, ♀ ad.

83. Junco caniceps, (Woodh.) Gray-headed Snowbird. a, ad.; (variety, see note on page ——); b, ad.; (normal style); c, juv.

84. Junco annectens, (Baird.) Pink-sided Snowbird. a, ad.; (normal style); b, ad.; (variety, see note on page ——).

85. Spizella socialis, β. arizonæ, (Coues.) Western Chipping Sparrow. a, ♂ ad.; b, ♀ ad.

86. Spizella monticola, (Gm.) Tree Sparrow. a, ♂ ad.; b, ♀ ad.

87. Spizella breweri, (Cass.) Brewer's Sparrow. a, ad.

88. Spizella pallida, (Swains.) Clay-colored Sparrow. a, ad.

89. Zonotrichia leucophrys, (Forst.) White-crowned Sparrow. a, ♂ ad.; b, ♀ ad.

90. Zonotrichia intermedia, (Ridgw.) Ridgway's White-crowned Sparrow. a, ♂ ad.; b, ♀ ad.; c, juv., in winter plumage.

91. Melospiza fasciata, γ. fallax, (Baird.) Rocky Mountain Song Sparrow. a, b, c, adults.

92. Melospiza lincolni (Aud.) Lincoln's Sparrow. a, ♂ ad.; b, ♀ ad.; c, juv.

93. Coturniculus passerinus, β. perpallidus, (Ridgw.) Western Yellow-winged Sparrow.

94. Passerella iliaca, (Merrem.) Fox-colored Sparrow. a, ♂ ad.; b, ♀ ad. [Typical *iliaca.*]

95. Calamospiza bicolor, (Towns.) Black Lark Bunting. a, ♂ ad.; b, ♀ ad.

96. Euspiza americana, (Gm.) Black-throated Bunting. a, ♂ ad.

96a. Hedymeles melanocephalus, (Swains.) Black-headed Grosbeak. a, ♂ ad.; b, ♀ ad.

97. Guiraca cærulea, (Linn.) Blue Grosbeak. a, ♂ ad.

98. Cyanospiza amœna, (Say.) Lazuli Bunting. a, ♂ ad.; b, ♀ ad.

99. Pipilo maculatus, δ. megalonyx, (Baird.) Long-clawed Ground Robin. a, ♂ ad.; b, ♀ ad.

100. Pipilo chlorurus, (Towns.) Green-tailed Ground Robin. a, ♂ ad.; b, ♀ ad.; c, juv.

101. Piplio fuscus, y. mesoleucus, (Baird.) Cañon Bunting. a, ♂ ad.

102. a, Cyanospiza cyanea, (Lin.) Indigo Bird. a, ♂ ad.

Family ICTERIDÆ: American Starlings; Hang-nests.

98. Dolichonyx oryzivorous, (L.) Bobolink. a, ♂ ad.

99. Molothrus aster, (Bodd.) Cow Blackbird. a, ♂ ad.; b, ♀ ad.

100. Xanthocephalus icterocephalus, (Bonap.) Yellow-headed Blackbird. a, ♂ ad.; b, ♀ ad.; c, pullus.

101. Agelæus phœniceus, (Linn.) Red-and-buff-shouldered Blackbird. a, ♂ ad.; b, ♀ ad.

102. Sturnella neglecta, (Aud.) Western Meadow Lark. a, ♂ ad.; b, ♀ ad.

103. Icterus bullocki, (Swains.) Bullock's Oriole. a, ♂ ad.; b, ♀ ad.; c. juv.

104. Icterus baltimore, (Linn.) Baltimore Oriole. a, ♂ ad.

105. Scolecophagus cyanocephalus, (Wagl.) Brewer's Blackbird. a, ♂ ad.; b, ♀ ad.

Family CORVIDÆ: Ravens, Crows and Jays.

106. Corvus corax, β. carnivorus, (Bartram.) American Raven. a, ad.; b, juv.

107. Corvus cryptoleucus, (Couch.) White-necked Raven. a, ad.; b, c, juv.

108. Corvus americanus, (Aud.) Common Crow. a, b, c. [Breeds in Colorado!]

109. Picicorvus columbnianus, (Wils.) Clarke's Nutcracker. a, ♂ ad.; b, ♀ ad.

110. Gymnokitta cyanocephala, (Max.) Maximilian's Nutcracker. a, ♂ ad.

111. Pica rustica, β. hudsonica, (Sabine.) American Black-billed Magpie. a, ♂ ad.; b, ♀ ad.; c, juv.

112. Perisoreus canadensis. β. capitalis, (Baird.) White-headed Gray Jay. a, ♂ ad., winter pl.; b, ♀ ad., summer pl.; c, juv.

113. Cyanocitta macrolopha, (Baird.) Long-crested Jay. a, ♂ ad.; b, ♀ ad.; c, d, e, juv.

114. Aphelocoma woodhousii. (Baird.) Woodhouse's Jay. a, ad.

Family ALAUDIDÆ: Larks.

115. Eremophila alpestris, (Forst.) Shore-Lark. a, b, adults.

116. Eremophila alpestris, γ, leucolæma, (Coues.) White-throated Shore Lark. a, b, c, adults; d, ♀ ad.; e, juv.

Family TYRANNIDÆ: Tyrant Flycatchers.

117. Tyrannus carolinensis, (Linn.) Eastern Kingbird. a, ♂ ad.; b, ♀ ad.

118. Tyrannus verticalis, (Say.) Western Kingbird. a, ♂ ad.; b, ♀ ad.

119. Tyrannus vociferans, (Swains.) Cassin's Kingbird. a, ♂ ad.

120. Contopus borealis, (Swains.) Olive-sided Flycatcher. a, ♂ ad.; b, ♀ ad.

121. Contopus richardsoni, (Swains.) Richardson's Pewee. a, ♂ ad.; b, ♀ ad.

122. Sayornis sayus, (Bonap.) Say's Pewee. a, ♂ ad.

123. Empidonax pusillus, (Swains.) Little Flycatcher; Trail's Flycatcher. a, ♂ ad.; b, ♀ ad.; c, juv.

124. Empidonax difficilis, (Baird.) Western Flycatcher. a, ♂ ad.; b, ♀ ad.

125. Empidonax obscurus, (Swains.) Wright's Flycatcher. a, ♂ ad.

126. Empidonax hammondi, (Xantus.) Hammond's Flycatcher. a, ♂ ad.

127. Empidonax minimus, (Baird.) Least Flycatcher.

Family CAPRIMULGIDÆ: Night-jars.

128. Antrostomus nuttalli, (Aud.) Poorwill. a, ♂ ad.; b, ♀ ad.

129. Chordeiles popetue, β. henryi, (Cass.) Western Night Hawk. a, ♂ ad.; b, ♀ ad.; c, d, juv.

Family TROCHILIDÆ: Humming Birds.

130. Selasphorus platycercus, (Swains.) Broad-tailed Hummer. a, ♂ ad.; b, ♀ ad.; c, ♂ ad. With nest and two young.

131. Selasphorus rufus, (Gmel.) Rufous-backed Hummer.

Family CUCULIDÆ: Cuckoos.

132. Coccyzus americanus, (Lin.) Yellow-billed Cuckoo. a, ♂ ad.; b, ♀ ad.

133. Geococcyx californianus, (Less.) Chaparral Cock; Road-runner. a, ♂ ad.

Family PICADÆ: Woodpeckers.

134. Picus harrisi, (Aud.) Harris's Woodpecker. a, ♂ ad.; b, ♀ ad.

135. Picus gairdneri, (Aud.) Gairdner's Woodpecker. a, ♂ ad.; b, ♀ ad.

136. Picodes americanus, β. dorsalis, (Baird.) White-backed three-toed Wood-pecker. a, ♂ ad.; b, ♀ ad.

137. Sphyrapicus varius, (Linn.) Red-throated Woodpecker. a, ♂ ad.

138. Sphyrapicus nuchalis, (Baird.) Red-naped Woodpecker. a, ♂ ad.; b, ♀ juv.

139. Sphyrapicus thyroideus, (Cass.) Black-breasted Woodpecker. a, ♂ ad.; b, ♀ ad.; c, ♂ juv.; d, ♀ juv.

140. Centurus carolinus, (L.) Red-bellied Woodpecker. a, ♂ ad.; b, ♀ ad.

141. Melanerpes erythrocephalus, (Linn.) Red-headed Woodpecker. a, ♂ ad.; b, ♀ ad.

142. Melanerpes torquatus, (Wils.) Lewis's Woodpecker. a, ♂ ad.; b, ♀ ad.

143. Colaptes mexicanus, (Swains.) Red-shafted Flicker. a, ♂ ad.; b, ♀ ad.; c.

144. Colaptes "hybridus," (Baird.) "Hybrid Flicker." a, ♂ ad.; b, ♀ juv.

Family ALCEDINIDÆ: Kingfishers.

145. Ceryle alcyon, (Linn.) Belted Kingfisher. a, ♂ ad.; b, ♀ juv.

Family COLUMBIDÆ: Pigeons or Doves.

146. Columba fasciata, (Say.) Band-tailed Pigeon. a, ♂ ad.

147. Zenædura carolinensis, (Linn.) Mourning Dove. a, ♂ ad.

Family TETRAONIDÆ: Grouse.

148. Centrocercus urophasianus, (Bonap.) Sage Hen. a, ♂ ad.; b, ♀ ad.

149. Pediœcetes columbianus, (Ord.) Sharp-tailed Grouse. a, ♂ ad.; b, ♀ ad.

150. Canace obscura, (Say.) Dusky Grouse. a, ♂ ad.; b, ♀ ad.; and nine chicks.

151. Lagopus leucurus, (Swains.) White-tailed Ptarmigan. a, d, adult, winter pl.; b, ♂ adult, summer pl.; c, ♀ ad., summer pl.; and 3 chicks.

Family STRIGIDÆ: Owls.

152. Bubo virginianus, β. subarcticus, (Hoy.) Western Great Horned Owl. a, b, adults.

153. Otus brachyotus (Gmel.) Short-eared Owl. a, adult. [Apparently the typical form, and evidently different from the usual American style.]

154. Otus brachyotus, β. cassini, (Brewer.) American Short-eared owl. a, b, adults.

155. Otus wilsonianus, (Less.) American Long-eared Owl. a, b, adults; c, d, pullus.

156. Scops asio, θ. maxwelliæ, (Ridgw.) Mrs. Maxwell's Owl. a, ♂ ad.; b, ♀ ad.; c, d, pullus. [See description at end of catalogue.]

157. Scops flammeola, (Licht.) Flammulated Owl. a, adult. [Boulder, Col., March. *Iris umber brown!*]

158. Nyctale acadica, (Gm.) Saw-whet Owl. a, adult; b, c, juv.

159. Glaucidium gnoma, (Wagl.) Pigmy owl. a, ♂ ad.; b, ♀ ad.

160. Speotyto cunicularia, y. hypogæa, (Bonap.) North American Burrowing Owl. a, ♂ ad.; b, ♀ ad.; c, d, pullus.

Family FALCONIDÆ: Falcons, Kites, Hawks and Eagles.

161. Falco saker, y. polyagrus, (Cass.) Prairie Falcon. a, "♀" ad.; b, "♂" juv. (2nd yr.); c, "♀" juv. (2nd yr.).

162. Falco richardsoni, (Ridgw.) Richardson's Merlin. a, ♀ (? ad.).

163. Falco sparverius, (Linn.) American Kestril. a, ♂ ad.; b, ♀ juv.

164. Pandion haliætus, β. carolinensis, (Gm.) American Osprey. a, b, juv.

165. Circus hudsonius, (Linn.) Marsh Hawk. a, ♂ ad.; b, ♀ juv.

166. Nisus cooperi, (Bonap.) Cooper's Hawk. a, ♂ juv.; b, ♀ juv.

167. Nisus fuscus, (Gm.) Sharp Skinned Hawk. a, ♂ juv.; b, ♀ juv.

168. Astur artricapillus, (Wils.) American Gos-hawk. a, ♂ ad.; b, ♀ ad.; c, juv.; d, e, pullus.

169. Buteo borealis, β. calurus, (Cass.) Western Red-tailed Buzzard. a, b, ad.; c, d, juv.

170. Buteo swainsoni, (Bonap.) Swainson's Buzzard. a, ♂ ad.; b, ♀ ad.; c, ♀ juv.

171. Archibuteo lagopus, β. sancti-johannis, (Gmel.) American Rough-legged Buzzard. a, ad.; b, c, juv.

172. Archibuteo ferrugineus, (Licht.) Ferruginous Rough-legged Buzzard; "California Squirrel Hawk." a, ♂ ad.; *melanistic*. [See description on page 212]; b, ♀ ad.; c, d, pullus.

173. Aquila chrysætos, β. canadensis, (Linn.) American Golden Eagle. a, ad.; b, juv., in 2nd or 3rd year; c, juv. in 1st year.

174. Haliætus leucocephalus, (Linn.) Bald Eagle. a, ad.

Family CATHARTIDÆ: American Vultures.

175. Rhinogryphus aura, (Linn.) Turkey Vulture. a, ad.

Family LARIDÆ: Jaegers, Gulls, and Terns.

176. Stercorarius parasiticus, (Brunn.) Parasitic Jaeger. a, juv. [Boulder, December].

177. Rissa tridactyla, (Linn.) Kittiwake Gull, winter pl. [Boulder, December].

178. Zema sabinii, (Prev. et des Murs.) Sabine's Gull. a, juv. [Boulder, December].

179. Chrœcocephalus Philadelphia, (Ord.) Bonaparte's Gull. a, juv., transition pl.

180. Larus delawarensis, (Ord.) Ring-billed Gull. a, adult; b, juv., transition pl.; c, juv., first yr.

Family CHARADRIIDÆ: Plovers.

181. Squatarola helvetica, (Linn.) Black-bellied Plover. a, juv.

182. Ægialitis montanus, (Towns.) Mountain Plover. a, ♂ ad.; b, ♀ ad.; c, pullus.

183. Ægialitis vociferus, (Linn.) Killdeer Plover. a, b, adult; c, d, pullus.

Family RECURVIROSTRIDÆ: Avocets and Stilts.

184. Recurvirostra americana, (Gmel.) American Avocet. a, adult.

185. Himantopus mexicanus, (Muller.) American Stilt.

Family PHALAROPODIDÆ: Phalaropes.

186. Steganopus wilsoni, (Sabine.) Wilson's Phalarope. a, ♀ ad.

Family ARDEIDÆ: Herons.

187. Ardea herodias, (Linn.) Great Blue Heron. a, ♀ ad.; b, juv.

188. Garzetta candidissima, (Jacq.) Snowy Heron. a, ad., breeding plumage.

189. Nyctherodias violaceus, (Linn.) Yellow-crowned Night Heron. a, ad., breeding plumage.

190. Botaurus minor, (Gmel.) American Bittern. a, b, adults; c, juv.

Family TANTALIDÆ: Ibises.

191. Tantalus loculator, (Linn.) Wood Ibis. a, juv.

192. Falcinellus guarauna, (Linn.) Bronzed Ibis. a, juv.

Family SCOLOPACIDÆ: Snipe, Sandpipers, etc.

193. Macrorhamphus griseus, (Gmel.) Red-breasted Snipe. a, b, adult, summer plumage.

194. Tringa aplina, β. americana, (Cassin.) American Dunlin. a, adult, winter plumage.

195. Tringa maculate, (Vieill.) Pectoral Sandpiper. a, adult.
196. Tringa bairdi, (Coues.) Baird's Sandpiper. a, juv.
197. Tringa minutilla, (Vieill.) Least Sandpiper. a, juv.
198. Ereunetes pusillus, (Linn.) Seipalmated Sandpiper. a, juv.
199. Totanus melanoleucus, (Gmel.) Greater Tell-tale. a, adult.
200. Totanus flavipes, (Gmel.) Yellow-legs. a, juv.
201. Totanus solitarious, (Wils.) Solitary Sandpiper.
202. Tringoides macularius, (Linn.) Spotted Sandpiper. a, b, ad.; c, d, juv.
203. Actiturus bartramius, (Wils.) Bartram's Tattler. a, ♂ ad.; b, ♀ ad.
204. Numenius longirostris, (Wils.) Long-billed Curlew. a, ♂ ad.

Family RALLIDÆ: Rails, Gallinules, and Coots.

205. Rallus virginianus, (Linn.) Virginia Rail. a, ♂ ad.
206. Porzana carolina, (Linn.) Sora Rail. a, ad.
207. Fulica americana, (Gmel.) American Coot. a, ad.; b, c, pullus.

Family ANATIDÆ: Swans, Geese and Ducks.

208. Cygnus americanus, (Sharpless.) Whistler Swan. a, b, adults.
209. Branta canadensis, (Linn.) Canada Goose. a, b, adults.
210. Anser gambeli, (Hartl.) White-fronted Goose. a, adult.
211. Anser albatus, (Cassin.) Lesser Snow Goose. a, b, adults.
212. Anas boschas, (Linn.) Mallard. a, ♂ ad.; b, ♀ ad.; c, d, e, pullus.
213. Chaulelasmus streperus, (Linn.) Gadwall. a, ♂ ad.
214. Mareca americana, (Gmel.) Baldpate. a, b, ♂ adult.
215. Querquedula discors, (Linn.) Blue-wing Teal. a, b, ♂ ad.; c, ♀ ad.
216. Nettion carolinensis, (Gmel.) Green-wing Teal. a, b, ♂ ad.; c, ♀ ad.
217. Dafila acuta, (Linn.) Pin-tail. a, ♂ ad.; b, ♀ ad.
218. Spatula clypeata, (Linn.) Shoveller. a, b, ♂ ad.; c, ♀ ad.
219. Aythya americana, (Eyton.) Red-head. a, ♂ ad.
220. Aythya vallisneria, (Wils.) Canvas-back. a, ♂ ad.
221. Bucephala clangula, β. americana, (Bonap.) American Golden-eye. a, ♂ ad.
222. Bucephala albeola, (Linn.) Butter-ball. a, ♂ ad.; b, ♀ ad.
223. Fulix affinis, (Eyton.) Lesser Black-head. a, ♂ ad.; b, ♀ ad.
224. Fulix collaris, (Donov.) Ring-bill. a, ♀ ad.
225. Œdemia americana, (Swains.) American Black Scoter. a, ♂ ad. [*Perfect adult plumage!*].

226. Erismatura rubida, (Wils.) Ruddy Duck. a, ♂ ad.

227. Mergus merganser, β. americanus. (Cass.) American Buff-breasted Sheldrake. a, ♂ ad.

228. Mergus serrator, (Linn.) Red-breasted Sheldrake. a, ♂ juv., transition pl.

229. Lophodytes cucullatus, (Linn.) Hooded Sheldrake. a, ♂ ad.; b, ♀ ad.

Family PELECANIDÆ: Pelicans.

230. Pelecanus erythrorhynchus, (Gmel.) American White Pelican. a, juv.

Family GRACULIDÆ: Cormorants.

231. Graculus dilophus, (Swains.) Double-crested Cormorant. a, juv.

Family COLYMBIDÆ: Loons.

232. Colymbus torquatus, (Brunn.) Great Northern Diver. a, juv.

Family PODICIPITIDÆ: Grebes.

233. Podiceps auritus, β californicus, (Lawr.) California Grebe. a, ad.; b, juv.

234. Podilymbus podiceps, (Linn.) Thick-billed Grebe. a, ad.; b, ♀ ad.; c, d, e, pullus.

NOTES

ARCHIBUTEO FERRUGINEUS, (Licht.)—The collection contains a melanistic specimen of this species, which is a fact of very great interest, since this condition is very rarely assumed by the species; indeed, this example is the first I have ever seen, although very numerous specimens in normal plumage have been examined by me. The following is a description of this remarkable specimen:

General color very dark chocolate brown, nearly uniform above, where faintly relieved by rufous spots, these most conspicuous on the inner lesser wing-coverts; occipital feathers snow-white at the base, those of the nape conspicuously edged with ferruginous; upper tail-coverts irregularly spotted with white and pale rufous; secondaries crossed by wide but indistinct bands of silvery plumbeous; outer webs of primaries bright silvery-gray, more obscure on the inner quills. Tail, pearl-gray, (the middle portion of each feather whitish, the inner webs chiefly white,) finely sprinkled at the end and toward base with darker gray; the shafts pure white for their whole length.

Entire head, throat, jugulum and breast quite uniform dark chocolate-brown, or soot-color, the feathers white at extreme bases; whole abdomen, sides and lining of wings ferruginous-rufous, with shaft-streaks and variously formed spots and bars of dusky [*sic*]; flank-plumes similar, but with the dusky markings prevailing; tribiæ dusky, the longer plumes variegated with ferruginous; tarsel feather uniform dusky; lower tail-coverts with exposed ends pale ferruginous, the concealed portion whitish. Whole under surface of primaries anterior to the emarginations, pure white, *immaculate*; under surface of tail also uniform white. Wing, 18.80; tail 10.50; culmen, 1.10; tarsus, 3.25; middle toe, 1.50.

In general aspect, this specimen bears a close resemblance to the rufous-chested examples of melanistic *Buteo borealis* (β. *calurus,*) the tail being the only very obvious difference so far as colors are concerned, though close inspection soon reveals other marked discrepancies, most important of which are the bright silver-gray of the outer surface and the immaculate snow-white of the under surface of the primaries. There is little resemblance to the melanistic examples of *A. lagopus* (β. *sancti-johannis,*) the general color being much too rufous, while the tail is conspicuously different. The great breadth of the gape and other peculiarities of structure only recognizable in *A. ferrugineus*, also immediately refer this specimen to that species.

Scops Asio, ε. Maxwelliæ, Ridgway, MSS.—Mrs. Maxwell's collection contains a number of specimens of what is evidently a local form of the common North American *Scops asio*, representing the opposite extreme of the var. *B. kennicotti*,[141] and quite as strongly marked as that form. These specimens and others that I have since seen, all agree in possessing with unusual uniformity the distinctive characters of the race, there being apparently much less of individual variation than in other forms of the species. This new race is a mountain bird, and possesses the distinctive features of alpine or boreal races in general, the size being larger and the colors very much

---

141. Ridgway's note: Naming the several marked geographical races of this species in the order of their date of publication, they may be arranged in the following sequence: a. asio (Strix asio, Linn., S. N., 1758, 92,) B. kennicotti (Scops kennicotti, Elliot, Pr. Phila. Acad. 1867, 69;) γ. floridanus (Scops asio, var. floridanus, Ridgway bull. Essex Inst. & Dec. 1873, 200;) γ. enano (Scops asio, var. enano Lawr., Bull. Essex Inst., Dec. 1873, 200,) and ε maxwelliæ, nobis.

paler than in the low-land races, even from much higher latitudes. In the colors, there is in all specimens an entire absence or but faint indication of any rufous tints, while the rufous phase of other forms is never assumed, as indeed, curiously enough, seems to be the case with the species throughout the western half of the continent, even where (as in California) the gray birds cannot be distinguished from individuals in corresponding plumage from the Atlantic States.

From its allies, *Scops maxwelliæ*, may be distinguished as follows:— Ch.—Ground-color above pale gray or grayish brown, relieved by the usual ragged mesial streaks of black, and irregular mottlings or vermiculations of lighter and darker shades; the ground-color, however never inclining strongly to reddish, and no darker in shade than a *very light* ash-gray or brown. The white spots on the outer webs of the primaries frequently confluent along the edge of the feathers, the darker spots being in extreme cases hardly visible on the basal portion of the quills when the wing is closed. Face grayish white, with faint vermiculations of darker grayish. No rusty gular collar, but in its stead, sparse, narrow bars of brown or rusty, on a white ground. Lower parts with white very largely predominating. Wing, 6.80–6.90; tail, 3.90–4.10; culmen, .60; tarsus, 1.45–1.50; middle toe, .80–.85.[142] Hab.—Mountains of Colorado (Mus. Mrs. Maxwell; also collection of R. Ridgway.) I name this new form in honor of Mrs. M. A. Maxwell, not only as a compliment to an accomplished and amiable lady, but also as a deserved tribute to her high attainments in the study of natural history.

JUNCO CANICEPS, (Woodh.)—A very remarkable specimen of this bird is in the collection. It differs from the usual, and we may say almost constant, plumage of the species, in having two well-defined bars of white on the wings, and in having a conspicuous tinge of bright rufous on the pileum, the plumage being otherwise normal. None of the species of *Junco* now known are characterized, even in part, by having rufous on the crown; but several

---

142. Ridgway's note: Before me are three specimens of the typical form (a. asio) in gray plumage which are so much alike that if the labels were removed they could scarcely be distinguished. Two of these, a pair, are from the coast of California; the other, an adult ♀, is from Virginia. Their measurements are as follows:

♀ (Fairfax CO., Va.): 6.50., 3.70.
♂ (Nicasio, Cal.): 6.30., 3.50.
♀ (" "): 6.60., 3.65.

tend in their variations to the other character, *i.e.* the white wing-bars; this feature being almost constant in *J. aikeni.* We have frequently seen this variation in *J. annectens*, and adult male of *J. oregonus* in our own collection exhibits the same remarkable feature. The fact that this barring of the wings has become a permanent feature of one species, while it occasionally, but very rarely, occurs in three or more others, suggests the question of whether we do not see in this evidence of the present genesis of species; and whether these characters, now unstable, may not through accelerated hereditary transmittal become permanent, thus characterizing, in due time, new forms.

JUNCO ANNECTENS, (Baird.)—An adult specimen, probably a female, since it is smaller than the males in the National Museum and other collections, differs from typical examples in having the pinkish of the sides invading the whole breast and strongly tinging the throat. In other respects, however, it does differ from ordinary specimens. Its measurements are as follows: Wing, 3.20; tail, 2.80; bill, from nostril, .35; tarsus, .78.

ROBERT RIDGWAY.

THE END.

Appendix

————

ADDITIONAL PHOTOGRAPHS OF MARTHA MAXWELL'S TAXIDERMY

FIGURE 29.1. Close-up of Maxwell sitting among her *Woman's Work* exhibit at Philadelphia International Centennial Exposition. *Courtesy,* Boulder Historical Society / Museum of Boulder.

FIGURE 29.2. Close-up from another angle of Maxwell sitting among her *Woman's Work* exhibit at Philadelphia International Centennial Exposition. *Courtesy,* Boulder Historical Society / Museum of Boulder.

FIGURE 29.3. Martha Maxwell in the Rocky Mountain Museum. *Courtesy,* Boulder Historical Society / Museum of Boulder.

FIGURE 29.4. Example of Maxwell's anthropomorphic taxidermy at the Rocky Mountain Museum. *Courtesy*, Boulder Historical Society / Museum of Boulder.

FIGURE 29.5. Taxidermy bird specimens at the Rocky Mountain Museum. *Courtesy, Boulder* Historical Society / Museum of Boulder.

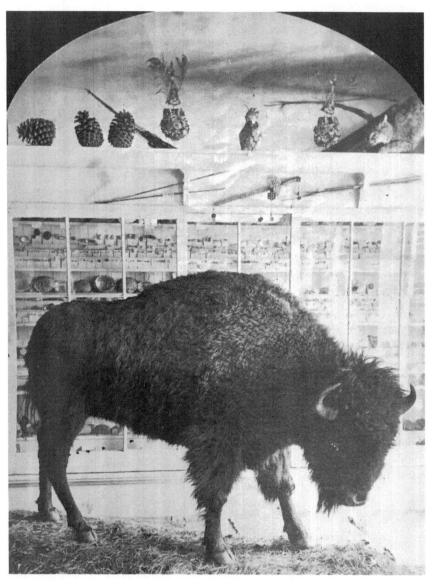

FIGURE 29.6. Taxidermied buffalo in the Rocky Mountain Museum. *Courtesy*, History Colorado Center, Denver.

FIGURE 29.7. Bird specimens at the Rocky Mountain Museum. *Courtesy*, History Colorado Center, Denver.

FIGURE 29.8. Taxidermy specimens at Rocky Mountain Museum. *Courtesy,* History Colorado Center, Denver.

Index

About the Editor

Julie McCown is an assistant professor of English at Southern Utah University. She specializes in early American literature, animal studies, women writers, and digital humanities. Her recent publications have focused on early African American literature, nineteenth-century American poetry, and nineteenth-century women's periodicals.